THE PSYCHOLOGY
OF LEARNING AND MOTIVATION

Advances in Research and Theory

VOLUME 8

CONTRIBUTORS TO THIS VOLUME

Alan D. Baddeley

Gordon H. Bower

Helen B. Daly

Edmund Fantino

Paul E. Gold

Graham Hitch

James L. McGaugh

Douglas Navarick

Lance J. Rips

Edward J. Shoben

Edward E. Smith

David R. Thomas

Endel Tulving

THE PSYCHOLOGY
OF LEARNING AND MOTIVATION

Advances in Research and Theory

EDITED BY GORDON H. BOWER

STANFORD UNIVERSITY, STANFORD, CALIFORNIA

Volume 8

1974

ACADEMIC PRESS   New York · San Francisco · London
A SUBSIDIARY OF HARCOURT BRACE JOVANOVICH, PUBLISHERS

ACADEMIC PRESS, INC.
111 Fifth Avenue, New York, New York 10003

United Kingdom Edition published by
ACADEMIC PRESS, INC. (LONDON) LTD.
24/28 Oval Road, London NW1

LIBRARY OF CONGRESS CATALOG CARD NUMBER: 66-30104

ISBN 0–12–543308–5

PRINTED IN THE UNITED STATES OF AMERICA

CONTENTS

SEMANTIC MEMORY AND PSYCHOLOGICAL SEMANTICS

Edward E. Smith, Lance J. Rips, and Edward J. Shoben

WORKING MEMORY

Alan D. Baddeley and Graham Hitch

THE ROLE OF ADAPTATION-LEVEL IN STIMULUS GENERALIZATION

David R. Thomas

THE LOGIC OF MEMORY REPRESENTATIONS

Endel Tulving and Gordon H. Bower

LIST OF CONTRIBUTORS

Numbers in parentheses indicate the pages on which the authors' contributions begin.

Alan D. Baddeley,[1] University of Stirling, Stirling, Scotland (47)

Gordon H. Bower, Stanford University, Stanford, California (265)

Helen B. Daly, State University of New York College at Oswego, Oswego, New York (187)

Edmund Fantino, University of California, San Diego, La Jolla, California (147)

Paul E. Gold, Department of Psychobiology, University of California, Irvine, California (233)

Graham Hitch,[1] University of Stirling, Stirling, Scotland (47)

James L. McGaugh, Department of Psychobiology, University of California, Irvine, California (233)

Douglas Navarick, California State University, Fullerton, California (147)

Lance J. Rips, Stanford University, Stanford, California (1)

Edward J. Shoben, Stanford University, Stanford, California (1)

Edward E. Smith, Stanford University, Stanford, California (1)

David R. Thomas, University of Colorado, Boulder, Colorado (91)

Endel Tulving, University of Toronto, Toronto, Ontario, Canada, and Yale University, New Haven, Connecticut (265)

[1] Present address: Medical Research Council, Applied Psychology Unit, 15 Chaucer Road, Cambridge, England.

CONTENTS OF
PREVIOUS VOLUMES

Volume 4

Volume 5

SEMANTIC MEMORY AND PSYCHOLOGICAL SEMANTICS[1]

Edward E. Smith, Lance J. Rips, and Edward J. Shoben

STANFORD UNIVERSITY, STANFORD, CALIFORNIA

I. Introduction

It was only about five years ago that the term semantic memory was introduced into the psychological literature (Collins & Quillian, 1969). It was intended to describe that system which contains the psychological representations of the meanings of words (a subjective lexicon), along with the processes that operate on such representa-

[1] We are indebted to Tom Schumacher and Linda Barrick for their assistance in carrying out the research reported here and to Herbert Clark, Susan Haviland, and Daniel Osherson for their helpful comments on an earlier version of this manuscript. The research was supported by United States Public Health Service Grant MH-19705.

1

tions. In this chapter we will present a theoretical approach to semantic memory which seems specific enough to explain most recent findings, yet general enough to be applicable to a wide range of semantic phenomena. But, before doing so, it seems best to set the topic of semantic memory in some psycholinguistic perspective.

A.   THE NATURE OF PSYCHOLOGICAL SEMANTICS

We first need to consider psychological semantics in relation to other approaches to meaning, namely, philosophical and linguistic semantics. Psychological semantics is concerned with psychological aspects of meaning, but this is not to say that every aspect of meaning can be handled by an exclusively psychological approach. To illustrate, consider an approach to semantics that equates the meanings of words with the mental processes that mediate comprehension. In such a theory, the central issues in semantics (e.g., synonymy, lexical ambiguity) are explicated only in terms of these mediating processes. In these terms, synonymy occurs when a single mental process is triggered by two distinct words, while lexical ambiguity occurs when distinct processes are occasioned by the same word. This exclusively psychological approach to meaning has been criticized on a number of grounds (Frege, 1892; Quine, 1960). For example, Frege argued that there is a constant aspect to word meanings that cannot be captured by variable psychological processes. In attempting to capture this inviolate core meaning, philosophical semanticists (e.g., Montague, 1973) have developed formal systems in which meaning is characterized by abstract functions. These functions are such as to assign referents (objects, sets of objects, other meaning functions, or truth values) to phrases on the basis of the nonlinguistic contexts in which these phrases might occur. In a similar vein, linguistic semantics also concerns itself with an abstract and invariant description of the language, in contrast to the psychological approach.

Although an exclusively psychological approach to meaning is placed in doubt by these criticisms, we can still ask how meanings are represented psychologically. In the same way that a psychologist may study how people perform arithmetic operations without making claims that he is contributing to our knowledge of number theory, we may study the psychological representations and processes that correspond to these abstract meanings, for it is the psychological representations that allow us to answer questions and verify statements. Thus the study of words and numbers as abstract systems does not vitiate the need to investigate these topics from the point of view of a psychological system. In taking this psychological approach, however, there is no guarantee that the abstract functions of philosophers and linguists will be isomorphic to psychological processes, even though both may assign the correct referents to the phrases of a language.

The above issue should not obscure what psychological semantics can gain from the approaches taken by other disciplines. The methods used by linguistic semantics may prove useful for psychologists as well. For example, one variation of this approach (Katz & Fodor, 1963) assumes that the meaning of a word can be analyzed into a set of fundamental semantic features. Given this assumption, problems relating to the synonymy and ambiguity of words can be explicated in terms of overlap among semantic features. Similarly, the meaning of larger linguistic units, like phrases and sentences, are derived from the semantic features of individual words by specific combination rules. But although semantic features are useful in many ways, there is a major problem in applying this approach to the study of meaning. As Lewis (1972) has pointed out, linguists until recently have neglected the notions of reference and truth. Thus linguistic semantics has provided a set of rules whereby one language (e.g., English) can be translated into another (the language of semantic features) without making contact with the objects referred to. Though this problem is a serious one for certain linguistic theories, it may be resolved by noting that semantic features may, at some psychological level, correspond to perceptual elements. For this permits one to compare representations of linguistic expressions to those of perceptual experiences (e.g., Bierwisch, 1971; Clark, Carpenter, & Just, 1973).

Psychological semantics, then, deals with the internal representation and processing of linguistic inputs, where such representations are capable of interfacing with perceptual encodings. Furthermore, such representations are memorial elements, and it is the nature of this semantic memory that is at issue in the present chapter.

B. The Scope of Semantic Memory Research

Clearly the semantic memory system must enter into the understanding of any natural language statement, for such a system contains the representations of word meanings. But thus far, the research that goes by the name semantic memory has been more confined. In particular, it has dealt with the verification of what we will call semantic propositions as contrasted with episodic propositions. This distinction, based on a proposal by Tulving (1972), holds that semantic propositions (e.g., *An apple is a fruit*) are verified against our knowledge of the constituent words in the stated proposition together with general world knowledge, while episodic propositions (e.g., *The apple in my kitchen is green*) are verified in relation to temporally marked, personal episodes and their interrelations. One means of illuminating this distinction is to consider how a hypothetical subject might verify the pair of sentences given in (1) and (2):

1. Some Mongolians you know are women.
2. Some Mongolians are women.

If our hypothetical subject knows only Mongolian men, then he should respond *False* to sentence (1). But this same subject will almost certainly respond *True* to sentence (2). Why the difference in response? Because (1) demands an answer on the basis of some personal episode, while (2) can be answered solely on the basis of the meaning of its constituent words and general world knowledge. That is, (1) is an episodic proposition while (2) is a semantic one. And the fact that the two questions can lead to different answers indicates that certain semantic knowledge cannot be directly tied to any discrete episode, thus supporting the proposed semantic versus episodic distinction. In this chapter we deal only with semantic propositions.[2]

With this background, we can now turn to the organization of this chapter. In the next section (II) we will present our semantic feature representation of word concepts, and combine it with a specific set of processing assumptions. The resulting model—called the Feature Comparison model—is intended to account for how subjects verify subset statements of the form S *is a* P (e.g., *A robin is a bird*), where S and P denote subject and predicate nouns, respectively. Some of these arguments are available elsewhere (Smith, Shoben, & Rips, 1974) and our discussion will be brief on these points. Section III

---

[2] Our semantic versus episodic distinction differs from the traditional Kantian distinction between analytic and synthetic statements. The latter dichotomy, a controversial one in contemporary philosophy (Quine, 1960, Section 14), segregates those statements which are true solely on the basis of the meanings of the constituent words (analytic truths) from statements which cannot be confirmed in this way (synthetic truths). The difference between the two distinctions is that while all analytic truths are semantic propositions, synthetic truths can be either semantic or episodic; synthetic statements are classified as semantic when the knowledge of the world needed to assess the proposition is generally available, and as episodic when the requisite knowledge is not generally available. Thus, sentence (2) is semantically true, but not analytically true since it is logically possible for all Mongolians to be male. Although the semantic versus episodic distinction may best be conceptualized as a continuum, we use the dichotomy here for the simple purpose of differentiating the kinds of propositions used in semantic memory research from those used in more traditional studies of memory.

extends the Feature Comparison model to a related paradigm, the Same-Different task, which also involves the verification of subset statements. In Section IV we will apply the model to the verification of statements that assert property relations (e.g., *A robin has wings*), rather than subset relations. To deal with property relations, it will be necessary to amend our structural and processing assumptions somewhat, though we will show that the basic Feature Comparison model can account for most of the relevant findings. Section V considers how the model can handle explicitly quantified statements (e.g., *Some reptiles are dangerous*), and here it will again prove necessary to amend our processing assumptions though our representational assumptions are kept intact. In Section VI we consider inductive, analogical, and metaphorical reasoning. While our representational assumptions once more remain unchanged, new processing assumptions are again called for. Thus what holds our approach together across this range of semantic phenomena is the means by which we represent semantic knowledge.

II. The Feature Comparison Model and Subset Statements

A. Some Empirical Rationale for the Model

To understand our theoretical model, it is helpful to consider first some experimental findings we have attempted to capture in the model. In earlier work (Rips, Shoben, & Smith, 1973) we presented a subject with *S is a P* sentences (e.g., *A robin is a bird*) and required him to decide (by pushing a button) whether each sentence was True or False. Unsurprisingly, subjects made few errors in this task, and our primary concern was with the reaction times (RTs). Two classes of RT were of interest: the average time taken to respond correctly to a True statement (True RT) and the mean time taken to respond correctly to a False sentence (False RT). For True RTs, the most salient aspect of our results was a typicality effect: for any given category, say birds, subjects were consistently faster in verifying some instances (e.g., *sparrow, pigeon*) than others (e.g., *chicken, goose*), where the faster instances were those that had been independently judged to be more typical of that category. That is, the judged typicality of an instance in a category is a good predictor of the speed with which it can be verified as a member of that category, with more typical instances being verified about 60 msec faster than atypical ones. Rosch (1973) had earlier obtained the same typicality result, and prior work by Wilkins (1971) can also be interpreted as demonstrating the same effect.

Another way to describe the typicality effect is to state that True RT decreased with the semantic relatedness of the subject and predicate nouns, as *bird* is more related to *sparrow* than to *chicken*. This sets the stage for considering the major finding for False RTs in this paradigm. Specifically, False RT increases with the semantic relatedness of the subject and predicate nouns (e.g., Rips *et al.*, 1973; Wilkins, 1971). For example, statements like *A robin is a mammal* (where both subject and predicate nouns are animal terms and hence somewhat related) take more than 200 msec longer to disconfirm than statements like *A robin is a car* (Rips *et al.*, 1973). Thus the fundamental findings are that True RT decreases with semantic relatedness while False RT increases with relatedness.

At a general level, our model explains these two results by assuming that the subjects' decisions in this task are based on a two-stage process. The first stage assesses the degree to which the subject and predicate nouns have similar semantic features, regardless of whether the shared features are essential for defining category membership or not. The second stage considers only those features essential for category membership and determines whether the essential features of the predicate noun are shared by the subject noun. It is further assumed that, if the first stage indicates either a very high or very low degree of similarity, then one can decide immediately whether the subject noun is an instance of the predicate without engaging in second-stage processing. That is, subject-predicate noun pairs with sufficiently high and low degrees of semantic relatedness will be classified as True and False, respectively, without any second-stage processing. If the first stage indicates an intermediate level of similarity, then the second stage is utilized. Since this second stage must take some time, it follows that related True items will be responded to faster than unrelated ones, while the reverse holds for False items.

B.   STRUCTURAL AND PROCESSING ASSUMPTIONS

Given this overview of the model, it is time to flesh out its details. Consider first the specific structural assumptions of the model. As noted earlier, the concept denoted by each lexical item is represented by a set of semantic features. Within each set, it is assumed that the features may vary continuously in the degree to which they confer category membership, with features at one extreme being those that are essential for defining the concept, while features at the other extreme are only characteristic of the concept. In situations that demand accurate categorization, like a sentence verification task, the feature set for an item may be partitioned into two subsets which correspond to the defining and characteristic features of an item. To illustrate, take the term *robin*. Defining features of this item might include mention of its wings and distinctive coloring, while its characteristic features might include indications that it is undomesticated and tends to perch in trees. This proposed contrast between defining and characteristic features applies to all terms including superordinates like *bird* and *animal*. For example, the characteristic features of *bird* might include a particular average size. Thus even abstract terms like *bird* are represented psychologically in a relatively concrete manner, and this suggestion seems to capture the notion of a prototype for each category (Rosch, 1973).

Consider now the processing assumptions of the Feature Comparison model. These assumptions, which are partly based on the work of Atkinson and Juola (1973), are contained in the multistage model presented in Fig. 1. The first stage compares both the defining and characteristic features of the subject and predicate nouns, and yields a measure, x (a random variable), of the overall similarity between the two nouns. This measure, x, reflects the proportion of all predicate features shared by the subject noun. If the resulting x is greater than a high criterion of similarity, c_1, a True decision is made immediately, while if x is less than a low criterion, c_0, a False decision is executed immediately. If x falls between the two criteria, i.e., $c_0 \leq x \leq c_1$, then the second stage is needed before a True-False decision can be reached. This second stage isolates the defining features of the predicate noun and then compares them to the defining features of the subject noun. Here, a True decision is made if the defining features of the predicate noun are in sufficient agreement with features of the subject noun, while a False decision is made otherwise. (See Smith *et al.*, 1974, for a fuller description of the model.)

C. Applications of the Model

Clearly this model offers a specific explanation of why semantic relatedness speeds True RTs but slows False RTs. Let us repeat these explanations with more detail. For True statements, the greater the semantic relatedness or typicality of a subject-predicate pair, the greater the probability that x will exceed c_1, and hence the greater the probability that a fast, single-stage, True decision can be made. For

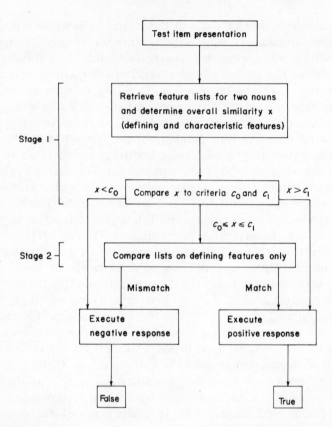

Fig. 1. The Feature Comparison model for the verification of subset statements. (After Smith *et al.,* 1974.)

False statements, the less the semantic relatedness of a subject-predicate pair, the greater the probability that x will be less than c_0, and hence the greater the probability that a fast, single-stage, False decision can be arrived at.

While the Feature Comparison model reflects rather nicely these two basic findings, there are other semantic memory effects that must be accounted for. Chief among these is the so-called category size effect. To illustrate this effect, consider the following two True statements:

3. A robin is a bird.
4. A robin is an animal.

Clearly the predicate of (4) designates a larger category than that of (3), and the general finding is that True RT increases with category size (e.g., Collins & Quillian, 1969; Meyer, 1970). The question is, how can the Feature Comparison model account for such a result? Our answer is that the category size effect may be nothing more than another illustration of the beneficial effect of semantic relatedness on True RT. That is, for the statements typically used in experiments on category size, there appears to be a confounding of size and relatedness—the subject and predicate nouns may have been more semantically related in statements involving smaller than larger categories. Hence the faster responses to smaller categories are really due to relatedness rather than size *per se*. As support for this argument, Rips *et al.* (1973) and Smith *et al.* (1974) showed that a category size effect obtained only when the subject noun was judged to be more related to the smaller than to the larger predicate category. Indeed in these studies, the category size effect actually reversed (i.e., larger categories were responded to faster than smaller ones) when the subject noun was judged to be more related to the larger predicate category. This latter finding is to be expected if relatedness is the crucial factor in these experiments.[3]

D. CHARACTERISTIC FEATURES AND THE REPRESENTATION OF CONCEPTS

The above description illustrates our model's ability to handle sentence verification results, but it does not indicate many of the ramifications of our proposed distinction between defining and characteristic features. Here we explore some implications of this proposal for alternative ways of representing the structure of categories and propositions.

1. Representation of Category Structure by Multidimensional Scaling

A category (e.g., *bird*) may be said to be structured when its members bear systematic relations to one another and to the category term itself. Such relations must, in our terms, be reducible to similarity of semantic features. Since the members of a given category

---

[3] We are oversimplifying here. Our model predicts some effect of category size *per se*, because as predicate category size is increased fewer features are needed in its representation. This means that the duration of the second stage should decrease. But it appears that this effect of size is generally overwhelmed by the effect of relatedness when the two factors are in opposition (see Smith *et al.*, 1974).

should differ more on the characteristic than the defining features of that category, a primary determinant of categorical structure should be the similarity of characteristic features. So if one could make manifest the structure of a category, then the relation between any pair of category members should be well described by their similarity with respect to certain characteristic features of the category term.

To depict the structure of the categories corresponding to birds and mammals, we (Rips *et al.,* 1973) have employed a multidimensional scaling procedure developed by Carroll and Chang (1970). This scaling procedure—referred to as INDSCAL—takes as input the semantic relatedness ratings of all possible pairings of the relevant items, and yields as output a Euclidean solution in n dimensions where the orientation of these dimensions is fixed by the scaling procedure itself. Some of our earlier results are shown in Figs. 2a and b. These results suggest that the structure of each of the two categories can be represented by two dimensions. In both cases, the dimension spanning the horizontal axis appears to represent a size continuum and the vertical axis seems to order the items in terms of their predatory relations (with predators at the bottom and farm animals at the top). Assuming that size and predacity are characteristic features for both birds and mammals, the solutions in Fig. 2 indicate that, as claimed, the relation between any two category

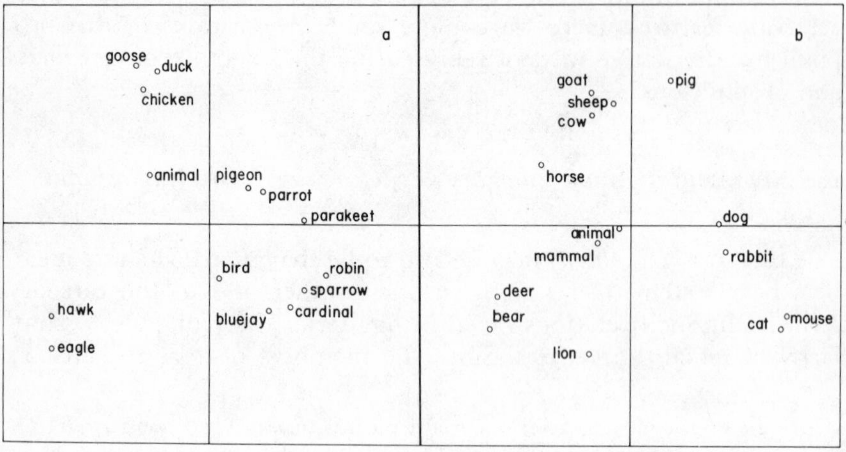

Fig. 2.   Multidimensional scaling solutions for birds, Panel a, and mammals, Panel b. (After Rips *et al.,* 1973, Experiment II.)

members can be described by their similarity with respect to certain characteristic features of the category term.

The obvious question is whether the structures in Fig. 2 really tell us anything new, for we have already assumed that category members are related to one another mainly in terms of the characteristic features of the category term. We suggest that Fig. 2 does indeed offer new insights, one methodological and the other substantive. First, consider the methodological point. It may be that for any pair of items from the same category, the interitem Euclidean distance given by the multidimensional solution provides a less noisy measure of the semantic relatedness of that pair than does the rated relatedness. Rips *et al.* (1973) went part of the way in demonstrating this when they found that Euclidean distances surpassed the ratings in predicting performance in certain semantic memory tasks. And the next section of this paper contains further support for the methodological importance of scaling analyses.

The substantive contribution of the solutions in Fig. 2 is that they offer a method for recovering the characteristic features of the category term. Specifically, in interpreting the dimensions to be size and predacity, we are suggesting that size and predacity may be characteristic features of the relevant animal concepts. An unpublished scaling study by Shoben supports this interpretation. The purpose of this experiment was to demonstrate that the structure of Fig. 2 was indeed due to variations of size and predacity, and not to variations of other features. On each trial a subject rated the similarity of a pair of birds with respect to a single feature. The rated pairs were all possible pairings of the terms in Fig. 2a and the single features to be judged included size, predacity, behavior, legs, wings, shape, beak, color, number of colors, and frequency (*i.e.*, how often one sees them). A total of 50 subjects participated, and, in accordance with a latin square design, each subject gave ratings for three of the above single features. Each feature thus produced a similarity matrix for the bird instances, and using our original solution (Fig. 2a) as a target configuration, we scaled each of our single-feature matrices to determine how much each of them resembled the target. If our original interpretation of the axes of Fig. 2a is valid, then the matrices associated with the features of size and predacity should most resemble the appropriate dimensions of the target configuration, while the matrices associated with other features should not necessarily be tied to one of the two dimensions in the target.

To execute this analysis we again used INDSCAL. When employed in this fashion, INDSCAL yields as output for each single-feature matrix its correlation with each dimension of the target configuration, as well as the total variance of the target configuration accounted for by the single feature. Our results showed that all of our single-feature matrices correlated positively with the target configuration. With two important exceptions, all of the single features correlated about equally with the size and predacity axes of the target. The two exceptions were, happily, size and predacity. The size feature correlated highly (.91) with the size axis of the target, minimally with the predacity axis (.15), and accounted for 86.4% of the variance in the target configuration. Similarly, the predacity feature correlated highly (.74) with the predacity axis of the target, less with the size axis (.34), and accounted for 68.3% of the variance in the target. These results are thus completely in line with our initial interpretation of the structure of Fig. 2a.

2. Representation of Propositions by Fuzzy Logic

Our distinction between defining and characteristic features, in conjunction with our assumption that characteristic features play a role in semantic categorization, indicates that category membership is a matter of degree rather than an all-or-none affair. This has implications for the type of logic needed to represent natural language. Specifically, the standard two-value logic of Propositional and Predicate Calculus cannot capture the fuzziness of natural language, and a multivalued system is needed instead. Such multivalued systems have been available for awhile (see, e.g., Rosser & Turquette, 1952), and recently Zadeh (1965) has developed a multivalued "fuzzy" logic that promises to be particularly useful for psychological representations.

In Zadeh's fuzzy logic a proposition can be assigned as a truth value (or degree of truth) any real number in the interval from 0 to 1. As examples, the proposition *A robin is a bird* might be assigned the value .9, *A chicken is a bird*, .7, *A bat is a bird*, .3, and *A car is a bird*, .1. This way of describing propositions is consistent with the previously discussed semantic relatedness effects in sentence verification. The typicality effect may be described as showing that the time needed to make a True decision decreases as the truth value of the sentence increases, e.g., True RT is faster for the *robin-bird* than the *chicken-bird* pair. It is also possible to accommodate the False RT results in a similar fashion. For in Zadeh's fuzzy logic, the degree of falsehood of a proposition is simply 1.0 minus the truth value of that proposition. Hence, the degree of falsehood of the sample *bat-bird* and *car-bird* propositions given above would be .7 and .9, respectively. And it seems natural to expect that the time needed to falsify a sentence decreases as the falsehood of the sentence increases. This would explain why False RT increases with semantic relatedness, since lower relatedness means higher degrees of false-hood. These relations between fuzzy truth value on the one hand and verification RTs on the other, have their correspondences in the processing model of Fig. 1 where, for a given proposition, the expected value of x may be directly proportional to truth value. That is, the fuzziness of natural language propositions is reflected in the first stage of the Feature Comparison model. We note that while the second stage of this model, as currently stated, contains no "fuzzi-ness," this may be an oversimplification of natural language proc-essing.

III.   Same-Different Decisions

While the Feature Comparison model was designed to deal with explicit subset statements of the form *A robin is a bird,* it can easily be extended to cover the results obtained in a Same-Different para-digm. In this task, a subject is presented with two test nouns simul-taneously and is required to decide if they both belong to the same prespecified category (a Same response), or not (a Different re-sponse). As an example, Rips *et al.* (1973) specified *bird* as the target category and then presented pairs like *eagle-hawk* (a Same pair) and *eagle-lion* (a Different pair).

A.   Structural and Processing Assumptions

There are several ways in which the Feature Comparison model can be extended to account for the results from the Same-Different task, and the treatment most consistent with empirical findings is shown in Fig. 3. The basic idea behind this extended model is that, in evaluating a Same-Different test pair the subject actually verifies two subset statements. Using the above example, where the test pair is *eagle-hawk* and the target category is *bird,* the subject would first confirm the implicit proposition *An eagle is a bird* and then verify *A hawk is a bird.* A Same response is made if both implicit proposi-tions are confirmed while a Different response is executed whenever one of the implicit propositions is disconfirmed. Thus a Same-Differ-

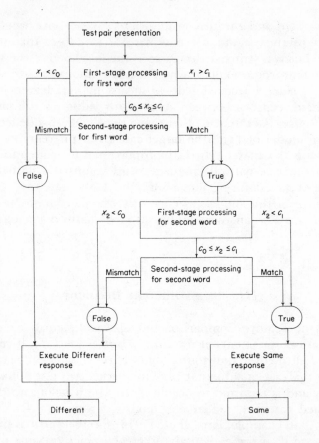

Fig. 3. An extended Feature Comparison model for Same-Different decisions.

ent task is merely a compounding of the simple verification task we have been considering so far.

The predictions from this extended model are straightforward in the case of Same RTs. Since a correct Same response indicates that each test word has been verified as an instance of the specified category, we would expect Same RT to decrease with the relatedness of each test word to the category. For Different RT, the predictions are a bit more complicated. To illustrate, consider a case where again the target category is *bird* and the test words are *eagle* and *lion*. It is now essential to distinguish between the order of processing of the test words, for two possible Different pairs may be formed from the sample pair, one in which the first word mismatches the category (*lion-eagle*) and the other in which the second word provides the mismatch (*eagle-lion*). We deal only with the latter case here, as that is the only case for which relevant data are available. For the *eagle-lion* case, the subject presumably first confirms the implicit proposition *An eagle is a bird,* and then disconfirms the proposition *A lion is a bird.* From the Feature Comparison model, we know that confirmation time decreases with relatedness while disconfirmation time increases with relatedness. It therefore follows directly from the extended model that, vis-à-vis the target category, Different RT should decrease with the relatedness of the first item (the confirmed proposition) but increase with the relatedness of the second item (the disconfirmed proposition).

B. Applications of the Model

Consider first the results for Same RT. Using bird as the specified category, Rips *et al.* (1973) found that, as predicted, Same RT decreased with the rated relatedness of each test word to bird. When mammal was the target category, however, the expected effects were not significant. But this apparent failure appears to be chiefly due to the use of ratings. For when Euclidean distance was used as a measure of semantic relatedness, the predictions for the mammal category also received some support. Further, in an unpublished study that will be described more fully below, Shoben (1973) used Euclidean distance as a measure of relatedness and found that Same RT decreased with the relatedness of both instances for both bird and mammal categories.

Turning now to Different RT, the relevant predictions have been tested by Shoben (1973). The Same-Different task used by Shoben differs from the paradigm discussed previously, in that on each trial of Shoben's task there were four target categories (birds, mammals, fruits, and vegetables) rather than one. Shoben's task is identical to one used by Schaeffer and Wallace (1970), and here a subject responds *Same* if the test words both belong to any one of the prespecified categories, and *Different,* otherwise. Our extended Feature Comparison model is directly applicable to this task, though the confirmation of the first proposition might include a testing of the first instance against all four categories. To illustrate, when the test pair *eagle-lion* is presented, a subject would presumably first compare *eagle* to the four target categories either sequentially or simultaneously; then, having confirmed that *An eagle is a bird,* the subject would disconfirm that *A lion is a bird.* Since a major determinant of the speed of the confirmation step is the semantic relatedness between the test word and its confirmed category, the predictions stated above will hold; i.e., Different RT should decrease with the relatedness of the confirmed proposition, but increase with the relatedness of the disconfirmed proposition.

In Shoben's experiment, one test word was presented above the other and the 12 subjects were instructed to process the top word first. About 60% of the test pairs required a Different response, and the majority of these involved items from related categories (birds and mammals or fruits and vegetables). It is the pairs generated from such related categories that we are concerned with, and in particular those that involve a bird and a mammal instance. For such pairs, the relevant indices of semantic relatedness (i.e., the relatedness between the first test word and its confirmed category and the relatedness between the second test word and its disconfirmed category) were measured by Euclidean distances in a solution that scaled all bird and mammal instances together. Shoben's results for Different RT confirmed both predictions of interest: Different RT decreased with the relatedness of the confirmed proposition but increased with the relatedness of the disconfirmed one. This constitutes rather striking evidence for our extended model when one notes that these differential effects of relatedness were obtained within a single response class. It is also worth noting that the second of Shoben's predictions is supported by the results of Schaeffer and Wallace (1970). Their experiments on Different RT varied the relatedness of what we have termed the disconfirmed proposition, and showed that Different RT increased with the more related propositions.

Shoben's experiment also demonstrates a certain asymmetry in Different RTs which is consistent with the Feature Comparison model, but problematic for alternative models of semantic memory. The asymmetry can best be explained by reference to Fig. 4. The top part of this figure contains two of Shoben's Different pairs. The pairs vary only in the order of the test items, where I_1 designates the first instance processed and I_2 the second instance. The rest of the figure depicts the semantic relations, as measured by Euclidean distance, between the relevant concepts. Here the greater the distance, the less the semantic relatedness. For the *goat-goose* pair it is assumed that the subject first confirms the proposition *A goat is a mammal* and then disconfirms *A goose is a mammal,* and so the relevant factors include the semantic relatedness of the confirmed (*goat-mammal*) and the disconfirmed (*goose-mammal*) propositions. For the other pair, *goose-goat,* the subject presumably confirms *A goose is a bird*

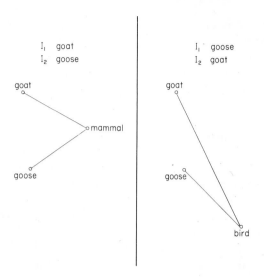

Fig. 4. An illustration of the asymmetry effect in Different decisions. (After Shoben, 1973.)

and then disconfirms *A goat is a bird,* and the relevant factors include the relatedness of the confirmed (*goose-bird*) and disconfirmed (*goat-bird*) propositions. But as Fig. 4 indicates, these pairs are asymmetric: while the relatedness of the confirmed propositions are roughly equal for the two pairs, the relatedness of the disconfirmed proposition is less in the second pair (*goose-goat*). Since the time to disconfirm a proposition decreases as relatedness decreases, it follows that the second pair should be responded to faster than the first. Selecting for study those Different pairs that had this form, Shoben tested and confirmed this predicted asymmetry. Note that this result rules out an interpretation of Same-Different relatedness effects based solely on the encodability or comprehensibility of the test words, for we have just demonstrated a relatedness effect where the identical words are used in the two pairs of interest.

While consistent with the extended Feature Comparison model, Shoben's asymmetry result is troublesome for some alternative hypotheses about semantic memory. First, it is incompatible with a theory proposed by Schaeffer and Wallace (1970) to account for Same-Different decisions. Their theory assumes, in part, that a subject reaches his decision by comparing the feature sets of the two test words in a pair. Such a symmetric theory clearly predicts that the order of the test words should not matter, but it does matter in

Shoben's experiment. Second, the asymmetry result causes problems for models in which semantic knowledge is represented in a network based on hierarchically ordered subset-superset relations (e.g., Collins & Quillian, 1969, 1972). To see this, consider Fig. 4 again. If, in the underlying semantic network, the hierarchical distance between *goat* and *mammal* is the same as that between *goose* and *bird* (a reasonable assumption since both relations involve direct superordination), then it is unclear why there should be any difference between the two pairs given in Fig. 4. For a network modeler to insure that the *goat-goose* pair takes longer, he must assume that the hierarchical distance between *goat* and *mammal* is greater than that between *goose* and *bird*. But this assumption leads to the prediction that, other things being equal, pairs involving the implicit propositions *A goat is a mammal* should be responded to slower than those involving *A goose is a bird,* and this prediction is disconfirmed in Shoben's data. In short, the asymmetry exemplified in Fig. 4 reflects the fact that a goat is less of a bird than a goose is a mammal. This is a very fuzzy fact indeed, perhaps too fuzzy for the strict confines of hierarchical networks. But we hasten to add that, if the assumptions of a network model are relaxed so that strict hierarchical organization is not required and/or pathways between properties are permitted, then such a model may well be made consistent with the asymmetry in question.

IV. Property Statements

Thus far we have considered only propositions of the form *S is a P* that assert simple category relations, like *A robin is a bird*. We now wish to extend our treatment to include other statement types, especially those which have played some role in previous studies of semantic memory. The latter sentences have been termed property statements by Collins and Quillian (1969). As we shall soon see, "property statement" is but a cover term for a variety of propositions with quite different semantic structures.

A. STRUCTURAL AND PROCESSING ASSUMPTIONS

We will consider three different types of property statements, where their forms may be designated as *S has P* (e.g., *An ostrich has a beak*), *S is* P_A (e.g., *An ostrich is brown*), and *S is* P_R (e.g., *An ostrich is large*). Here, *S* and *P* again denote subject and predicate nouns, respectively, while P_A and P_R designate two types of adjectives. The latter types are absolute adjectives (P_A), like *brown* and *square,* and relative adjectives (P_R) like *large* and *tall.* One way to express the distinction here is to observe that absolute adjectives denote the same property regardless of the noun they modify, while relative adjectives denote somewhat different properties in the context of different nouns (see Martin, 1969). Thus the meaning of *brown* in *brown ostrich* and *brown building* is more similar than the meaning of *large* in *large ostrich* and *large building.* While this difference in denotative specificity is probably a continuous one, we will simplify matters here by treating the distinction as a dichotomy.

Let us start with absolute adjectives, that is, with statements of the form S *is* P_A. Such property sentences are similar to the category statements (S *is a* P) we have considered earlier. This similarity is particularly noticeable from a set-theoretic perspective. For an S *is a* P proposition is true if and only if the set denoted by S is a subset of the set designated by P, and similarly, an S *is* P_A proposition is true if and only if S is a subset of P_A things. For example, *An ostrich is a bird* is true if ostriches are a subset of birds, and *An ostrich is brown* is true if ostriches are a subset of brown things. This similarity suggests that S *is* P_A statements can be treated by the Feature Comparison model in the same way as S *is a* P statements. Thus, for an absolute adjective like *brown,* we have a semantic feature list containing both defining features and characteristic ones (since brown things may have other incidental properties), and this property feature list may be compared to the feature list of the subject noun in the usual manner. Specifically, in the first stage the defining and characteristic features of the property would be compared to the features of the subject noun, while the second stage (when executed) would isolate the defining features of the predicate and determine whether they match the defining features of the subject. Again, we are interested in the effects of semantic relatedness, and again related True statements and unrelated False statements may be processed solely by the first stage because of very extensive or very minimal feature overlap. This leads to the predictions that when verifying S *is* P_A statements, semantic relatedness decreases True RT but increases False RT.[4]

---

[4] A recent study by Glass, Holyoak, and O'Dell (1974) suggests another means by which relatedness may affect the time to verify property statements that use the *is* construction. This proposal, when couched in our terminology, assumes that the second stage is a self-terminating process, and that the features of a related property may be found earlier than the features of an unrelated property, perhaps because the former are more defining.

Consider now S is P_R statements (e.g., *An ostrich is large,* considered in the generic sense that every ostrich is large). These statements containing relative adjectives are unlike those we have dealt with until now, which can be seen by noting the set-theoretic characteristics of relative adjective constructions. Unlike previous cases, an S is P_R statement is not true if and only if S is a subset of P_R things, since how can one determine if ostriches are a subset of large things? Rather, *An ostrich is large* may be true if and only if ostriches are a subset of large birds. Generally, a statement S is P_R will be true if S is a member of that subset of its immediate superordinate determined by P_R (Bierwisch, 1971). Thus to handle property statements containing relative adjectives, we must consider a new theoretical procedure.

One possible procedure for verifying S is P_R statements is as follows. In the first step, one retrieves the feature sets for both S and its immediate superordinate concept, S'. Since only S is presented in the statement, we need to specify a mechanism that will derive S' from S. This may be accomplished by dropping the least important defining features of S, and finding a new concept that best matches the reduced feature set. This new concept will be S'. For example, when the least important defining features of *ostrich* (S) are removed, the remaining defining features should be similar to those that define *bird* (S'). In the second step of this verification procedure, one compares the values which S and S' have on the dimension denoted by P_R. This comparison will determine whether the difference between these two values indicates a True or a False decision. To illustrate the entire procedure, given *An ostrich is large,* one would retrieve the features of *ostrich* and *bird* and ascertain whether the value of *ostrich* on the size dimension is greater than that of *bird* (leading to a True decision), or not (a False decision). We note that, while this procedure seems capable of determining correct responses for many S is P_R statements, the procedure is probably oversimplified. For in some situations, one might compare the subject noun to a concept other than its immediate superordinate. For example, if animals in general were the topic of conversation, the statement *An ostrich is large* might lead to a comparison of *ostrich* and *animal* on the size dimension. There may well be other determinants of what exact concept is compared to the subject noun, but any attempt to deal with these added complexities would take us too far afield.

The above processing procedure differs from the Feature Comparison model in several respects. A crucial difference is that the above procedure does not involve a direct comparison of the overall similarity between the features of the subject noun and the predicate adjective. Since such a comparison process has thus far been the basis for predicting semantic relatedness effects, it is possible that semantic memory tasks using property statements with relative adjectives may produce different results than those tasks using absolute adjectives. We know of no relevant data on this point. But, our suspicion is that S is P_R statements provide another basis for making differential predictions about RTs in a verification task. Following the lead of Clark, Carpenter, and Just (1973), we note that some relative adjectives seem to be more defining of certain concepts than others, and that statements containing more defining adjectives can be verified faster than those containing less defining ones. Thus height may be a more defining feature of *ostrich* than is width. And statements asserting height relations with *ostrich* as subject may be judged as more semantically related, and be verified faster, than comparable statements involving width. This is because the more defining features may be accessed faster than less defining ones in the feature list of the subject noun. (Note the similarity of this suggestion to that given for absolute adjectives in footnote 4.) To the extent that this proposal has merit, one should obtain an effect that looks like the usual relatedness effect on True RT, though in this case the effect would be mediated by a different mechanism than that usually responsible.[5]

We turn now to property statements of the form S has P (e.g., *An ostrich has a beak*). Here, we face new problems regarding the best way to represent the proposition of interest. From the set-theoretic perspective, we note that S has P statements of this form do not assert that S is a subset of P, but rather that S is a subset of those things that have P as a part. For example, *An ostrich has a beak* is true if and only if ostriches are a subset of those things that have beaks as parts. The problem posed by such statements is how to supply a

---

[5] We note that it is possible to develop alternative procedures for verifying S is P_R statements. For example, rather than assuming that the superordinate concept *bird* must be retrieved to evaluate *An ostrich is large*, one could assume that the size feature of *ostrich* indicates its value with respect to the superordinate. Given this type of representation, one can access the information needed for verification directly from the stated concept, though new processes must be introduced to handle cases where the subject noun is compared to a concept other than its superordinate. The main reason we did not develop this hypothesis in the text is simply that there are no relevant data on relative adjectives which would enable us to distinguish between the various proposals.

suitable representation for the verb *has*. A plausible solution is to assume that verbs are also represented in terms of semantic features. But now we must contend with the perhaps even more difficult problem of how the complex predicate *has P* (e.g., *has a beak*) can be composed from the features of *has* and those of the property noun. The type of theoretical device needed here is one that combines the two relevant sets of features in such a way that the complex predicate is itself represented in an appropriate way.

To gain some footing on these problems, let us first assume that, in the statements of interest, the verb *has* can be represented by a single feature that designates inalienable possession, or roughly the "has-as-a-part" relation. We then assume that this feature is prefixed to the entire list of defining and characteristic features that represent the property noun (e.g., *beak*). The resulting compound feature-list represents the complex predicate *has P* (e.g., *has a beak*). This compound list is such that the features designating *P* compose an integral set, and it is this entire set that is indexed by the feature denoting *has*. Finally, we assume that the features of a subject noun may contain some indication of whether they are "has-as-a-part" features, i.e., some of the features of a subject noun may be compound feature lists like the ones just described. Given these representational assumptions, it is now possible to apply the Feature Comparison model directly to *S has P* statements. In the first stage, the compound feature list of the entire predicate would be compared to the list of subject features, while the second stage would consider only the defining features of the predicate's feature set and determine whether they match the comparable features of the subject. So once more we would expect related True and unrelated False statements to be verified rapidly, since they often require only first-stage processing.

To summarize, we have argued that two types of property statements (S is P_A and S has P) are compatible with the Feature Comparison model and its predictions that semantic relatedness decreases True RT and increases False RT. In contrast, S is P_R statements require a different processing routine though they may show some similar effects. Thus if all three of these statement types are indiscriminately mixed together, as they have been in semantic memory research, then the best prediction is simply that property statements will show the usual semantic relatedness effects. And it is this simple prediction that we will explore in the following. However, the theoretical descriptions given above suggest the need for future research to consider the different types of property statements in detail. There is a limit to what can be learned from analyses that treat all property statements as if they had the same semantic structure.

B. APPLICATIONS OF THE MODEL

1. Basic Findings

Perhaps the clearest test of the relatedness predictions is contained in a recent study we conducted (with Keith Wescourt). In this experiment, 12 subjects verified 60 statements of the *S has P* form, where half the statements were True and half False, and within each response class, half had been independently judged to be related and the remainder had been judged as unrelated. Sample True statements include *Lions have manes* (related) and *Lions have eyes* (unrelated), while sample False statements are *Lions have stripes* (related) and *Lions have dials* (unrelated). The results were entirely as expected. True RT was some 200 msec faster for related than unrelated statements, and False RT was about 200 msec slower for related than unrelated statements.

The same effects of relatedness are quite evident in prior studies of property verification (Kintsch, Crothers, & Berman, 1971; Kosslyn & Nelson, 1973). In the Kintsch *et al.* study, subjects responded *True* to semantically acceptable statements, and *False* otherwise. Acceptable statements were either related, like *Water is wet,* or unrelated like *Water is frozen.* Similarly, False statements were either related, e.g., *A shark is meek,* or unrelated, e.g., *A shark is vacant.* Again the results showed that related True statements were responded to faster than unrelated ones, while related False statements were slower than their unrelated counterparts.

2. Alternatives to Semantic Relatedness

While these findings make the case for the importance of semantic relatedness, there are other proposed determinants of property statement verification. Here we will consider three such proposals, and in each case we will argue that semantic relatedness may really be the crucial factor.

a. Imagery. Jorgensen and Kintsch (1973) have suggested that while some sentences are verified by a semantic system, others are evaluated by imagery processes. In an attempt to document this contention, Jorgensen and Kintsch showed that, for both True and

False sentences of the form *S has P* or *S verb P,* statements rated high in imagery value were verified faster than those rated low in imagery. The obvious question is: Is this imagery manipulation confounded with semantic relatedness? Holyoak (1974) has recently provided an affirmative answer. Holyoak had the Jorgensen and Kintsch sentences rated for subject-property semantic relatedness, and found that the True high-imagery statements were more related than their low-imagery counterparts, while False high-imagery statements were less related than their low-imagery equivalents. This means that the Jorgensen and Kintsch result may reflect nothing more than the familiar differential effect of relatedness on True and False judgments.

We caution the reader that the above should not be taken as an argument against any role of imaginal processes in the verification of semantic propositions. There may well be such a role (see Kosslyn & Nelson, 1973, for some suggestive evidence), but no unambiguous argument in its favor has, to our knowledge, yet been published.

b. Property Generality. Perhaps the best-known work on the verification of property statements is that introduced by Collins and Quillian (1969). In their model, nouns are represented as nodes in a hierarchically organized semantic network. Properties are stored at the highest (most general) node in the hierarchy to which the property truly applies. To illustrate, consider statements (5) and (6).

5. A bird has wings.
6. A bird has a heart.

Wings would be stored directly with *bird,* but *heart,* a more general property, would be stored only with a higher level superordinate like *animal.* This implicates property generality as a determinant of verification RT. That is, for True property statements containing a fixed subject noun [e.g., statements (5) and (6)], RT should be longer for the more general properties since these properties cannot be directly retrieved from the stated noun.

This predicted effect was supported in the experiments of Collins and Quillian (1969). But it was soon pointed out (Conrad, 1972; Smith, Haviland, Buckley, & Sack, 1972) that the Collins and Quillian variation in property generality was confounded with other aspects of noun-property pairs. While these critics focused on co-occurrence frequency, from the present point of view the critical confounding is between property generality and semantic relatedness. Clearly the noun and property in statement (5) appear to be more related than their counterparts in (6), and this could account for why the former statement was verified faster. This is not to say that there is a perfect correlation between property generality and semantic relatedness, but rather that these two factors were confounded in the statements actually used by Collins and Quillian. Indeed, when Conrad (1972) used a wider variety of property statements, sampling them so that factors like relatedness were taken into account, she failed to find any substantial RT increase with property generality.[6]

    c. Co-occurrence Frequency. As noted above, several authors have suggested that the critical factor in the verification of property statements is the frequency with which the subject and property nouns co-occur in natural language. Conrad (1972) has provided the best-known evidence for this frequency hypothesis. In her experiment, she first had one group of subjects produce properties for a given set of nouns, and assumed that the resulting production frequencies provided measures of the co-occurrence frequencies of the noun-property pairs. Conrad then presented the relevant noun-property pairings to another group of subjects for verification, and found that True RT decreased with production frequency.

    While Conrad's result is quite straightforward, we suggest that production frequency is partially determined by semantic relatedness. This is supported by the fact that production frequencies and ratings of semantic relatedness for the same set of items are highly correlated (Rips *et al.*, 1973). If Conrad's frequency measure did reflect relatedness, then her results merely reaffirm our claim that sentence confirmation time decreases with the relatedness of the constituent concepts.

    Now it is one thing to dismiss the somewhat exotic effects of imagery and property generality, but it is another to argue against the time-honored frequency variable. Advocates of frequency (e.g., Anderson & Bower, 1973) would propose that relatedness ratings of any sort merely reflect co-occurrence, and that it is for this reason that relatedness and production frequency are so highly correlated. Such advocates might further attempt to bolster their position by showing that production frequencies, or other ratings, accurately reflect co-occurrence frequencies tabulated from a representative sample of printed English, although to our knowledge, no such co-occurrence count has ever been performed. But our rejoinders to such argu-

---

[6] In an unpublished study by Kosslyn and Nelson, semantic relatedness and property generality were varied orthogonally, and True RT actually decreased with generality. This effect is consistent with the Feature Comparison model. When the confounding with relatedness is removed, more general properties should contain fewer semantic features, and this means that the duration of the second stage will be briefer.

ments, including even a co-occurrence count, would be that semantic relatedness may be the more fundamental factor in that it may determine why certain noun-property pairs are used more frequently than others. That is, while many psychologists are satisfied with any explanation that ultimately reduces to co-occurrence frequency— in part, a carryover from the halcyon days of general behavior theory —we are here suggesting that certain frequency variations may themselves be reducible to semantic factors. A similar position has been advocated previously by Clark (1970) in his analysis of free association data, and by Klatzky, Clark, and Macken (1973) in their study of marked and unmarked adjectives.

Three phenomena are relevant to this frequency versus semantics issue. First, the scaling configurations presented in Fig. 2 are readily interpretable in terms of variations among characteristic features, but it is unclear how to interpret the configurations with reference to co-occurrence frequencies. The second phenomenon of interest is Lakoff's (1972) analysis of hedges, and this requires a bit of exposition. Hedges (e.g., *a true, technically speaking*) are modifiers which qualify predicates, and a particular hedge can only be used with certain subject-predicate pairings. For example, the statements *A robin is a true bird* and *Technically speaking, a chicken is a bird* are acceptable, but recombining either of these subject-predicate pairings with the other hedge results in a less acceptable statement. Lakoff explains this aspect of hedges in terms of defining and characteristic features. To illustrate Lakoff's argument, some hedges are used when the subject and predicate nouns share both defining and characteristic features (e.g., *A robin is a true bird*), others are employed when only the defining features are shared (e.g., *Technically speaking, a chicken is a bird*), and still others are used when only characteristic features are shared (e.g., *A decoy is a fake duck*). Now the point of all this for our present purposes is simply that one would be hard pressed to come up with an account of hedges that dealt only with co-occurrence frequency, in contrast to Lakoff's semantic account which utilizes the defining versus characteristic feature distinction. The third matter of concern to the frequency versus semantics issue is the finding that False RT increases with semantic relatedness. While we have explained this result in terms of shared semantic features, a frequency-oriented explanation would presumably argue that False RT increases with the co-occurrence frequency of the subject-predicate pair. However, the latter argument is problematic. For it is possible that the co-occurrence frequencies of even the more related subject-predicate pairings used in semantic memory experiments are in the neighborhood of zero, and this precludes the variation in frequency needed to explain the variation in False RTs. For example, the False statements *Lions have stripes* and *A shark is meek* have been considered to be highly related, but for both cases it is doubtful that any subjects had recently experienced a co-occurrence of the subject and predicate terms. Thus the three phenomena we have described all suggest the primacy of a semantic-based explanation over one derived from frequency considerations.

In a recent experiment, Anderson and McGaw (1973) have obtained evidence which supports our semantic position. In this experiment, subjects learned sentences, each of which contained a category name (e.g., *animal*). In recalling the sentences, subjects were cued with one of two instances drawn from that category. These instances (e.g., *wolf* and *squirrel*) were equated for production frequency; however, one of the instances (*wolf*) was closely related to a high production frequency item (*dog*), while the second instance (*squirrel*) was not related in this way. Results showed that the more related item consistently provided the better cue for recall. While the authors argue this effect as support for an imagery interpretation, it is easily explained on the basis of shared semantic features between category and instance. Most important, this experiment provides evidence of semantic relatedness, even when production frequency is controlled.

V. Quantified Statements

We turn now to the processing of explicitly quantified statements. In discussing such statements we return to the simple subset statements we treated in Section II. There we proposed our basic Feature Comparison model for sentences of the form *A robin is a bird*. We now wish to argue that this model is sufficient to account for the processing of universally quantified statements, like *All robins are birds,* while the processing of other quantifiers (e.g., *many, some*) can best be accounted for by adding some processing assumptions to the basic model. To motivate these arguments, it is helpful to consider first an alternative theoretical approach to quantification, called the Exemplar model.

A. THE EXEMPLAR MODEL

According to this model, one verifies a statement like *All robins are birds* by checking whether each robin exemplar stored in memory is also a stored bird exemplar. If this stipulation is met, then one can respond *True;* otherwise one can respond *False.* To make this model consistent with our emphasis on features, we could suppose that each exemplar is represented by a set of defining and characteristic features. It seems clear that we can find specific features (or conjunctions of features) which will allow us to describe any individual uniquely, be he real like Richard Nixon or fictitious like Mack the Knife. It should be noted, however, that one will generally have to rely on episodic rather than semantic memory to determine whether or not an individual exists as the referent of a particular description.

But although any real or imaginary individual can be represented by means of features, limitations of our experience are such that only a few exemplars of any given category are so represented. That is, most natural categories are open sets (Carbonell & Collins, 1973) in the sense that their exemplars cannot be enumerated in memory. This places bounds on the manner in which we can process quantified statements. To verify that *All robins are birds,* one cannot check all possible robin exemplars, since one knows only a small subset of robins. If only this small subset of exemplars is considered, it is doubtful that one could have much confidence in any of his correct True decisions, and it is likely that one would often reach incorrect True decisions about a False proposition (like, *All pilots are men*). Yet judgments about semantic propositions seem to be characterized by high confidence and accuracy. These considerations argue strongly against the plausibility of an Exemplar model for the verification of universally quantified semantic propositions, and we note that Meyer (1970) has earlier provided experimental evidence inconsistent with this model. Thus to understand quantified semantic propositions, we need processing routines that do not depend upon the examination of any given instance, but rather operate as if such sentences were in a class of lawlike statements such as *Water boils at 212°F* (see Goodman, 1955, and p. 34 below). The desired processing routines can best be developed within the context of the Feature Comparison model.

B. STRUCTURAL AND PROCESSING ASSUMPTIONS

1. *Universal Quantification*

We are interested in the full range of quantifiers, including *all, most, many, some, a few, none.* The easiest of these for us to deal with is the universal quantifier *all,* for the Feature Comparison model is already sufficient to handle this case. In particular, the second stage of this model involves a comparison of the defining features of the predicate (e.g., *bird*) with those of the subject noun (e.g., *robin*). If these predicate features are a subset of the subject noun's defining features, then *a fortiori* all robins are birds. It should come as no surprise that the same process insures both that *All robins are birds* and that *A robin is a bird,* for the indefinite article in the latter, generic, statement is probably interpreted as *every* or as some other expression of universal quantification. Thus universal quantification can be conceptualized as a procedure which operates on sets of features stored in semantic memory.

2. *Other Quantifiers*

We wish to extend this model to deal with a wider variety of quantifiers, as in sentences (7)–(10):

7. All men are mammals.
8. Most men are bipeds.
9. Many men are workers.
10. Some / A few / Several } men are senators.

Observe that the set of quantifiers in these sentences is ordered by the size of the domain that they apply to (e.g., *all* applies to a larger domain than *most*), and, as Horn (1972) points out, this is reflected in the fact that the above quantifiers are partially ordered by the adverbial phrase *if not.* . . . To see this, note that sentences (11) and (12) are perfectly acceptable, while (13) and (14) are less so.

11. A few men, if not many, are chauvinists.
12. Many men, if not most, are generous.
13. *Many men, if not a few, are chauvinists.
14. *Most men, if not many, are generous.

In general then, the quantifier within the *if not* phrase must have a larger domain than the initial quantifier.

The above observations suggest a means by which different quantifiers may be represented in the Feature Comparison model. Basically, we propose that quantifiers with different domains specify different ranges of relevant features to be considered during the second processing stage, with quantifiers of lesser domains specifying greater ranges of relevant features. To be more explicit, first recall that we had earlier assumed that the features of nouns can be ordered along a continuum depending on how essential each feature is for the concept in question. Here, we explicitly assume that a very defining feature will tend to be possessed by all instances of a given category, while, at the other extreme, weakly characteristic features will be possessed by only some of the instances. We further assume that while the second-stage processing of a sentence like (7) considers only the most defining features of the subject noun, the comparable processing of statements like (8)–(10) allows matches to characteristic features as well. We can conceive of *most, many,* and *some* as specifying a successively larger range of relevant, second-stage, features of the subject noun. Thus quantifiers with larger domains (e.g., *all* and *most*) pick out a small range of relevant features, while quantifiers with smaller domains (*a few, several*) will specify a larger range of relevant features. If the predicate's defining features are included in this specified range, then the second stage will lead to a True decision, and otherwise, a False decision. In this way different quantifiers can be represented in the Feature Comparison model, with all quantifiers represented as processing routines.

Some further remarks should be made about the above "feature range" formulation for quantifiers. First, in the verification of a sentence such as *Some men are senators,* it may be too strong to require that the defining features of *senator* match even weakly characteristic features of *man.* In this case it may be that the second stage reaches a True decision whenever no defining feature of the predicate contradicts any defining feature of the subject noun. This is sufficient to disconfirm the False statements encountered in most of the verification tasks we have considered, and amounts to the assumption that we should take statements like *Some men are senators* to be true unless we have strong semantic evidence to the contrary. Second, our general formulation about quantifiers ignores presuppositions of existence which are conveyed by the quantifiers. This, however, is in line with the notion that semantic memory be concerned with description, and not with the question of whether the descriptions refer to real world entities. Third, other quantifiers, like *none* or *no,* can be represented as the negations of the corresponding positive quantifier (*some*). Evidence that negative quantifiers are, in fact, comprehended in terms of their positive counterparts can be found in some recent studies (e.g., Just & Carpenter, 1971).

Finally, we note that the implications of our formulation for the expected duration of the second stage will depend on the exact manner in which this stage is accomplished. To illustrate this point, consider a base proposition *Men are mammals* which is quantified by either *all* or *many.* Suppose that the second stage is a serial, self-terminating, search process, where the search always begins with the most defining feature of the subject noun and then proceeds to the next most defining element. In this case, the search will always find matching features among the subject noun's most defining entries, regardless of whether the quantifier is *all* or *many*. Hence the prediction for this case is that there should be no effect of the feature range of a quantifier on True RT. But now consider a case that is identical to the preceding, except that the search of the features of the subject noun is random rather than governed by definingness. Here, the fact that *many* results in a greater range of relevant features than *all*, might slow down search times for the *many* statement. This is because most of the matching features may be found among the more defining ones of the subject noun, and these defining features will be found sooner in the smaller search set specified by *all* than in the larger set determined by *many*. In this case, our best prediction is that True RT will be longer for *many* than *all* statements. In view of these complexities and the paucity of relevant data, our applications of the Feature Comparison model to quantification experiments will emphasize other aspects of the model. But the importance of our formulation about the feature range of quantification should not be overlooked, as this formulation provides a natural means by which the Feature Comparison model can elucidate the processing of natural language quantifiers.

C. Applications of the Model

Thus far the only published research on quantification and semantic memory is contained in an important paper by Meyer (1970). Meyer's finding of current interest is that the time needed to verify certain quantified statements increased when the quantifier was changed from *some* to *all*. In particular, both True and False RT were longer for *all* than *some* statements when either (a) the subject noun denoted a subset of the predicate (these are called subset statements and are exemplified by *Chairs are furniture*), (b) the subject noun denoted a superset of the predicate (superset statements, exemplified by *Furniture are chairs*), or (c) the subject and predicate nouns denoted partially overlapping categories (overlap statements, e.g., *Women are writers*). In contrast, there was no RT difference between the two quantifiers for statements where the subject and predicate nouns denoted disjoint categories (disjoint statements, e.g., *Birds are vehicles*).

In considering how the Feature Comparison model might explain Meyer's results, we note that there are three aspects of the model that can function as explanatory mechanisms. First, there is the factor of semantic relatedness, which governs the probability that the second stage will be executed. While we have previously used this mechanism extensively in explaining experimental results, we would not expect the relatedness of a subject-predicate pair to be in any way influenced by the quantifier it is used with. The second relevant aspect of the model concerns variations in the number of relevant features considered in the second stage, where such variations are due in part to the choice of quantifier. But, as previously noted, no precise predictions can be generated here because of the dependence of such predictions on the exact nature of the second stage. Finally, placement of the decision criteria, c_0 and c_1 (see Fig. 1), may serve as an explanatory device, and it is this device that we will use to handle Meyer's *all-some* differences.

To make this explanation clear, we first note two aspects of Meyer's experiments, one methodological and the other conceptual. The methodological point is simply that *all* and *some* statements were presented in different blocks of trials. This suggests that subjects might have used different criteria placements for the different blocks. The conceptual issue arises from the possible correlation between semantic relatedness and sentence type (subset, superset, overlap, or disjoint). Specifically, from the examples given by Meyer, it appears that relatedness was quite high for both subset and superset statements, somewhat lower for overlap statements, and lower still for disjoint statements. This means that, in the block of trials where *all* statements were presented, some of the False statements (i.e., the superset statements) were as related as the True statements (i.e., the subset statements). For this reason, the relatedness of the subject-predicate pair was not a good indication of its truth value, and consequently, second-stage processing was frequently needed on both True and False *all* statements in order to yield accurate responses. The means by which subjects could insure frequent second-stage processing were stringent decision criteria, i.e., relatively large distances between c_0 and c_1. In contrast, for the block of *some* statements, only disjoint statements are False and these are the least related. Hence the relatedness of the subject-predicate pairs offered a good indication of its truth value, so that first-stage processing would often suffice for accurate *some* decisions. Subjects could insure single-stage (only) processing by using lenient decision criteria, i.e., by making the distance between c_0 and c_1 relatively small. Thus Meyer's *all-some* results may well reflect differences in how often the second stage was needed, where such differences were mediated by criteria placements. The reason Meyer did not obtain an *all-some* difference for disjoint sentences may simply be that such statements were so unrelated that most of them required only first-stage processing regardless of criteria placement.

Though our explanation of Meyer's results seems plausible, it is also *ad hoc*. But this explanation leads to two new predictions about verifying *all* and *some* statements which Rips (1973) has tested in some unpublished experiments. The first prediction pertains to *some* statements in the Meyer paradigm. Specifically, highly related False (disjoint) statements should slow both True and False RT. The rationale for this prediction is that the use of more related Falses makes it unwise for subjects to use relatedness as an indication of the truth value of a *some* statement. Consequently, more stringent criteria will be used, leading to more second-stage processing and longer RTs for both True and False *some* statements. Rips tested this in an experiment similar to Meyer's. *All* and *some* statements were presented in separate blocks, where the *all* items included subset (True) and superset (False) statements, while the *some* items were composed of subset (True), superset (True), and disjoint (False) statements. For both types of quantifiers, half the statements were True and half False. The major variation of interest was the relatedness of the disjoint *some* statements. One group of 24 subjects received unrelated disjoint statements (e.g., *Some congressmen are cars*), while a second group of the same size received related disjoint sentences (e.g., *Some congressmen are presidents*). Most important, both groups received the identical subset and superset statements as True *some* sentences, as well as the identical *all* sentences. The results were as predicted. RTs to *some* statements were substantially slower for the subjects receiving related Falses than for those receiving unrelated Falses. This finding obtained for True RT (as well as False RT) even though the True statements were identical for both groups, which constitutes strong evidence that the effect is mediated by a change in decision criteria. Further results indicated that there was no difference between the two groups with respect to RT to *all* statements. This was expected since there is no reason for criteria change in the block of *all* trials. Lastly, for both groups, *all* statements took longer to process than *some* statements, though the *all-some* difference was, of course, greater for the subjects presented with unrelated Falses.

As noted, in both the study just described and in the Meyer experiment, *all* and *some* statements were presented in separate blocks. It was this aspect that permitted the subjects to adopt different criteria for the two types of trials, particularly when the False *some* sentences were unrelated. This line of reasoning leads to the second prediction of interest. If *all* and *some* statements are randomly intermixed over trials then subjects should not be able to adopt different criteria for the different quantifiers. This should eliminate Meyer's *all-some* difference even when the false *somes* are unrelated. Rips tested this prediction in a second experiment, where the *all* and *some* statements used in the previous study were now presented to a new group of 24 subjects in random order. As expected, the intermixing of quantifiers eliminated the *all-some* difference. Furthermore, the elimination of the *all-some* difference was entirely due to increased RTs for *some* statements, as it should be since it was these statements which could no longer benefit from lenient criteria. Taken together, Rips' two experiments provide strong support for the role of decision processes in semantics.

VI. Induction, Analogy, and Metaphor

One virtue of the semantic features approach we have adopted is that it allows us to make some contact with the neglected issues of inductive and analogical thought. Indeed, inductive and analogical thought seem quite continuous with the type of intellectual processes utilized in verifying sentences, especially in the role played by characteristic features.

A. INDUCTION

To understand the relation of induction to the preceding section, it is instructive to revive the Exemplar model for a moment. Recall that the Exemplar model runs into problems in accounting for how one verifies a statement like *All robins are birds,* for how can one confirm this generalization on the basis of the small subset of positive instances (i.e., exemplars) he has actually remembered? Now this problem is the classical one of justifying inductive inference, i.e., of justifying a categorization on the basis of partial information. For the quantified statements considered in the previous section, we offered the Feature Comparison model as a solution to this problem.

This model allows verification of such generalizations on the basis of the features of the subject and predicate terms, where the assignment of features to terms is based on the linguistic usage of the terms, rather than on the induction of these features. We note that it seems impossible to get any foothold at all on the problem of induction if linguistic rules of this type are ignored (Goodman, 1955).

But our solution has its limitations. For there are many cases where linguistic usage alone fails to provide clear-cut guides to the validity of propositions. In particular, we are concerned with semantic categorization situations where the category involved is a novel one, though based on some familiar semantic concepts. An example of this would be the category of all birds that have some special property X. Here, categorization should depend on one's previous knowledge of the familiar concept *bird* (given by linguistic knowledge), and on whatever information is provided about the exemplars of the new category. Cases like these have been extensively investigated in studies of concept attainment.

1. Concept Attainment and Related Studies

Typical studies of concept attainment require a subject to induce a category like red triangles on the basis of only a sample of the category's exemplars (Hunt, Marin, & Stone, 1966). Thus, these studies have the format of the type of induction situation we are interested in. A new concept (red triangles) is built upon older ones (red things and triangles), and a limited number of exemplars of the new category is given. But beyond this superficial similarity, there is little resemblance between natural language concepts and those employed in standard concept attainment studies (Rosch, 1974). That is, the concepts employed in the latter studies generally involve discrete values of attributes, and classification rules with clear-cut necessary and sufficient criteria. Consequently, there is no basis for any internal structure of the concept, and any one exemplar is as typical a category member as any other. In contrast, we have argued in the preceding sections that natural language concepts often involve continuous values as features (e.g., size), have fuzzy criteria for membership, are structured on the basis of characteristic features, and manifest extensive typicality differences. So we must look elsewhere for results that bear directly on natural language induction.

There are several recent studies that deal with categories which do have the earmarks of natural language concepts. For example, in recent pattern recognition experiments (Posner & Keele, 1968; Reed,

1972), a subject first learns how to classify a set of exemplar patterns into a few mutually exclusive categories, where these patterns involve variations along relatively continuous features and the classification rules are ill-defined. The subject is then tested on his ability to classify new test patterns. The results indicate that the subject uses the exemplars to form a prototype of the category (where the prototype might represent the mean values of its exemplars on each relevant attribute), and then classifies the new patterns on the basis of their overall similarity to the prototypes. These results are strikingly similar to the description of semantic categorization given by the first stage of the Feature Comparison model. There, categorizations were sometimes based on the overall similarity of an exemplar to a category prototype, where the prototype was the set of defining and characteristic features for the category term. What all of this suggests is that inductive classifications rely heavily on the overall similarity between the to-be-classified item and some representative of the category. This same suggestion has been proposed by Kahneman and Tversky (1973) for cases where individuals must produce either nominal or numerical categorizations of uncertain events. In what follows we explore the implications of this induction-by-similarity principle in tasks involving natural language concepts.

2. Structural and Processing Assumptions

Our studies of natural language induction (Rips, unpublished) employ the following task. Subjects are provided with a problem concerning a hypothetical island populated by different animals, say six species of mammals. They are then told that all members of one of these species (e.g., bears) have a certain property, and their task is to estimate for each of the other species (e.g., lions) what percentage of its members also have that property. Thus a new concept (mammals-having-the-property) is created from familiar semantic concepts, and the insufficiency of the given information demands the use of induction.

The structural and processing assumptions for this task are simple. We assume the usual semantic feature representations for the animal terms that we have previously used. With respect to processing, it is assumed that a subject makes his decision in the above task by determining the overall similarity between those items he knows to be category members (e.g., bears) and the item he has to classify (e.g., lions). That is, the greater the overall similarity of defining and characteristic features between the known exemplar and the unknown test item, the greater the percentage assigned to the test item.

3. Applications of the Model

In the first experiment, the hypothetical island was populated by pigs, lions, horses, deer, dogs, mice, bats, and chickens. The first six of these terms were chosen from the scaling solution for mammals in Fig. 2b. The two outliers, bats and chickens, were added to emphasize the range of typicality among the mammal instances. Each subject was told that all of the animals in one of these species had a new type of contagious disease, and he was then asked to estimate the percentage of animals in each of the remaining seven species that had also contracted the disease. We refer to the latter seven species as target instances, and to the species known to have the disease as the given instance. Six different groups of about forty subjects each were tested, with each group receiving a different given instance. Bats and chickens were not used as given instances, and only data from the six instances selected from the scaling solution were considered in analyzing the results.

To determine the effects of overall similarity on subjects' responses, we again used Euclidean distances from the scaling solution (Fig. 2b) as measures of similarity. The percentage assigned to a target was found to increase significantly with the similarity between the given and target instances, the correlation between similarity and assigned percentage being .55. While this result is as predicted, our analysis also indicated a second effect. The percentage assigned to a target increased with the typicality of the given instance. That is, the greater the similarity of the given instances (e.g., bear) to its superordinate (mammal), the greater the estimated percentages to all targets, with the correlation between these two variables being .43 when the effect of the similarity of target and given instance is partialed out. In contrast, the typicality of the targets had no effect on estimated percentages. Intuitively, our typicality effect means that typical instances have greater inductive power than less typical ones, for information about the former is more likely to be generalized to other instances. Thus, given a typical instance, say, horse, subjects will produce a higher estimate for an atypical target, say, mouse, than if they were given mouse and asked to estimate the number of horses with the disease.

These findings have been replicated in a second experiment, which differed from the first primarily in that the instances used were selected from the scaling solution for birds (Fig. 2a). The instances chosen were sparrows, robins, eagles, hawks, geese, and ducks. As before, the percentage assigned to a target increased with the overall similarity between the target and given instance (the correlation being .88), and further increased with the typicality of the given instance (with a partial correlation of .47). Thus, both experiments offer some support for the hypothesis that natural language induction is tied to the overall semantic similarity between the concepts involved, where such similarity is a matter of shared defining and characteristic features. Further, it appears that the similarity between the two instances must be weighted by the typicality of the given instance. This latter finding is reminiscent of the previously described results for straightforward classification judgments, and it suggests that when we combine well-established concepts to form new ones, we carry along aspects of the internal structure of the older concepts.

B. Structure of Analogy and Metaphor

We have suggested that interesting cases of induction build upon concepts already in use. Thus our experiments on induction demonstrate the influence of the semantic structure of the category bird (or mammal) on the new concept animals-having-disease. In a more obvious way, analogies, like *bear:bug::Cadillac:Volkswagen,* as well as metaphors, also involve the interaction of features from two semantic domains.

1. Structural and Processing Assumptions for Cross-Category Analogies

How then are two semantic categories (say, our standards, birds and mammals) compared in an analogy? It is helpful to treat this question in the context of the sample analogy, *mouse:bear::blue-jay:—?—,* where either *eagle* or *hawk* constitutes an acceptable answer (Rips *et al.,* 1973). We assume our usual semantic feature representation for these animal terms, and again the characteristic as well as defining features must be involved. For, although defining features must be considered in processing cross-category analogies, there is not always enough variation among these features to support such analogies. Characteristic features must therefore play a major role in analogical reasoning, just as they did in induction. For the above example, inspection of Fig. 2 indicates that the first two terms (*mouse* and *bear*) differ mainly in terms of size, and this, along with a consideration of other features, provides a basis for selecting an acceptable answer to the problem. That is, either *eagle* or *hawk* differs from *bluejay* on the features of size and predacity in the same way that *bear* differs from *mouse*. Thus, solving cross-category analogies like the one above involves comparisons of features which are common to both domains.

The comparison process used to solve such analogies has been described by Rips *et al.* (1973), where this description is based on the earlier work of Rumelhart and Abrahamson (1973). Basically, the process includes three steps. To illustrate, consider again the analogy *mouse:bear::bluejay:*—?—, and the alternative responses, *cardinal, goose, duck,* and *eagle*. First, the subject determines the differences between the first two terms in the analogy mainly with respect to characteristic features of the category term, noting both the direction and extent of the differences (e.g., *mouse* is much smaller than *bear*). Second, the subject determines the corresponding differences between the third term (*bluejay*) and each alternative. Finally, he selects that alternative whose differences from the third term most closely match the corresponding differences between the first two terms, where this matching considers both direction and extent. Notice that in this case, the subject cannot rely on the absolute value of the size or predacity of the animals, since the difference in size between a bluejay and an eagle is much less than that between a mouse and a bear. Rather, the subject must somehow normalize the differences along the characteristic feature dimensions of the category term, over the range of animals in each category; this process might use the category term (e.g., *bird*) as a focal point, and normalize differences in terms of it.

2. Applications of the Model

In a study reported in Rips *et al.* (1973), subjects solved analogies of the form $A:B::X:$—?—by selecting an answer from a set of six alternatives. Here, A and B were animal terms drawn from one of the scaling solutions in Fig. 2 (say, the mammal space), and X was an animal term drawn from the other space (birds). For each analogy, we selected the items so that the third term (e.g., *bluejay*) occupied approximately the same position as the first term (e.g., *mouse*) in their respective spaces. Given this correspondence, we expected subjects to select as an answer an item (e.g., *eagle*) that occupied roughly the same position as the second term (e.g., *bear*) in their respective spaces. For if such an answer were chosen, then the feature difference between the third term and answer would be equivalent to that between the first two terms, and this is in accord with the prediction from the three-step process described earlier. This prediction was reliably supported for 9 of the 12 analogies studied.

In an unpublished follow-up, 14 subjects were given analogies of the form $A:B::$—?—:—?—. Here, A and B were simply the first two terms from each of the 12 analogies used in the previous experiment. If A and B were mammals (birds), subjects were asked to choose two birds (mammals) from a set of six alternatives so that the resulting analogy would be valid. In this task, our expectation was that subjects would select those two terms which occupied the same regions in their space that the first two terms occupied in the other space. For this would maintain the correspondence in features required by our postulated three-step process. For example, the expected answers for *bear*:*mouse*::—?— were *eagle* and *bluejay*. In this experiment the prediction was confirmed for all analogies tested.

It is worth noting that although the approach taken here invokes the same representational assumptions we have used throughout, our processing routine for analogies is quite different from the one we used in the Feature Comparison model. But such processing differences are to be expected when one moves to markedly different tasks. That is, we consider it a reasonable goal to specify a general-purpose semantic representation, and then to attach more specific processing routines that operate on this representation. It is perhaps instructive that computer modelers of language comprehension have also had to settle for numerous processing routines operating on a common semantic structure (see, e.g., Carbonell & Collins, 1973).

3.   *Metaphor*

We know of no systematic, psychological approach to the problem of metaphor. Nor are we about to present one. Rather, we merely wish to comment here on how one might begin to view metaphors in terms of the ideas we have already presented.

A traditional view, traceable to Aristotle's *Poetics,* is that metaphor is a kind of implicit analogy. However, as Black (1954–55) and Beardsley (1958) have pointed out, such a view seems to be valid for only a restricted set of relatively tame metaphors, like *Richard is a lion.* To see the limitations of this view, consider the rather complex metaphors in (15)–(17):

15. . . . and the blessed sun himself, a fair hot wench in flame-coloured taffeta. (Shakespeare, *1 Henry IV*)

16. Where is the summer, the unimaginable Zero summer? (Eliot, *Four Quartets*)

17. You know, you haven't stopped talking since I came here. You must have been vaccinated with a phonograph needle. (Groucho Marx, *Duck Soup*)

These metaphors appear to defy analysis by simple analogy. Rather, as Black notes, there is a more radical reorganization of one semantic domain by means of another.

In a recent attempt to characterize metaphor, Bever and Rosenbaum (1970) suggested that metaphoric reorganization can take place when the hierarchical structure of one semantic domain is imposed on another. For example, in order to understand the expression *colorful idea,* one makes use of a semantic hierarchy in which a node *colorful object* is connected by the *is* relation to the nodes for *green, red, blue,* etc. This tree structure, but not the concept nodes themselves, is transferred from *colorful object* to the node for *idea.* In this way, we come to conceive of a colorful idea as one with many different qualities. But although this proposal views metaphor as structural reorganization, it appears that simple hierarchies cannot account for more than a limited set of examples, as Bever and Rosenbaum themselves note. Inspection of the metaphors in (15)–(17) illustrates the difficulties in finding such a hierarchical interpretation.

How then to characterize metaphors? Beardsley (1958) has presented a promising account of this problem which is easily translatable into our terminology of defining and characteristic features. To start, it is first necessary to distinguish the subject of the metaphor [e.g., the sun, in (15)] from the metaphorical predicates (e.g., being a wench in flame-coloured taffeta). Now, if one attributes these predicates to the subject literally, then contradictions on defining features arise. In (15), a contradiction occurs since properties of animate objects are ascribed to an inanimate one (the sun) and no sensible attribution can be made at the literal level. However, characteristic features of metaphoric predicates can emphasize, or increase the definingness of features of the subject. Thus, in (15) we temporarily increase the definingness of color and temperature, where these features are already among the features of *sun.* Alternatively, those characteristic features of the predicate which do not contradict subject features can be added to the features of the subject. In (16) for example, *zero* suggests an origin or beginning of experience, which we temporarily ascribe to our concept of a given summer. These proposals are quite similar to notions we have already encountered, and at least offer some inkling of what might be involved in understanding metaphor. But only an inkling.

VII. Summary and Conclusions

After setting the problem of semantic memory in psycholinguistic perspective, we began our account of how semantic propositions are verified. We first assumed a semantic feature representation which distinguished between defining and characteristic features. This representation was then coupled with a two-stage processing model, and we applied the resulting Feature Comparison model to the results of studies requiring the verification of simple subset statements. This model offered an explicit explanation of semantic relatedness and category size effects in this paradigm, while our assumption about characteristic features further suggested some new insights about the representation of natural language concepts and propositions. The Feature Comparison model was then extended to accommodate findings from recent Same-Different experiments. Here, the extended model proved capable of encompassing a range of semantic relatedness findings, including some newly reported effects which seem problematic for other models. We next applied the basic Feature Comparison model to the verification of simple property statements. While the representation of property information necessitated several new structural and processing considerations, the basic model again provided an explanation of many of the semantic effects on verification. Further, it suggested alternative interpretations of findings originally attributed to nonsemantic factors. We then considered the model in relation to explicitly quantified statements, and extended our processing assumptions so as to include several different natural language quantifiers. Once more the Feature Comparison model, when suitably augmented, was consistent with the existant data, including some new results which highlighted the decision component of the model. In the last section, we explored the utility of our semantic feature representation for understanding the nature of induction, analogy, and metaphor. Here, the processing routines differed from our usual two-stage model, and these new procedures offered a promising account of our experimental results on induction and analogy.

Thus, we have been able to provide a systematic account of a diverse range of semantic phenomena in terms of a fixed representational scheme and a limited set of processes that compare feature sets. But although we consider these results very promising, we note that there are several gaps. First among these is the fact that we have not offered a sufficiently detailed account of the second stage of the Feature Comparison model. This was particularly noticeable in our treatment of quantified statements (Section V), where our lack of detail about the second stage precluded us from drawing any strong predictions from our range-of-features hypothesis about quantifiers. Secondly, although we provided a detailed account of property statements containing *is* and *has* constructions (Section IV), we did not deal with those statements that involve more complex verbs. Third, our treatment of induction and analogy (Section VI) was limited to a restricted set of problems and data, while our handling of metaphor was confined to but a few remarks. Lastly, throughout this chapter we have emphasized the verification of single propositions and have not concerned ourselves with the semantic integration problems posed by multiproposition statements. While this is a formidable list of omissions, all of them seem, in principle, to be amenable to a semantic features approach. They therefore constitute topics for future work, rather than indications that our theoretical orientation is misdirected. Indeed, we consider the semantic feature direction taken here to be the most profitable one for understanding the domain called semantic memory, and for relating it to other domains of natural language processing.

REFERENCES

Anderson, J. R., & Bower, G. H. *Human associative memory.* Washington: Winston, 1973.

Anderson, R. C., & McGaw, B. On the representation of meanings of general terms. *Journal of Experimental Psychology,* 1973, **101,** 301–306.

Atkinson, R. C., & Juola, J. F. Factors influencing speed and accuracy of word recognition. In S. Kornblum (Ed.), *Attention and performance.* Vol. 4. New York: Academic Press, 1973.

Beardsley, M. C. *Aesthetics.* New York: Harcourt, 1958.

Bever, T. G., & Rosenbaum, P. S. Some lexical structures and their empirical validity. In R. A. Jacobs & P. S. Rosenbaum (Eds.), *Readings in English transformational grammar.* Waltham, Mass.: Ginn, 1970.

Bierwisch, M. On classifying semantic features. In D. D. Steinberg & L. A. Jakobovits (Eds.), *Semantics: An introductory reader in philosophy, linguistics and psychology.* London & New York: Cambridge Univ. Press, 1971.

Black, M. Metaphor. *Proceedings of the Aristotelian Society,* 1954–1955, **60,** 273–294.

Carbonell, J. R., and Collins, A. M. Natural semantics in artificial intelligence. *Proceedings of the Third International Joint Conference on Artificial Intelligence,* 1973, 344–351.

Carroll, J. D., & Chang, J. J. Analysis of individual differences in multi-dimensional scaling via an n-way generalization of "Eckart-Young" decomposition. *Psychometrika*, 1970, **36**, 283–319.

Clark, H. H. Word associations and linguistic theory. In J. Lyons (Ed.), *New horizons in linguistics*. Baltimore: Penguin Books, 1970.

Clark, H. H., Carpenter, P. A., & Just, M. A. On the meeting of semantics and perception. In W. G. Chase (Ed.), *Visual information processing*. New York: Academic Press, 1973.

Collins, A. M., & Quillian, M. R. Retrieval time from semantic memory. *Journal of Verbal Learning and Verbal Behavior*, 1969, **8**, 240–248.

Collins, A. M., & Quillian, M. R. Experiments on semantic memory and language comprehension. In L. W. Gregg (Ed.), *Cognition in learning and memory*. New York: Wiley, 1972.

Conrad, C. Cognitive economy in semantic memory. *Journal of Experimental Psychology*, 1972, **92**, 149–154.

Frege, G. On sense and reference. *Zeitschrift für Philosophie und Philosophische Kritik*, 1892, **100**, 25–50.

Glass, A. L., Holyoak, K., & O'Dell, C. Production frequency and the verification of quantified statements. *Journal of Verbal Learning and Verbal Behavior*, 1974, in press.

Goodman, N. *Fact, fiction and forecast*. (2nd ed.) New York: Bobbs-Merrill, 1955.

Holyoak, K. The role of imagery in the evaluation of sentences: Imagery or semantic factors. *Journal of Verbal Learning and Verbal Behavior*, 1974, **13**, 163–166.

Horn, L. R. On the semantic properties of logical operators in English. Unpublished doctoral dissertation, Linguistics Department, University of California at Los Angeles, 1972.

Hunt, E. B., Marin, J., & Stone, P. J. *Experiments in induction*. New York: Academic Press, 1966.

Jorgensen, C. C., & Kintsch, W. The role of imagery in the evaluation of sentences. *Cognitive Psychology*, 1973, **4**, 110–116.

Just, M. A., & Carpenter, P. A. Comprehension of negation with quantification. *Journal of Verbal Learning and Verbal Behavior*, 1971, **10**, 244–253.

Kahneman, D., & Tversky, A. On the psychology of prediction. *Psychological Review*, 1973, **80**, 237–251.

Katz, J. J., & Fodor, J. A. The structure of a semantic theory. *Language*, 1963, **39**, 170–210.

Kintsch, W., Crothers, E. J., & Berman, L. N. The effects of some semantic and syntactic properties of simple sentences upon the latencies of judgments of semantic acceptability. *Studies in mathematical learning theory and psycholinguistics*. University of Colorado, Quantitative Psychology Program, Computer Laboratory for Instruction in Psychological Research, Report No. 4, 1971.

Klatzky, R. L., Clark, E. V., & Macken, M. Asymmetries in the acquisition of polar adjectives: Linguistic or conceptual? *Journal of Experimental Child Psychology*, 1973, **16**, 32–46.

Kosslyn, S. M., & Nelson, K. E. Imagery use in the verification of sentences. Paper presented at the meetings of the American Psychological Association, Montreal, September, 1973.

Lakoff, G. Hedges: A study in meaning criteria and the logic of fuzzy concepts. *Papers from the eighth regional meeting, Chicago Linguistics Society*, 1972, 183–228.

Lewis, D. General semantics. In D. Davidson & G. Harman (Eds.), *Semantics of natural language*. Dordrecht: Reidel, 1972.

Martin, J. E. Semantic determinants of preferred adjective order. *Journal of Verbal Learning and Verbal Behavior*, 1969, **8**, 697–704.

Meyer, D. E. On the representation and retrieval of stored semantic information. *Cognitive Psychology*, 1970, **1**, 242–299.

Montague, R. The proper treatment of quantification in ordinary English. In J. Hintikka, J. Moravcsik, & P. Suppes (Eds.), *Approaches to natural language.* Dordrecht: Reidel, 1973.

Posner, M. I., & Keele, S. W. On the genesis of abstract ideas. *Journal of Experimental Psychology*, 1968, **77**, 353–363.

Quine, W. V. O. *Word and object.* Cambridge, Mass.: MIT Press, 1960.

Reed, S. K. Pattern recognition and categorization. *Cognitive Psychology*, 1972, **3**, 382–407.

Rips, L. J. Quantification and semantic memory. Unpublished manuscript, Stanford University, 1973.

Rips, L. J., Shoben, E. J., & Smith, E. E. Semantic distance and the verification of semantic relations. *Journal of Verbal Learning and Verbal Behavior*, 1973, **12**, 1–20.

Rosch, E. On the internal structure of perceptual and semantic categories. In T. E. Moore (Ed.), *Cognitive development and acquisition of language.* New York: Academic Press, 1973.

Rosch, E. Universals and cultural specifics in human categorization. In R. Breslin, W. Lonner, & S. Bochner (Eds.), *Cross-cultural perspectives on learning.* London: Sage Press, 1974, in press.

Rosser, J. B., & Turquette, A. R. *Many-valued logics.* Amsterdam: North-Holland Publ., 1952.

Rumelhart, D. E., & Abrahamson, A. A. A model for analogical reasoning. *Cognitive Psychology*, 1973, **5**, 1–28.

Schaeffer, B., & Wallace, R. The comparison of word meanings. *Journal of Experimental Psychology*, 1970, **86**, 144–152.

Shoben, E. J. The verification of semantic relations in a same-different paradigm: An asymmetry in semantic memory. Unpublished manuscript, Stanford University, 1973.

Smith, E. E., Haviland, S. E., Buckley, P. B., & Sack, M. Retrieval of artificial facts from long-term memory. *Journal of Verbal Learning and Verbal Behavior*, 1972, **11**, 583–593.

Smith, E. E., Shoben, E. J., & Rips, L. J. Structure and process in semantic memory: A featural model for semantic decisions. *Psychological Review*, 1974, **81**, 214–241.

Tulving, E. Episodic and semantic memory. In E. Tulving & W. Donaldson (Eds.), *Organization and memory.* New York: Academic Press, 1972.

Wilkins, A. T. Conjoint frequency, category size, and categorization time. *Journal of Verbal Learning and Verbal Behavior*, 1971, **10**, 382–385.

Zadeh, L. Fuzzy sets. *Information and Control*, 1965, **8**, 338–353.

WORKING MEMORY

Alan D. Baddeley[1] and Graham Hitch[1]

UNIVERSITY OF STIRLING, STIRLING, SCOTLAND

I. Introduction

Despite more than a decade of intensive research on the topic of short-term memory (STM), we still know virtually nothing about its role in normal human information processing. That is not, of course, to say that the issue has completely been neglected. The short-term store (STS)—the hypothetical memory system which is assumed to be responsible for performance in tasks involving short-term memory paradigms (Atkinson & Shiffrin, 1968)—has been assigned a crucial role in the performance of a wide range of tasks including problem solving (Hunter, 1964), language comprehension (Rumelhart, Lindsay, & Norman, 1972) and most notably, long-term learning (Atkinson & Shiffrin, 1968; Waugh & Norman, 1965). Perhaps the most cogent case for the central importance of STS in general information processing is that of Atkinson and Shiffrin (1971) who attribute to STS the role of a controlling executive system responsible for coordinating and monitoring the many and complex subroutines that are responsible for both acquiring new material and retrieving old. However, despite the frequency with which STS

[1] *Present address:* Medical Research Council, Applied Psychology Unit, 15 Chaucer Road, Cambridge, England.

47

has been assigned this role as an operational or working memory, the empirical evidence for such a view is remarkably sparse.

A number of studies have shown that the process of learning and recall does make demands on the subject's general processing capacity, as reflected by his performance on some simultaneous subsidiary task, such as card sorting (Murdock, 1965), tracking performance (Martin, 1970), or reaction time (Johnston, Griffith & Wagstaff, 1972). However, attempts to show that the limitation stems from the characteristics of the working memory system have proved less successful. Coltheart (1972) attempted to study the role of STS in concept formation by means of the acoustic similarity effect, the tendency for STM to be disrupted when the material to be remembered comprises items that are phonemically similar to each other (Baddeley, 1966b; Conrad, 1962). She contrasted the effect of acoustic similarity on concept formation with that of semantic similarity, which typically effects LTM rather than STM (Baddeley, 1966a). Unfortunately for the working memory hypothesis, her results showed clear evidence of semantic rather than acoustic coding, suggesting that the long-term store (LTS) rather than STS was playing a major role in her concept formation task.

Patterson (1971) tested the hypothesis that STS plays the important role in retrieval of holding the retrieval plan, which is then used to access the material to be recalled (Rumelhart *et al.*, 1972). She attempted to disrupt such retrieval plans by requiring her experimental group to count backwards for 20 seconds following each item recalled. On the basis of the results of Peterson and Peterson (1959), it was assumed that this would effectively erase information from STS after each recall. Despite this rather drastic interference with the normal functioning of STS however, there was no reliable decrement in the number of words recalled.

The most devastating evidence against the hypothesis that STS serves as a crucially important working memory comes from the neuropsychological work of Shallice and Warrington (Shallice & Warrington, 1970; Warrington & Shallice, 1969; Warrington & Weiskrantz, 1972). They have extensively studied a patient who by all normal standards, has a grossly defective STS. He has a digit span of only two items, and shows grossly impaired performance on the Peterson short-term forgetting task. If STS does indeed function as a central working memory, then one would expect this patient to exhibit grossly defective learning, memory, and comprehension. No such evidence of general impairment is found either in this case or in subsequent cases of a similar type (Warrington, Logue, & Pratt, 1971).

It appears then, that STS constitutes a system for which great claims have been made by many workers (including the present authors), for which there is little good evidence.

The experiments which follow attempt to answer two basic questions: first, is there any evidence that the tasks of reasoning, comprehension, and learning share a common working memory system?; and secondly, if such a system exists, how is it related to our current conception of STM? We do not claim to be presenting a novel view of STM in this chapter. Rather, our aim is to present a body of new experimental evidence which provides a firm basis for the working memory hypothesis. The account which follows should therefore be regarded essentially as a progress report on an on-going project. The reader will notice obvious gaps where further experiments clearly need to be performed, and it is more than probable that such experiments will modify to a greater or lesser degree our current tentative theoretical position. We hope, however, that the reader will agree that we do have enough information to draw some reasonably firm conclusions, and will feel that a report of work in progress is not too out of place in a volume of this kind.

II. The Search for a Common Working Memory System

The section which follows describes a series of experiments on the role of memory in reasoning, language comprehension, and learning. An attempt is made to apply comparable techniques in all three cases in the hope that this will allow a common pattern to emerge, if the same working memory system is operative in all three instances.

In attempting to assess the role of memory in any task, one is faced with a fundamental problem. What is meant by STS? Despite, or perhaps because of, the vast amount of research on the characteristics of STS there is still little general agreement. If our subsequent work were to depend on a generally acceptable definition of STS as a prerequisite for further research, such research would never begin. We suspect that this absence of unanimity stems from the fact that evidence for STS comes from two basically dissimilar paradigms. The first is based on the traditional memory span task. It suggests that STS is limited in capacity, is concerned with the retention of order information, and is closely associated with the processing of speech. The second cluster of evidence derives from the recency effect in free recall. It also suggests that STS is limited in capacity; however, its other dominant feature is its apparent resistence to the effects of other variables, whether semantic or speech-based (Glanzer, 1972). Rather than try to resolve these apparent discrepancies, we decided to begin by studying the one characteristic that both approaches to STS agreed on, namely its limited capacity. The technique adopted was to require S to retain one or more items while performing the task of reasoning, language comprehension, or learning. Such a concurrent memory load might reasonably be expected to absorb some of the storage capacity of a limited capacity working memory system, should such a system exist. The first set of experiments describes the application of this technique to the study of a reasoning task. To anticipate our results, we find a consistent pattern of additional memory load effects on all three tasks that we have studied: reasoning, language comprehension, and free recall. Additionally, all three tasks show evidence of phonemic coding. From this evidence we infer that each of the tasks involves a spanlike component, which we refer to as working memory. Further evidence from the free recall paradigm shows that the recency effect is neither disrupted by an additional memory span task nor particularly associated with phonemic coding. We therefore suggest a dichotomy between working memory and the recency effect, in contrast to the more usual view that both recency and the memory span reflect a single limited capacity short-term buffer store (STS).

A. The Role of Working Memory in Reasoning

The reasoning task selected was that devised by Baddeley (1968) in which S is presented with a sentence purporting to describe the order of occurrence of two letters. The sentence is followed by the letters in question, and S's task is to decide as quickly as possible whether the sentence correctly describes the order in which the letters are presented. For example, he may be given the sentence *A is not preceded by B-AB,* in which case he should respond *True.* A range of different sentences can be produced varying as to whether they are active or passive, positive or negative, and whether the word *precedes* or *follows* is used. This task is typical of a wide range of sentence verification tasks studied in recent years (Wason & Johnson-Laird, 1972). Its claim to be a reasoning task of some general validity is supported by the correlation between performance and

intelligence (Baddeley, 1968) and its sensitivity to both environ-
mental and speed-load stress (Baddeley, De Figuredo, Hawkswell-
Curtis, & Williams, 1968; Brown, Tickner, & Simmonds, 1969). The
first experiment requires S to perform this simple reasoning task
while holding zero, one, or two items in memory. If the task relies
on a limited capacity system, then one might expect the additional
load to impair performance.

1. Experiment I: Effects of a One- or Two-Item Preload

Subjects were required to process 32 sentences based on all possible combinations of sentence voice (active or passive), affirmation
(affirmative or negative), truth value (true or false), verb type (precedes or follows), and letter order (AB or BA). The experiment used
a version of the memory preload technique in which S is given one
or two items to remember. He is then required to process the sentence and having responded "True" or "False," he is then required
to recall the letters. A slide projector was used to present the sentences, each of which remained visible until S pressed the "True"
or "False" response key. Twenty-four undergraduate Ss were tested.
The order in which the three conditions were presented were determined by a Latin square. For half the Ss the preload was presented
visually, while the other half was given an auditory preload. In the
zero load condition, S was always presented with a single letter before
the presentation of the sentence. However, the letter was the same
on all trials, and S was not required to recall it subsequently. With
the one- and two-letter loads, the letters differed from trial to trial
but were never the same as those used in the reasoning problem.
All Ss were informed of this.

TABLE I

MEAN TIME (SEC) TO COMPLETE VERBAL REASONING PROBLEMS
AS A FUNCTION OF SIZE OF ADDITIONAL MEMORY LOAD AND
METHOD OF READING MEMORY ITEMS

Method of reading	Memory load		
	Zero	1-letter	2-letters
Silent	3.07	3.35	3.21
Aloud	3.33	3.26	3.41
Means	3.20	3.31	3.31

The results are shown in Table I. There was no reliable effect of memory load on solution time regardless of whether the load was one or two letters, and was presented visually or auditorily ($F < 1$ in each case). Since letter recall was almost always perfect, it appears to be the case that Ss can hold up to two additional items with no impairment in their reasoning speed. This result suggests one of two conclusions; either that the type of memory system involved in retaining the letters is not relevant to the reasoning task, or else that a load of two items is not sufficient to overtax the system. Experiment II attempts to decide between these two hypotheses by increasing the preload from two to six letters, a load which approaches the memory span for many Ss.

2. Experiment II: Effects of a Six-Digit Preload

Performance on the 32 sentences was studied with and without a six-letter memory preload. In the preload condition each trial began with a verbal "ready" signal followed by a random sequence of six letters spoken at a rate of one per second. The reasoning problem followed immediately afterwards, details of presentation and method of responding being the same as in Experiment I. After solving the problem, S attempted to recall verbally as many letters as possible in the correct order. In the control condition, the reasoning problem followed immediately after the "ready" signal. After completing the problem, and before being presented with the next problem, S listened to a six-letter sequence and recalled it immediately. This procedure varies the storage load during reasoning, but roughly equates the two conditions for total memorization required during the session.

Separate blocks of 32 trials were used for presenting the two conditions, each block containing the 32 sentences in random order. Half the Ss began with the control condition and half with the preload condition. Two groups of 12 undergraduate Ss were tested. The two groups differed in the instructions they were given. The first group (equal stress) was told to carry out the reasoning task as rapidly as possible, consistent with high accuracy, and to attempt to recall all six letters correctly. The second group (memory stress) was told that only if their recall was completely correct could their reasoning time be scored; subject to this proviso, they were told to reason as rapidly as they could, consistent with high accuracy. All Ss were given a preliminary three-minute practice session on a sheet of reasoning problems, and were tested individually.

TABLE II

MEAN REASONING TIMES AND RECALL SCORES FOR THE "EQUAL STRESS"
AND "MEMORY STRESS" INSTRUCTIONAL GROUPS

Instructional emphasis	Mean reasoning time (sec)		Mean no. items recalled (max = 6)	
	Control	Memory preload	Control	Memory preload
"Equal stress"	3.27	3.46	5.5	3.7
"Memory stress"	2.73	4.73	5.8	5.0

Mean reasoning times (for correct solutions) and recall scores for both groups of subjects are shown in Table II. For the "equal stress" Ss memory load produced a slight but nonsignificant slowing down in reasoning time (on a Wilcoxon test, $T = 31$, $N = 12$, $P > .05$), while for the "memory stress" Ss memory load slowed down reasoning considerably ($T = 4$, $N = 12$, $P < .01$). There appears to have been a trade-off between reasoning and recall in the memory load condition. The equal stress Ss achieved their unimpaired reasoning at the expense of very poor recall compared with that of the memory stress Ss.

The results show then, that there is an interaction between additional short-term storage load and reasoning performance. In comparison with the results of Experiment I these suggest that the interaction depends on the storage load since, up to two items can be recalled accurately with no detectable effect. Thus the reasoning task does not seem to require all the available short-term storage space. The results show additionally that the form of the interaction depends on the instructional emphasis given to S. It seems likely therefore that interference was the result of the active strategy that Ss employed. One possibility is that the "memory stress" Ss dealt with the memory preload by quickly rehearsing the items, to "consolidate" them in memory before starting the reasoning problem. If this were the case, then reasoning times ought to be slowed by a constant amount (the time spent rehearsing the letters), regardless of problem complexity. Figure 1 shows mean reasoning time for the memory stress group for different types of sentence. Control reaction times (RTs) show that problems expressed as passives were more difficult than those expressed as actives, and that negative forms were more difficult than affirmatives. However, the slowing down in reasoning produced by the memory preload was roughly constant regardless of problem difficulty. Analysis of variance showed significant effects

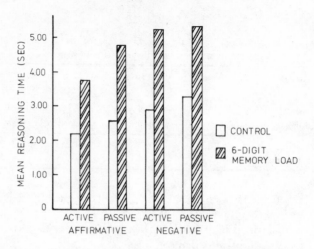

Fig. 1. Mean reasoning time for different forms of the problem for the "memory stress" group of subjects.

of memory load [$F(1,10) = 8.51, P < .025$], sentence voice [$F(1,10 = 7.34, P < .025$], and negation [$F(1,10 = 34.9, P < .001$]. None of the interaction terms involving the load factor approached significance.

The results of this experiment do not adequately demonstrate that the verbal reasoning task involves a short-term storage component. Subjects seem to have adopted a strategy of time-sharing between rehearsal of the memory letters and reasoning. While the time-sharing may have been forced by competition between the tasks for a limited storage capacity, this is not necessarily the case. The tasks may, for example, have competed for use of the articulatory system, without having overlapping storage demands.

Experiment III attempts to prevent the strategy of completely switching attention from the memory task to the reasoning test by changing from a preload to a concurrent load procedure. In the concurrent load procedure, S is required to continue to rehearse the memory load items aloud while completing the reasoning task. Since the process of articulation has itself been shown to impair performance in both memory (Levy, 1971; Murray, 1967, 1968) and reasoning (Hammerton, 1969; Peterson, 1969), two additional conditions were included to allow a separation of the effects of memory load and of articulation.

3. Experiment III: Effects of a Concurrent Memory Load

All Ss performed the 32 reasoning problems under each of four conditions, the order in which the conditions were tested being determined by a Latin square. In the control condition, a trial began with a verbal warning signal and the instruction "say nothing." The problem was then presented and solved as quickly and accurately as possible. The second condition used the articulatory suppression procedure devised by Murray (1967). Subjects were instructed to say the word "the" repeatedly, at a rate of between four and five utterances per second. After S had begun to articulate, the problem was presented, whereupon he continued the articulation task at the same high rate until he had pressed the "True" or "False" response button. The third condition followed a procedure adopted by Peterson (1969) in which the articulation task consisted of the cyclic repetition of a familiar sequence of responses, namely the counting sequence "one-two-three-four-five-six." Again, a rate of four to five words per second was required. In the fourth condition, S was given a random six-digit sequence to repeat cyclically at a four- to five-digit per second rate. In this condition alone, the message to be articulated was changed from trial to trial. The three articulation conditions therefore range from the simple repetition of a single utterance, through the rather more complex articulation involved in counting, up to the digit span repetition task, which presumably makes considerably greater short-term storage demands. Degree of prior practice and method of presentation were as in Experiment II.

Table III shows the performance of the 12 undergraduate Ss tested in this study. Concurrent articulation of "the" and counting up to six produced a slight slowing of reasoning time, but by far the greatest slowing occurred with concurrent articulation of random digit sequences. Analysis of variance showed a significant main effect of

TABLE III

MEAN REASONING TIMES AND ERROR RATES AS A FUNCTION OF CONCURRENT ARTICULATORY ACTIVITY

Concurrent articulation	Mean reasoning RT (sec)	Percent reasoning errors
Control	2.79	8.1
"The-The-The . . ."	3.13	10.6
"One-Two-Three . . ."	3.22	5.6
Random 6-digit No.	4.27	10.3

conditions $[F(3,33) = 14.2, P < .01]$. Newman-Keuls tests showed that the effect was mainly due to the difference between the random digit condition and the other three. The slight slowing down in the suppression-only and counting conditions just failed to reach significance.

These results suggest that interference with verbal reasoning is not entirely to be explained in terms of competition for the articulatory system, which may be committed to the rapid production of a well-learned sequence of responses with relatively little impairment of reasoning. A much more important factor appears to be the short-term memory load, with the availability of spare short-term storage capacity determining the rate at which the reasoning processes are carried out. Since difficult problems presumably make greater demands on these processes, one might expect that more difficult problems would show a greater effect of concurrent storage load. Figure 2 shows the mean reasoning times for problems of various kinds. As is typically the case with such tasks (Wason & Johnson-Laird, 1972), passive sentences proved more difficult than active sentences $[F(1,11) = 55.2, P < .01]$, and negatives were more difficult than affirmatives $[F(1,11) = 38.5, P < .01]$. In addition to the main effect of con-

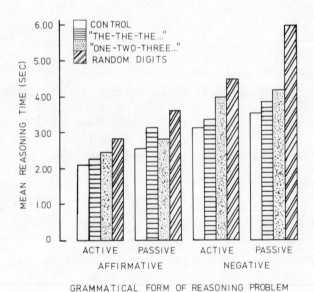

Fig. 2. Effects of concurrent articulatory activity on mean reasoning time for different types of problem.

current activity, activity interacted with sentence voice [$F(3,33) =$ 5.59, $P < .01$] and with negativity [$F(3,33) = 5.29, P < .01$]. Figure 2 shows that these interactions were due largely to performance in the random digit condition. Additional storage load seems to have slowed down solution times to passives more than actives and to negatives more than affirmatives. Thus the greater the problem difficulty, the greater the effect of an additional short-term storage load.

In summary, it has been shown that additional STM loads of more than two items can impair the rate at which reasoning is carried out. Loads of six items can produce sizable interference, but the effect may depend on the instructional emphasis given to Ss (Experiment II). The interference effects may be partly due to the articulatory activity associated with rehearsal of the memory items, but there is a substantial amount of interference over and above this which is presumably due to storage load (Experiment III). The trade-off between reasoning speed and additional storage load suggests that the interference occurs within a limited capacity "workspace," which can be flexibly allocated either to storage or to processing.

The effect of articulatory suppression in Experiment III was small and did not reach statistical significance. However, Hammerton (1969) has reported evidence that suppression can produce reliable interference in this task. His Ss repeated the familiar sentence "Mary had a little lamb" while carrying out the Baddeley reasoning task. Performance was impaired when contrasted with a control group who said nothing when reasoning. This result together with those of Peterson (1969) suggests that reasoning may resemble the memory span task in having an articulatory component. Experiment IV explores the relation between the memory span and working memory further by taking a major feature of the verbal memory span, namely its susceptibility to the effects of phonemic similarity, and testing for similar effects in the verbal reasoning task.

4. Experiment IV: Phonemic Similarity and Verbal Reasoning

One of the more striking features of the memory span for verbal materials is its apparent reliance on phonemic (either acoustic or articulatory) coding. This is revealed both by the nature of intrusion errors (Conrad, 1962; Sperling, 1963) and by the impairment in performance shown when sequences of phonemically similar items are recalled (Baddeley, 1966b; Conrad & Hull, 1964). As Wickelgren (1965) has shown, phonemic similarity has its disruptive effect principally on the retention of order information, and since the reasoning task employed depends on the order of the letters concerned, it seems reasonable to suppose that the manipulation of phonemic similarity might prove a suitable way of disrupting any STS component of the task. Experiment IV, therefore, studied the effect of phonemic similarity on the reasoning task and compared this with the effect of visual similarity, a factor which is typically found to have little or no influence on memory span for letters.

A group testing procedure was used in which Ss were given test sheets containing 64 reasoning problems printed in random order and were allowed three minutes to complete as many as possible. A 2×2 factorial design was used with phonemic and visual similarity as factors. There were two replications of the experiment, each using different letter pairs in each of the four conditions. The sets of letter pairs used were as follows: *MC, VS* (low phonemic similarity, low visual similarity); *FS, TD* (high phonemic, low visual similarity); *OQ, XY* (low phonemic, high visual similarity); and *BP, MN* (high phonemic, high visual similarity). Thirty-two undergraduate Ss were tested, half with one letter set and half with the other. All Ss were first given a preliminary practice session using the letter-pair *AB*. Each S then completed a three-minute session on each of the four types of problems. Problems were printed on sheets, and Ss responded in writing. The order of presenting the four conditions was determined using a Latin square.

Table IV shows the mean number of correctly answered questions in the various conditions. Since there were no important differences between results from the two replications, data from the two sets of letter pairs have been pooled. Only the effect of phonemic similarity was significant ($N = 32$, $Z = 2.91$, $P < .002$), while visual similarity appeared to have no effect ($N = 32$, $Z < 1$). It appears then that the verbal reasoning task does require the utilization of phonemically

TABLE IV

MEAN NUMBER OF REASONING PROBLEMS CORRECTLY
SOLVED IN THREE MINUTES AS A FUNCTION OF PHONEMIC
AND VISUAL SIMILARITY OF THE LETTERS
USED IN THE PROBLEMS

		Phonemic similarity of letters	
		Low	High
Visual similarity of letters	Low	43.2	40.9
	High	42.9	39.8

coded information, and, although the effect is small, it is highly consistent across Ss.

In summary then, verbal reasoning shows effects of concurrent storage load, of articulatory suppression, and of phonemic similarity. This pattern of results is just what would be expected if the task depended on the use of a short-term store having the characteristics typically shown in the memory span paradigm. However, the magnitude of the effects suggest that the system responsible for the memory span is only part of working memory. We shall return to this point after considering the evidence for the role of working memory in prose comprehension and learning.

B. Comprehension and Working Memory

While it has frequently been asserted that STS plays a crucial role in the comprehension of spoken language (e.g., Baddeley & Patterson, 1971; Norman, 1972), the evidence for such a claim is sparse. There is, of course, abundant evidence that language material may be held in STM (Jarvella, 1971; Sachs, 1967) but we know of no evidence to suggest that such storage is an essential function of comprehension under normal circumstances, and in view of the lack of any obvious defect in comprehension shown by patients with grossly defective STS (Shallice & Warrington, 1970), the importance of STS in comprehension remains to be demonstrated. Experiments V and VI attempt to do so using the memory preload and the concurrent memory load techniques.

1. Experiment V: Effects of a Memory Preload on Comprehension

In this experiment, S listened to spoken prose passages under each of two memory load conditions and was subsequently tested for retention of the passages. In the experimental condition, each sentence of the passage was preceded by a sequence of six digits spoken at a rate of one item per second. After listening to the sentence, S attempted to write down the digit sequence in the correct order in time to a metronome beating at a one-second rate. Hence S was required to retain the digit sequence while listening to the sentence. In the control condition the digit sequence followed the sentence and was recalled immediately afterward. Thus both conditions involved the same amount of overt activity, but only in the experimental condition was there a temporal overlap between the retention of the digits and sentence presentation. In both conditions the importance of recalling the digits accurately was emphasized. After each passage, S was allowed three minutes to complete a recall test based on the Cloze technique (Taylor, 1953). Test sheets comprised a typed script of each of the passages, from which every fifth word had been deleted. The passages contained approximately 170 words each, and hence there were about 33 blanks which S was instructed to try to fill with the deleted word. This technique has been shown by Rubenstein and Aborn (1958) to be a reasonably sensitive measure of prose retention. Three different types of passage were included in the experiment: descriptions, narratives, and arguments. Two examples of each type were constructed giving six passages in all, each of which contained ten sentences. Each of 30 Ss was tested on all six passages, comprising one experimental and one control condition for each of the three passage types. Subjects were tested in two separate groups, each receiving a different ordering of the six passages.

Table V shows the mean number of correctly completed blanks for the control and experimental conditions together with the mean number of digit sequences correctly reported in the two conditions. The digit preload impaired performance on the comprehension test for all three types of passage. Differences were significant for the descriptions ($Z = 2.81$, $P < .01$, Wilcoxon test) and the narratives ($Z = 2.91$, $P < .01$), but not for the arguments ($Z = 1.14$, $P > .05$). Thus, test performance is impaired when digits have to be held in store during presentation of the passage. Digit recall scores were

TABLE V

COMPREHENSION AND DIGIT RECALL SCORES WITH AND WITHOUT ADDITIONAL
MEMORY LOAD FOR THREE TYPES OF PASSAGE

Type of passage	Memory load condition	Comprehension score[a]	Digit recall score[b]
Description	No load	16.8	11.8
	Load	13.3	7.7
Narrative	No load	20.1	11.4
	Load	18.0	7.8
Argument	No load	14.5	11.4
	Load	13.6	8.1

[a] Mean no. of blanks correctly filled in—max = 33
[b] Mean no. of digit strings correctly reported—max = 14

also poorest in the experimental condition, but this was, of course, to be expected in view of the long filled retention interval in this condition.

While the results can be interpreted as showing that comprehension is impaired by an additional short-term storage load, this conclusion is not unchallengeable. Firstly, the Cloze procedure is probably a test of prompted verbatim recall and may not measure comprehension. Secondly, the control condition of the experiment may not have been entirely satisfactory. If the time *between* sentences is important for comprehension of the meaning of the passage as a whole, the control group itself may have suffered from an appreciable amount of interference. The next experiment goes some way to overcoming both these objections, using the concurrent memory load procedure instead of the preload technique.

2. Experiment VI: Effects of a Concurrent Memory Load on Comprehension

This experiment compared the effects of three levels of concurrent storage load on prose comprehension. In all three conditions, the memory items were presented visually at a rate of one per second using a TV monitor. The concurrent memory load tasks were as follows. In the three-digit load condition, S was always presented with sequences of three digits, each sequence being followed by a 2-second blank interval during which S attempted to recall and write down the three digits he had just seen. In the six-digit condition, the sequences all comprised six items and were followed by a 4-second blank interval. Again S was instructed not to recall the digits until the sequence had been removed. Time intervals were chosen so as to keep S busy with the digit memory task, and were also such that all conditions would require input and output of the same total number of digits. In the control condition, S was presented with sequences of three and six digits in alternation. After each three-digit list there was a 2-second blank interval, and after each six-digit list the blank interval was 4 seconds. In this case, however, S was simply required to copy down the digits while they were being presented. It was hoped that this task would require the minimal memory load consistent with the demand of keeping the amount of digit writing constant across conditions. The main difference between the three conditions was, therefore, the number of digits which S was required to store simultaneously. Instructions emphasized the im-

portance of accuracy on all three digit tasks, and an invigilator
checked that Ss were obeying the instructions.

Comprehension was tested using six passages taken from the Neale
Analysis of Reading Ability (Neale, 1958). Two passages (those
suited for 12- and 13-year-old children) were selected from each of
the three parallel test forms. Each passage comprised approximately
120 words and was tested by eight standardized questions. These
have the advantage of testing comprehension of the passage without
using the specific words used in the original presentation. They can,
therefore, be regarded as testing retention of the gist of the passage
rather than verbatim recall. Answers were given a score of one if
correct, half if judged almost correct, and zero otherwise. At the
start of each trial, the experimenter announced which version of the
digit task was to be presented before testing began. After a few
seconds of the digit processing task, the experimenter began to read
out the prose passage at a normal reading rate and with normal
intonation. At the end of the passage, the digit task was abandoned
and the experimenter read out the comprehension questions. A
total of 15 undergraduates were tested in three equal-sized groups,
in a design which allowed each passage to be tested once under each
of the three memory load conditions.

The mean comprehension scores for the three conditions are
shown in Table VI. The Friedman test showed significant overall
effects of memory load ($\chi_r^2 = 7.3$, $P < .05$). Wilcoxon tests showed
that the six-digit memory load produced lower comprehension scores
than either the control condition ($T = 19$, $N = 14$, $P < .05$), or the
three-digit condition ($T = 19.5$, $N = 15$, $P < .05$). There was no
reliable difference between the three-digit load and control conditions ($T = 44.5$, $N = 14$, $P > .05$). Thus, comprehension is not reliably affected by a three-item memory load, but is depressed by a
six-item load, a pattern of results which is very similar to that observed with the verbal reasoning task.

TABLE VI

MEAN COMPREHENSION SCORES AS A FUNCTION OF SIZE OF CONCURRENT
MEMORY LOAD

	Memory load		
	Control (1-digit)	3-digit	6-digit
Mean comprehension score (max = 8)	5.9	5.6	4.8

While Experiments IV and V present *prima facie* evidence for the role of working memory in comprehension, it could be argued that we have tested retention rather than comprehension. From what little we know of the process of comprehension, it seems likely that understanding and remembering are very closely related. It is, however, clearly desirable that this work should be extended and an attempt made to separate the factors of comprehension and retention before any final conclusions are drawn.

If comprehension makes use of STM, it should be possible to impair performance on comprehension tasks by introducing phonemic similarity into the test material. To test this hypothesis using the prose comprehension task of the previous experiment would have involved the difficult task of producing passages of phonemically similar words. We chose instead to study the comprehension of single sentences, since the generation of sentences containing a high proportion of phonemically similar words seemed likely to prove less demanding than that of producing a whole passage of such material.

3. Experiment VII: Phonemic Similarity and Sentence Comprehension

The task used in this experiment required S to judge whether a single sentence was impossible or possible. Possible sentences were both grammatical and meaningful, while impossible sentences were both ungrammatical and relatively meaningless. Impossible sentences were derived from their possible counterparts by reversing the order of two adjacent words near the middle of the possible sentence. Two sets of possible sentences were constructed, one comprising phonemically dissimilar words and the other one containing a high proportion of phonemically similar words. An example of each type of possible sentence together with its derived impossible sentence is shown in Table VII. In order to equate the materials as closely as

TABLE VII

Examples of the Sentences Used in Experiment VIII

	Possible version	Impossible version
Phonemically dissimilar	Dark skinned Ian thought Harry ate in bed	Dark skinned Ian Harry thought ate in bed
Phonemically similar	Red headed Ned said Ted fed in bed	Red headed Ned Ted said fed in bed

possible, each phonemically similar sentence was matched with a phonemically dissimilar sentence for number of words, grammatical form, and general semantic content. There were nine examples of each of the four conditions (phonemically similar possible; phonemically similar impossible; phonemically dissimilar possible, and phonemically dissimilar impossible), giving 36 sentences in all.

Each sentence was typed on a white index card and was exposed to S by the opening of a shutter approximately half a second after a verbal warning signal. The sentence remained visible until S had responded by pressing one of two response keys. Instructions stressed both speed and accuracy. Twenty students served as Ss and were given ten practice sentences before proceeding to the 36 test sentences which were presented in random order.

Since reading speed was a potentially important source of variance, 13 of the 20 Ss were asked to read the sentences aloud at the end of the experiment and their reading times were recorded. The 36 sentences were grouped into four sets of nine, each set corresponding to one of the four experimental conditions and were typed onto four separate sheets of paper. The order of presenting the sheets was randomized across Ss, and the time to read each was measured by a stopwatch.

Table VIII shows mean reaction times for each of the four types of sentence, together with reading rate for each condition. It is clear that phonemic similarity increased the judgment times for both possible and impossible sentences $[F(1,9) = 8.77, P < .01]$, there being no interaction between the effects of similarity and grammaticality $[F(1,9) < 1]$. An interaction between the effects of phonemic similarity and sentence type $[F(8,152) = 4,38, P < .001]$ suggests that the effect does not characterize all the sentences presented. Inspec-

TABLE VIII

RESULTS OF EXPERIMENT VIII

Sentence type	Mean RT for judgment of "possibility" (sec)			Mean reading time (sec)		
	Possible version	Impossible version	Average	Possible version	Impossible version	Average
Phonemically dissimilar	2.84	2.62	2.73	2.93	3.18	3.06
Phonemically similar	3.03	2.83	2.93	2.96	3.19	3.08

tion of the three sentence sets out of nine which show no similarity effect suggests that this is probably because the dissimilar sentences in these sets contained either longer or less frequent words than their phonemically similar counterparts. Clearly, future experiments should control word length and frequency.

Reading times did not vary appreciably with phonemic similarity $[F(1,12) < 1]$. It is, therefore, clear that phonemic similarity interfered with the additional processing over and above that involved in reading, required to make the possible/impossible judgment. As Table VIII suggests, although impossible sentences took longer to read than possible sentences $[F(1,12) = 41.6, P < .001]$, they were judged more rapidly $[F(1,19) = 17.3, P < .001]$. This contrast suggests that when judging impossible sentences, S was able to make his judgment as soon as an unlikely word was encountered and did not have to read the entire sentence.

To summarize the results of this section: first, comprehension of verbal material is apparently impaired by a concurrent memory load of six items but is relatively unimpaired by a load of three or less. Second, it appears that verbal comprehension is susceptible to disruption by phonemic similarity. It should be noted, however, that use of the term comprehension has necessarily been somewhat loose; it has been used to refer to the retention of the meaning of prose passages on the one hand and to the detection of syntactic or semantic "impossibility" on the other. Even with single-sentence material, Ss can process the information in a number of different ways depending on the task demands (Green, 1973). It should, therefore, be clear that the use of the single term "comprehension" is not meant to imply a single underlying process. Nevertheless, it does seem reasonable to use the term "comprehension" to refer to the class of activities concerned with the understanding of sentence material. Tasks studied under this heading do at least appear to be linked by the common factor of making use of a short-term or working memory system. As in the case of the verbal reasoning studies this system appears to be somewhat disrupted by the demands of a near-span additional memory load and by the presence of phonemic similarity.

It might reasonably be argued that the reasoning task we studied is essentially a measure of sentence comprehension and that we have, therefore, explored the role of working memory in only one class of activity. The next section, therefore, moves away from sentence material and studies the retention and free recall of lists of unrelated words. The free recall technique has the additional advantage of allowing us to study the effects that the variables which appear to have influenced the operation of working memory in the previous experiments have on the recency effect, a phenomenon which has in the past been regarded as giving a particularly clear indication of the operation of STS.

C. WORKING MEMORY AND FREE RECALL

1. Experiment VIII: Memory Preload and Free Recall

This experiment studied the free recall of lists of 16 unrelated words under conditions of a zero-, three-, or six-digit preload. The preload was presented before the list of words and had to be retained throughout input and recall, since S was only told at the end of the recall period whether to write the preload digit sequence on the right- or left-hand side of his response sheet. The experiment had two major aims. The first aim was to study the effect of a preload on the LTM component of the free recall task, hence giving some indication of the possible role of working memory in long-term learning. The second aim was to study the effect of a preload on the recency effect. Since most current views of STS regard the digit span and the recency effect as both making demands on a common short-term store, one might expect a dramatic reduction of recency when a preload is imposed. However, as was pointed out in the intro-duction, there does appear to be a good deal of difference between the characteristics of STS revealed by the digit span procedure (sug-gesting that it is a serially ordered speech-based store) and the char-acteristics suggested by the recency effect in free recall (which ap-pears to be neither serially ordered nor speech-based).

All lists comprised 16 high-frequency words equated for word length and presented auditorily at a rate of two seconds per word. Subjects were given a preload of zero, three, or six digits and were required to recall the words either immediately or after a delay of 30 seconds during which subjects copied down letters spoken at a one-second rate. In both cases, they had one minute in which to write down as many words as they could remember, after which they were instructed to write down the preload digits at the left- or right-hand side of their response sheets. Instructions emphasized the importance of retaining the preload digits.

The design varied memory load as a within S factor, and delay of recall between Ss. The same set of 15 lists were presented to both immediate and delayed recall groups. Within each group there were three subgroups across which the assignment of particular lists to particular levels of preload was balanced. For each group the 15

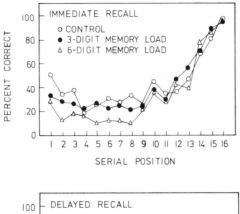

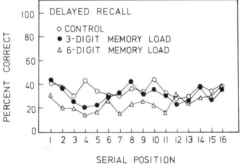

Fig. 3. Effects of additional short-term memory load on immediate and delayed free recall.

trials of the experiment were divided into blocks of three, in which each load condition occurred once. Subject to this constraint, the ordering of conditions was random. Twenty-one undergraduates served in each of the two subgroups. Figure 3 shows the serial position curves for recall as a function of size of preload for the immediate and delayed recall conditions. Analysis of variance showed significant effects due to delay [$F(1,40) = 9.85$, $P < .01$], serial position [$F(15,600) = 49.4$, $P < .001$], and the delay $\times$ serial position interaction [$F(15,600) = 33.4$, $P < .001$]. These correspond to the standard finding that delaying free recall abolishes the recency effect. There were also significant effects due to memory load [$F(2,80) = 35.8$, $P < .001$], to the memory load $\times$ serial position interaction, [$F(30,1200) = 1.46$, $P < .05$], and to the load $\times$ serial position $\times$ delay interaction [$F(30,1200) = 1.80$, $P < .01$].

The overall percentage of words recalled declined with increased

TABLE IX

PERCENTAGES OF WORDS RECALLED IN THE VARIOUS
CONDITIONS OF EXPERIMENT X

	Memory load		
	Zero	3-digits	6-digits
Immediate recall	43.9	41.6	35.2
Delayed recall	35.5	32.3	24.5

preload (see Table IX). Comparison between means using the New-man-Keuls procedure showed that the impairment due to a three-digit preload was just significant ($P < .05$) while the six-digit preload condition was significantly worse than both the control and the three-digit preload conditions at well beyond the .01 significance level.

It is clear from Fig. 3 that the load effect was restricted to the long-term component of recall and did not substantially influence the recency effect.

The first conclusion from this study is that performance on the secondary memory component of free recall is adversely effected by a digit preload, with the size of the decrement being a function of the size of the preload. A somewhat more dramatic finding is the apparent absence of a preload effect on the recency component. There are, however, at least two classes of interpretations of this result. The first is to conclude that an STM preload does not interfere with the mechanism of the recency effect. This would be a striking conclusion, since the "standard" account of recency assumes that the last few items are retrieved from the same store that would be used to hold the preload items. To accept this hypothesis would require a radical change of view concerning the nature of the recency effect. An alternative hypothesis is to assume that S begins to rehearse the preload items at the beginning of the list, and by the end of the list has succeeded in transferring them into LTS, freeing his STS for other tasks. Two lines of evidence support this suggestion: firstly, there was only a marginal effect of preload on recall of the last few items when recall was delayed (see Fig. 3). This suggests that the preload effect diminished as the list progressed. Secondly, when questioned after the experiment, 37 out of 39 Ss stated that they carried out some rehearsal of the digits, and 26 of these said that they rehearsed the digits mostly at the beginning of the word list. Clearly, our failure to control Ss, rehearsal strategies prevents our drawing any firm conclusions about the influence of preload on the recency effect. The next experiment, therefore, attempts to replicate the present results under better controlled conditions.

Before passing on to the next experiment, however, it is perhaps worth noting that the delayed recall technique for separating the long- and short-term components in free recall is the only one of the range of current techniques which would have revealed this potential artifact. Techniques which base their estimates of the two components entirely on immediate recall data assume that the LTS component for later items in the list can be estimated from performance on the middle items. In our situation, and possibly in many others, this assumption is clearly not valid.

2. Experiment IX: Concurrent Memory Load and Free Recall

This experiment again studied the effects of three levels of memory load on immediate and delayed free recall. In general, procedures were identical with Experiment VIII, except that the concurrent load rather than the preload technique was used. This involved the continuous presentation and test of digit sequences throughout the presentation of the memory list. In this way, it was hoped to keep the memory load relatively constant throughout the list and so avoid the difficulties of interpretation encountered in the previous study.

The concurrent load procedure was similar to that described for Experiment VI and involved the visual presentation of digit sequences. In the six-digit concurrent load condition, sequences of six digits were visible for four seconds, followed by a four-second blank interval during which S was required to recall and write down the six digits. The three-digit concurrent load condition was similar except that the three-digit sequences were presented for only two seconds and followed by a two-second blank interval, while in the control condition, S saw alternate sequences of three and six digits, followed, respectively, by gaps of two and four seconds. In this condition, however, he was instructed to copy down the digits as they appeared. The three conditions were thus equal in amount of writing required, but differed in the number of digits that had to be held in memory simultaneously.

The procedure involved switching on the digit display and requiring S to process digits for a few seconds before starting the auditory presentation of the word list. The point at which the word list began was varied randomly from trial to trial. This minimized the chance that a particular component of the digit task (e.g., input or recall) would be always associated with particular serial positions in the word list. After the last word of each list, the visual display was switched off and Ss immediately abandoned the digit task. In the immediate recall condition, they were allowed one minute for written recall of the words, while in the delayed condition they copied a list of 30 letters read out at a one-second rate before beginning the one-minute recall period.

The design exactly paralleled that used in the previous experiment, with 17 undergraduates being tested in the immediate recall condition and 17 in the delayed condition. High accuracy on the digit task was emphasized; each of the three-digit processing procedures was practiced before beginning the experiment, and behavior was closely monitored during the experiment to ensure that instructions were obeyed.

The immediate and delayed recall serial position curves are shown in Fig. 4. Because of the scatter in the raw data, scores for adjacent serial positions have been pooled, except for the last four serial positions. Analysis of variance indicated a significant overall effect of memory load [$F(2,64) = 45.2$, $P < .01$], with mean percentage correct scores being 31.8, 31.2, and 24.8 for the zero-, three- and six-item load conditions, respectively. The Newman-Keuls test indicated a significant difference between the six-digit load condition and both other conditions ($P < .01$), which did not differ significantly between themselves.

As Fig. 4 suggests, there were highly significant effects of serial position [$F(15,480) = 70.7$, $P < .01$], of delay [$F(1,32) = 26.6$, $P < .01$], and of their interaction [$F(15,480) = 29.1$, $P < .001$], indicating the standard effect of delay on the recency component. The analysis showed no evidence of a two-way interaction between memory load and serial position ($F < 1$) and very weak evidence for a three-way interaction among memory load, serial position, and delay [$F(30,960) = 1.32$, $P > .10$]. The general conclusion, therefore, is that an additional concurrent memory load, even of six items, does not significantly alter the standard recency effect.

This conclusion confirms the result of the previous experiment, but rules out one of the possible interpretations of the earlier data. With the preload technique, the absence of an effect of load on recency might have been due to a progressive decline in the "effort" or "difficulty" associated with the digit task during input of the word list. Such an explanation is not appropriate for the present results since the concurrent load procedure ensured that the digit memory task was carried out right through input of the word lists, a conclusion which is supported by the continued separation of the

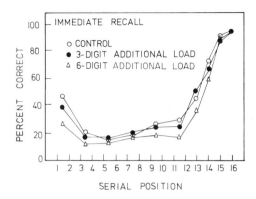

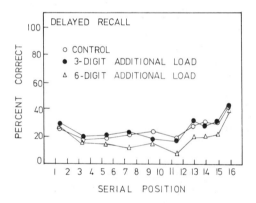

Fig. 4. Effects of concurrent short-term storage load on immediate and delayed free recall.

three- and six-digit load conditions over the last few serial positions in the delayed recall condition (see Fig. 3). Thus, even though six digits are concurrently being stored during the input of the final words of the list, the recency effect is unimpaired. To account for this, it must be assumed that the recency mechanism is independent from that involved in the memory span task. According to most dual-store theories, the digit span task ought to keep STS virtually fully occupied. Since the recency effect is commonly supposed to depend on output from this store, the digit span task should seriously reduce the amount of recency observed. It seems, therefore, that the buffer-storage account of recency is faced with a major difficulty.

Our data suggest then that a concurrent load of six items does impair the long-term component of free recall. Furthermore, as in the case of our reasoning task and prose comprehension studies, a load of three items has only a marginal effect. These results are consistent with the hypothesis of a working memory, which has some features in common with the memory span task. Since the memory load was present only during input of the words and not during recall, it is reasonable to conclude that working memory is concerned with the processes of transferring information to LTM. The absence of an effect of concurrent storage load on the recency effect suggests that working memory may have little or nothing to do with the recency effect. This hypothesis is discussed more fully in the concluding section of the chapter, when extra evidence against a buffer-storage account of recency is presented and an alternative interpretation suggested.

3. Experiment X: Speech Coding and Free Recall

In the case of both verbal reasoning and comprehension, we observed a similar effect of preload to that shown in the last two experiments, together with clear evidence of phonemic coding. This was revealed by effects of both acoustic similarity and articulatory suppression in the reasoning task, and by acoustic similarity effects in comprehension. There already exists evidence that phonemic similarity may be utilized in free recall (Baddeley & Warrington, 1973; Bruce & Crowley, 1970), provided at least that the phonemically similar items are grouped during presentation. The effects observed were positive, but since acoustic similarity is known to impair recall of order while enhancing item recall (Wickelgren, 1965), this would be expected in a free recall task. It is perhaps worth noting in connection with the dichotomy between span-based indicators of STS and evidence based on the recency effect suggested by the results of the last two experiments that attempts to show that the recency effect is particularly susceptible to the effects of phonemic similarity have proved uniformly unsuccessful (Craik & Levy, 1970; Glanzer, Koppenaal, & Nelson, 1972). Although there is abundant evidence that Ss may utilize phonemic similarity in long-term learning, this does not present particularly strong evidence in favor of a phonemically based working memory, since Ss are clearly able to utilize a very wide range of characteristics of the material to be learnt, possibly using processes which lie completely outside the working memory system. The next experiment, therefore, attempts to examine the role of articulatory coding in long-term learning more directly using the articulatory suppression technique. It comprises one of a series of unpublished studies by Richardson and Baddeley and examines the effect of concurrently articulating an irrelevant utterance on free recall for visually and auditorily presented word sequences.

Lists of ten unrelated high-frequency words were presented at a rate of two seconds per word either visually, by memory drum, or auditorily, which involved the experimenter reading out the words from the memory drum, which was screened from S. A total of 40 lists were used, and during half of these S was required to remain silent during presentation, while for the other half he was instructed to whisper "hiya" [an utterance which Levy (1971) found to produce effective suppression] at a rate of two utterances per second throughout the presentation of the word list. Half the Ss articulated for the first 20 lists and were silent for the last 20, while the other half performed in the reverse order. Manipulation of modality was carried out according to an *APBA* design, with half the Ss receiving visual as the first and last conditions, and half receiving auditory first and last. Each block of ten lists was preceded by a practice list in the appropriate modality and with the same vocalization and recall conditions. Following each list, S was instructed to recall immediately unless the experimenter read out a three-digit number, in which case he was to count backwards from that number by three's. Half the lists in each block of ten were tested immediately and half after the 20-second delay; in each case S was allowed 40 seconds for recall. Sixteen undergraduates served as Ss. The major results of interest are shown in Fig. 5, from which it is clear that articulatory suppression impaired retention [$F(1,1185) = 19.6$, $P < .001$]. The effect is shown particularly clearly with visual presentation and appears to be at least as marked for the earlier serial positions which are generally regarded as dependent on LTS, as for the recency component. This result is consistent with the suggestion of a working memory operating on phonemically coded information and transferring it to LTS. It further supports Glanzer's (1972) conclusion that the recency effect in free recall does not reflect articulatory coding and lends further weight to the suggestion that working memory is probably not responsible for the recency effect.

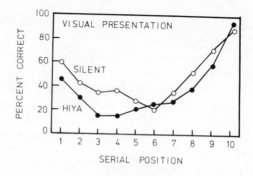

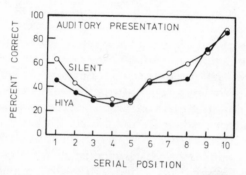

Fig. 5. Effect of concurrent articulation on free recall of visually and aurally presented word lists. (Data from Richardson and Baddeley, unpublished.)

III. A Proposed Working Memory System

We have now studied the effect of factors which might be supposed to influence a working memory system, should it exist, across a range of cognitive tasks. The present section attempts to summarize the results obtained and looks for the type of common pattern which might suggest the same system was involved across the range of tasks.

Table X summarizes our results so far. We have studied three types of task: the verbal reasoning test, language comprehension, and the free recall of unrelated words. As Table X shows, these have in all three cases shown a substantial impairment in performance when an additional memory load of six items was imposed. In contrast to this, a load of three items appears to have little or no decremental effect, an unexpected finding which is common to all three situations. In the case of phonemic similarity, we have found the type of

TABLE X

		Verbal reasoning	Comprehension	Free recall	
				LTS	Recency
Memory load				Small	
	1–3 items	No effect	No effect	decrement	No effect
	6 items	Decrement	Decrement	Decrement	No effect
Phonemic similarity		Decrement	Decrement	Enhancement	No effect
Articulatory suppression		Decrement	Not studied	Decrement	No effect

effect that would be expected on the assumption of a working memory system having characteristics in common with the digit span. Such effects are reflected in a performance decrement in those tasks where the retention of order is important (the reasoning and sentence judging tasks), coupled with a positive effect in the free recall situation for which the recall order is not required. Finally we have found that articulatory suppression, a technique which is known to impair digit span (Baddeley & Thomson, unpublished), has a deleterious effect in the two situations in which we have so far studied it, namely reasoning and free recall learning.

There appears then to be a consistent pattern of effects across the three types of task studied, strongly suggesting the operation of a common system such as the working memory initially proposed. This system appears to have something in common with the mechanism responsible for the digit span, being susceptible to disruption by a concurrent digit span task, and like the digit span showing signs of being based at least in part upon phonemic coding. It should be noted, however, that the degree of disruption observed, even with a near-span concurrent memory load, was far from massive. This suggests that although the digit span and working memory overlap, there appears to be a considerable component of working memory which is not taken up by the digit span task. The relatively small effects of phonemic coding and articulatory suppression reinforce this view and suggest that the articulatory component may comprise only one feature of working memory. Coltheart's (1972) failure to find an effect of phonemic similarity on a concept formation task is, therefore, not particularly surprising.

We would like to suggest that the core of the working memory system consists of a limited capacity "work space" which can be divided between storage and control processing demands. The next three sections comprise a tentative attempt to elaborate our view of the working memory system by considering three basic questions: how work space is allocated, how the central processing system and the more peripheral phonemic rehearsal system interact in the memory span task, and, finally, whether different modalities each have their own separate working memory system.

A. ALLOCATION OF WORK SPACE

Our data suggest that a trade-off exists between the amount of storage required and the rate at which other processes can be carried out. In Experiment III, for example, Ss solved verbal reasoning problems while either reciting a digit sequence, repeating the word *the,* or saying nothing. It is assumed that reciting a digit sequence requires more short-term storage than either of the other two conditions. Reasoning times, which presumably reflect the rate at which logical operations are carried out, were substantially increased in this condition. Furthermore, problems containing passive and negative sentences were slowed down more than problems posed as active and affirmative sentences. Since grammatically complex sentences presumably require a greater number of processing operations than simple sentences, this result is consistent with the assumed trade-off between storage-load and processing-rate.

The effect of additional memory load on free recall may be used to make a similar point. Experiments on presentation rate and free recall suggest that "transfer" to LTS proceeds at a limited rate. Since increasing memory load reduced transfer to LTS, it is arguable that this may result from a decrease in the rate at which the control processes necessary for transfer could be executed.

However, although our evidence suggests some degree of trade-off between storage-load and processing-rate, it would probably be unwise to regard working memory as an entirely flexible system of which any part may be allocated either to storage or processing. There are two reasons for this. In the first place, there may ultimately be no clear theoretical grounds for distinguishing processing and storage: they may always go together. Secondly, at the empirical level, a number of results show that it is difficult to produce appreciable interference with additional memory loads below the size of the span. This may mean that a part of the system that may be used for storage is not available for general processing. When the capacity of this component is exceeded, then some of the general-purpose work space must be devoted to storage, with the result that less space is available for processing. We shall discuss this possibility in more detail in the next section.

The final point concerns the factors which control the trade-off between the amount of work space allocated to two competing tasks. Results show that instructional emphasis is at least one determinant. In Experiment II, for example, Ss for whom the memory task was emphasized showed a very much greater effect of a six-digit preload on reasoning time than was shown by a second group who were instructed that both tasks were equally important. Evidence for a similar effect in free recall learning has been presented by Murdock (1965). He showed that a concurrent card-sorting task interfered with the long-term component of free recall and that the trade-off between performance on the two tasks was determined by the particular payoff specified in the instructions.

B. The Role of Working Memory in the Memory Span

We have suggested that the working memory system may contain both flexible work space and also a component that is dedicated to storage. This view is illustrated by the following suggested interpretation of the role of working memory in the memory span task. It is suggested that the memory span depends on both a phonemic response buffer which is able to store a limited amount of speechlike material in the appropriate serial order and the flexible component of working memory. The phonemic component is relatively passive and makes few demands on the central processing space, provided its capacity is not exceeded. The more flexible and executive component of the system is responsible for setting up the appropriate phonemic "rehearsal" routines, i.e., of loading up the phonemic buffer and of retrieving information from the buffer when necessary. Provided the memory load does not exceed the capacity of the phonemic buffer, little demand is placed upon the central executive, other than the routine recycling of the presumably familiar subroutines necessary for rehearsing digits. When the capacity of the phonemic buffer is exceeded, then the executive component of working memory must devote more of its time to the problem of storage. This probably involves both recoding in such a way as to reduce the length or complexity of the phonemic subroutine involved in rehearsal and also devoting more attention to the problem of retrieval. It is, for example, probably at this stage that retrieval rules

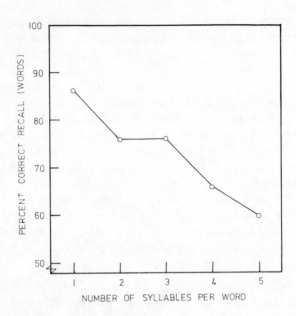

Fig. 6. Effect of word length on short-term serial recall. (Data from Baddeley and Thomson, unpublished.)

become useful in allowing S to utilize his knowledge of the experimental situation in order to interpret the deteriorated traces emerging from an overloaded phonemic buffer (Baddeley, 1972).

According to this account, the span of immediate memory is set by two major factors: the capacity of the phonemic loop, which is presumably relatively invariant, and the ability of the central executive component to supplement this, both by recoding at input and reconstruction at the recall stage. We have begun to study the first of these factors by varying word length in the memory span situation. Figure 6 shows the results of an experiment in which eight Ss were presented with sequences of five words from each of five sets. Each set comprised ten words of equal frequency of occurrence, but sets varied in word length, ranging in number of syllables from one through five. There is a clear tendency for performance to decline as word length increases. A similar result was independently obtained by Standing (personal communication) who observed a negative correlation between the memory span for a given type of material and the speed at which that material can be articulated. It is perhaps worth noting at this point that Craik (1968) reports that the recency effect in free recall is unaffected by the word length, suggesting once again a clear distinction between factors influencing the recency effect in free recall and those affecting the memory span. Watkins (1972) has further observed that word length does not influence the modality effect, but does impair the long-term component of verbal free recall. The former result would tend to suggest that the precategorical acoustic store on which the modality effect is generally assumed to rely (Crowder & Morton, 1969) lies outside the working memory system.

We, therefore, appear to have at least tentative evidence for the existence of a phonemic buffer, together with techniques such as articulatory suppression and the manipulation of word length which hopefully will provide tools for investigating this component in greater depth. It is possible that this component plays a major role in determining the occurrence of both acoustic similarity effects in memory and perhaps also of such speech errors as tongue twisters and spoonerisms. It seems likely that although it does not form the central core of working memory the phonemic component will probably justify considerably more investigation.

The operation of the central component of working memory seems likely to prove considerably more complex. It seems probable that it is this component that is responsible for the "chunking" of material which was first pointed out by Miller (1956) and has subsequently been studied in greater detail by Slak (1970), who taught subjects to recode digit sequences into a letter code which ensured an alternation between consonants and vowels. This allowed a dramatic reduction in the number of phonemes required to encode the sequence and resulted not only in a marked increase in the digit span, but also in a clear improvement in the performance of a range of tasks involving the long-term learning of digit sequences. A similar recoding procedure, this time based on prior language habits, is probably responsible for the observed increase in span for letter sequences as they approximate more closely to the structure of English words. This, together with the decreased importance of phonemic similarity, suggests that S is chunking several letters into one speech sound rather than simply rehearsing the name of the letter (Baddeley, 1971).

During retrieval, the executive component of the working memory system is probably responsible for interpreting the phonemic trace; it is probably at this level that retrieval rules (Baddeley, 1972) are applied. These ensure that a trace is interpreted within the constraints of the experiment, with the result that Ss virtually never produce completely inappropriate responses such as letters in an experiment using digits. We have unfortunately, however, so far done little to investigate this crucial central executive component; techniques aimed at blocking this central processor while leaving the peripheral components free should clearly be developed if possible.

C. ONE OR MANY WORKING MEMORIES?

Our work so far has concentrated exclusively on verbal tasks, and the question obviously arises as to how general are our conclusions. It seems probable that a comparable system exists for visual memory which is different at least in part from the system we have been discussing.

Brooks (1967, 1968) studied a number of tasks in which S is induced to form a visual image and use this in an immediate memory situation. He has shown that performance in such a situation is impaired by concurrent visual processing, in contrast to equivalent phonemically based tasks, which are much more susceptible to concurrent verbal activity. We have confirmed and extended Brooks' results using visual pursuit tracking (Baddeley, Grant, Wight, & Thomson, 1974) which was found to cause a dramatic impairment in performance on a span task based on visual imagery, while producing no decrement in performance on an equivalent phonemically based task. Further evidence for the existence of a visual memory system which may be unaffected by heavy phonemic processing demands comes from the study by Kroll, Parks, Parkinson, Bieber, and Johnson (1970), who showed that Ss could retain a visually presented letter over a period of many seconds of shadowing auditory material.

From these and many other studies, it is clear that visual and auditory short-term storage do employ different subsystems. What is less clear is whether we need to assume completely separate parallel systems for different modalities, or whether the different modalities may share a common central processor. Preliminary evidence for the latter view comes from an unpublished study by R. Lee at the University of St. Andrews. He studied memory for pictures in a situation where Ss were first familiarized with sets of pictures of a number of local scenes, for which they were taught an appropriate name. Several slightly different views of each scene were used although only half of the variants of each scene were presented during the pretraining stage. Subjects were then tested on the full set of pictures and were required in each case to name the scene, saying whether the particular version shown was an "old" view which they had seen before or a "new" one. Subjects' performance was compared both while doing this task alone and while doing a concurrent mental arithmetic task (e.g., multiplying 27 and 42). Subjects were able to name the scenes without error in both conditions, but made a number of errors in deciding whether or not they had seen any given specific view of that scene; these errors were markedly more frequent in the mental arithmetic condition, suggesting that the visual recognition process was competing for limited processing capacity with the arithmetic task. One obvious interpretation of this result is to suggest that the central processor which we have assumed forms the core of working memory in our verbal situations plays a similar role in visual memory, although this time with a separate peripheral memory component, based on the visual system. What little evidence there exists, therefore, suggests that the possibility of a single common central processor should be investigated further, before assuming completely separate working memories for different modalities.

D. WORKING MEMORY AND THE RECENCY EFFECT IN FREE RECALL

A major distinction between the working memory system we propose and STS (Atkinson & Shiffrin, 1968) centers on the recency effect in free recall. Most theories of STM assume that retrieval from a temporary buffer store accounts for the recency effect, whereas our own results argue against this view. It is suggested that working memory, which in other respects can be regarded as a modified STS, does not provide the basis for recency.

Experiment IX studied the effect of a concurrent digit memory task on the retention of lists of unrelated words. The results showed that when Ss were concurrently retaining six digits, the LTS component of recall was low, but recency was virtually unaffected. Since six digits is very near the memory span, the STS model would have to assume that STS is full almost to capacity for an appreciable part of the time during the learning of the words for free recall. On this model, both recency and LTS transfer should be lowered by the additional short-term storage load. As there was no loss of recency, it seems that an STS account of recency is inappropriate. Instead, it seems that recency reflects retrieval from a store which is different from that used for the digit span task. Perhaps the most important aspect of this interpretation is that the limited memory span and limited rate of transfer of information to LTS must be regarded as having a common origin which is different from that of the recency effect. It would be useful to consider briefly what further evidence there is for this point of view.

E. THE MEMORY SPAN, TRANSFER TO LTS, AND RECENCY

There is a wide range of variables which appear to affect the memory span (or short-term serial recall) and the LTS component of free recall in the same way, but which do not affect the recency component of free recall. In addition to the effects of word length and articulatory suppression which we have already discussed, which probably reflect the limited storage capacity of the working memory system or of one of its components, there are a number of variables which have been shown to affect the second limitation of the STS system, namely the rate at which it is able to transfer information to LTS. Several sets of experimental results show that the recency effect is not influenced by factors which interfere with LTS transfer. Murdock (1965), Baddeley, Scott, Drynan, and Smith (1969), and Bartz and Salehi (1970) have all shown that the LTS component of free recall is reduced when Ss are required to perform a subsidiary card-sorting task during presentation of the items for free recall. The effect is roughly proportional to the difficulty of the subsidiary task. However, there is no effect on the recency component of recall. Similar results have been reported by Silverstein and Glanzer (1971) using arithmetic varying in level of difficulty as the subsidiary task. As most of these authors concluded, the results suggest that there is a limited capacity system mediating LTS registration which is not responsible for the recency effect. On the present hypothesis, the subsidiary task is viewed as interfering with working memory and does not necessarily, therefore, interfere with recency as well. Hence the crucial difference in emphasis between the two theories (working memory-LTS, and STS-LTS) is that working memory is supposed to have both buffer-storage and control-processing functions, with recency explained by a separate mechanism.

IV. The Nature of the Recency Effect

So far, the most compelling argument for rejecting the buffer-storage hypothesis for recency has been the data from Experiment XI, in which a concurrent memory span task did not abolish recency in free recall. Clearly the argument needs strengthening.

Tzeng (1973) presented words for free recall in such a way that before and after each word, S was engaged in a 20-second period of counting backwards by three's. Under these conditions the serial position curve showed a strong recency effect. After learning four such lists, S was asked to recall as many words as possible from all four lists. Even on this final recall, the last items from each of the lists were recalled markedly better than items from earlier positions. Neither of these two recency effects is easily attributable to retrieval from a short-term buffer store. With the initial recall, the counting task ought to have displaced words from the buffer. In the case of the final recall the amount of interpolated activity was even greater. Tzeng's results, therefore, suggest at the very least that the recency effect is not always attributable to output from buffer storage. Tzeng cites further evidence (unpublished at the time of writing) from Dalezman and from Bjork and Whitten, in both cases suggesting that recency may occur under conditions which preclude the operation of STS.

Baddeley (1963) carried out an experiment in which Ss were given a list of 12 anagrams to solve. Anagrams were presented one at a time for as long as it took for a solution to be found, up to a limit of one minute, at which time the experimenter presented the solution. After the final anagram, S was questioned about his strategy and was then asked to freely recall as many of the solution words as possible. The results of the recall test are shown in Fig. 7 since they were not reported in the original paper. They show that despite the unexpected nature of the recall request and the delay while S discussed his strategy, a pronounced recency effect occurs. Since each item except the last was followed by up to a minute of problem-

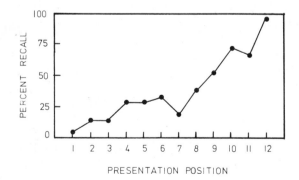

Fig. 7. Recall of anagram solutions as a function of order of presentation of the problems. (Data from Baddeley, 1963.)

solving activity and the last item was followed by a period of question-answering, it is difficult to explain this recency effect in terms of a temporary buffer store.

An experiment by Glanzer (1972) which we have successfully replicated (Baddeley & Thomson, unpublished) presents further problems for a simple buffer-store interpretation of the recency effect. Instead of unrelated words, Glanzer used proverbs as the material to be recalled. His results showed two striking phenomena: first, the recency effect extended over the last few proverbs rather than the last few words; and second, a filled delay reduced, but by no means eliminated, the marked recency effect observed. The extent of recency, therefore, seems to be defined in terms of "semantic units" rather than words. This is not, of course, incompatible with a buffer-storage account, although in this experiment, a good deal of semantic processing would presumably have to occur before entry of a proverb into this buffer. The assumption of a more central store does have the additional advantage of "explaining" the durable recency effect observed in this study, in terms of the suggestion by Craik and Lockhart (1972) that greater depth of processing is associated with greater durability. However, it is clearly the case that such a depth of processing is by no means essential to the recency effect. Indeed, the effect appears to be completely unaffected by factors such as presentation rate (Glanzer & Cunitz, 1966), concurrent processing load (Murdock, 1965), and type of material (Glanzer, 1972), all of which would be expected to have a pronounced influence on depth of processing.

A more promising alternative explanation of recency might be to elaborate the proposal made by Tulving (1968) that recency reflects the operation of a retrieval strategy, rather than the output of a specific store. Provided one assumes that ordinal recency may be one accessible feature of a memory trace, then it is plausible to assume that Ss may frequently access items on the basis of this cue. The limited size of the recency effect, suggesting that recency is only an effective cue for the last few items, might reasonably be attributed to limitations on the discriminability of recency cues. One might assume, following Weber's Law, that with the newest item as a reference point, discriminability of ordinal position ought to decrease with increasing "oldness." The advantage of assuming an ordinal retrieval strategy of this kind is that it can presumably be applied to any available store and possibly also to any subset of items within that store, provided the subset can be adequately categorized. Thus, when an interpolated activity is classed in the same category as the learned items, the interpolated events will be stored in the same dimension as the to-be-remembered items and will hence supersede them as the most recent events. When the interpolated activity is classed in a different category from the learned items, recency will be unaffected. This presumably occurred in the case of proverbs and the anagram solutions. It also seems intuitively plausible to assume that a similar type of recency is reflected in one's own memory for clearly specified classes of events, for example, football games, parties, or meals at restaurants, all of which introspectively at least appear to exhibit their own recency effect. It is clearly necessary to attempt to collect more objective information on this point, however.

The preceding account of recency is highly tentative, and although it does possess the advantage of being able to deal with evidence which presents considerable difficulties for the buffer-store interpretation, it does leave two very basic questions unanswered. The first of these concerns the question of what factors influence the categorization of different types of events; it seems intuitively unlikely that backward-counting activity should be categorized in the same way for example as visually presented words, and yet counting effectively destroys the recency effect in this situation. This is, of course, a difficult problem, but it is no less a problem for the buffer-store interpretation which must also account for the discrepancy between Tzeng's results and the standard effect of a filled delay on recency.

The second basic question is that of how ordinal recency is stored, whether in terms of trace-strength, in terms of ordinal "tags" of some kind, or in some as yet unspecified way. Once again, this problem is not peculiar to the retrieval cue interpretation of recency; it is clearly the case that we are able to access ordinal information in some way. How we do this, and whether ordinal cues can be used to retrieve other information, is an empirical question which remains unanswered.

V. Concluding Remarks

We would like to suggest that we have presented *prima facie* evidence for the existence of a working memory system which plays a central role in human information processing. The system we propose is very much in the spirit of similar proposals by such authors as Posner and Rossman (1965) and Atkinson and Shiffrin (1971). However, whereas earlier work concentrated principally on the memory system *per se,* with the result that the implications of the system for nonmemory tasks were largely speculative, our own work has been focused on the information processing tasks rather than the system itself. As a consequence of this, we have had to change our views of both working memory and of the explanation of certain STM phenomena.

To sum up, we have tried to make a case for postulating the working memory-LTS system as a modification of the current STS-LTS view. We would like to suggest that working memory represents a control system with limits on both its storage and processing capabilities. We suggest that it has access to phonemically coded information (possibly by controlling a rehearsal buffer), that it is responsible for the limited memory span, but does not underly the recency effect in free recall. Perhaps the most specific function which has so far been identified with working memory is the transfer of information to LTS. We have not yet explored its role in retrieval, so that the implications of Patterson's (1971) results for the nature of working memory are still unclear. Our experiments suggest that the phonemic rehearsal buffer plays a limited role in this process, but is by no means essential. The patient K.F., whom Shallice and Warrington (1970) showed to have grossly impaired digit span together with normal long-term learning ability, presents great difficulty for the current LTS-STS view, since despite his defective STS, his long-term learning ability is unimpaired. His case can, however, be handled quite easily by the view of working memory proposed, if it is assumed that only the phonemic rehearsal-buffer component of his working memory is impaired, while the central executive component is intact. Our experiments also suggest that working memory plays a part in verbal reasoning and in prose comprehension. Understanding the detailed role of working memory in these tasks, however, must proceed hand-in-hand with an understanding of the tasks themselves.

We began with a very simple question: *what is short-term memory for?* We hope that our preliminary attempts to begin answering the question will convince the reader, not necessarily that our views are correct, but that the question was and is well worth asking.

Acknowledgments

Part of the experimental work described in this chapter was carried out at the University of Sussex. We are grateful to colleagues at both Sussex and Stirling for valuable discussion and in particular to Neil Thomson whose contribution was both practical and theoretical. The financial support of both the British Medical Research Council and the Social Sciences Research Council is gratefully acknowledged.

References

Atkinson, R. C., & Shiffrin, R. M. Human memory: A proposed system and its control processes. In K. W. Spence & J. T. Spence (Eds.), *The psychology of learning and motivation: Advances in research and theory.* Vol. 2. New York: Academic Press, 1968. Pp. 89–195.

Atkinson, R. C., & Shiffrin, R. M. The control of short-term memory. *Scientific American,* 1971, **225,** 82–90.

Baddeley, A. D. A Zeigarnik-like effect in the recall of anagram solutions. *Quarterly Journal of Experimental Psychology,* 1963, **15,** 63–64.

Baddeley, A. D. The influence of acoustic and semantic similarity on long-term memory for word sequences. *Quarterly Journal of Experimental Psychology,* 1966, **18,** 302–309. (a)

Baddeley, A. D. Short-term memory for word sequences as a function of acoustic, semantic and formal similarity. *Quarterly Journal of Experimental Psychology,* 1966, **18,** 362–366. (b)

Baddeley, A. D. A three-minute reasoning test based on grammatical transformation. *Psychonomic Science,* 1968, **10,** 341–342.

Baddeley, A. D. Language habits, acoustic confusability and immediate memory for redundant letter sequences. *Psychonomic Science,* 1971, **22,** 120–121.

Baddeley, A. D. Retrieval rules and semantic coding in short-term memory. *Psychological Bulletin,* 1972, **78,** 379–385.

Baddeley, A. D., De Figuredo, J. W., Hawkswell-Curtis, J. W., & Williams, A. N. Nitrogen narcosis and performance under water. *Ergonomics,* 1968, **11,** 157–164.

Baddeley, A. D., Grant, S., Wight, E., & Thomson, N. Imagery and visual working memory. In P. M. Rabbitt & S. Dornic (Eds.), *Attention and performance.* Vol. 5. New York: Academic Press, 1974, in press.

Baddeley, A. D., & Patterson, K. The relationship between long-term and short-term memory. *British Medical Bulletin,* 1971, **27,** 237–242.

Baddeley, A. D., Scott, D., Drynan, R., & Smith, J. C. Short-term memory and the limited capacity hypothesis. *British Journal of Psychology,* 1969, **60,** 51–55.

Baddeley, A. D., & Warrington, E. K. Memory coding and amnesia. *Neuropsychologia,* 1973, **11,** 159–165.

Bartz, W. H., & Salehi, M. Interference in short- and long-term memory. *Journal of Experimental Psychology,* 1970, **84,** 380–382.

Brooks, L. R. The suppression of visualization in reading. *Quarterly Journal of Experimental Psychology,* 1967, **19,** 289–299.

Brooks, L. R. Spatial and verbal components in the act of recall. *Canadian Journal of Psychology,* 1968, **22,** 349–368.

Brown, I. D., Tickner, A. H., & Simmonds, D. C. V. Interference between concurrent tasks of driving and telephoning. *Journal of Applied Psychology,* 1969, **53,** 419–424.

Bruce, D., & Crowley, J. J. Acoustic similarity effects on retrieval from secondary memory. *Journal of Verbal Learning and Verbal Behavior,* 1970, **9,** 190–196.

Coltheart, V. The effects of acoustic and semantic similarity on concept identification. *Quarterly Journal of Experimental Psychology,* 1972, **24,** 55–65.

Conrad, R. An association between memory errors and errors due to acoustic masking of speech. *Nature* (London), 1962, **193,** 1314–1315.

Conrad, R., & Hull, A. J. Information, acoustic confusion and memory span. *British Journal of Psychology,* 1964, **55,** 429–432.

Craik, F. I. M. Two components in free recall. *Journal of Verbal Learning and Verbal Behavior,* 1968, **7,** 996–1004.

Craik, F. I. M., & Levy, B. A. Semantic and acoustic information in primary memory. *Journal of Experimental Psychology,* 1970, **86,** 77–82.

Craik, F. I. M., & Lockhart, R. S. Levels of processing: A framework for memory research. *Journal of Verbal Learning and Verbal Behavior,* 1972, **11,** 671–684.

Crowder, R. G., & Morton, J. Precategorical acoustic storage (PAS). *Perception & Psychophysics,* 1969, **5,** 365–373.

Glanzer, M. Storage mechanisms in free recall. In G. H. Bower (Ed.), *The psychology of learning and motivation: Advances in research and theory.* Vol. 5. New York: Academic Press, 1972. Pp. 129–193.

Glanzer, M., & Cunitz, A. R. Two storage mechanisms in free recall. *Journal of Verbal Learning and Verbal Behavior,* 1966, **5,** 351–360.

Glanzer, M., Koppenaal, L., & Nelson, R. Effects of relations between words on short-term storage and long-term storage. *Journal of Verbal Learning and Verbal Behavior,* 1972, **11,** 403–416.

Green, D. W. A psychological investigation into the memory and comprehension of sentences. Unpublished doctoral dissertation, University of London, 1973.

Hammerton, M. Interference between low information verbal output and a cognitive task. *Nature (London),* 1969, **222,** 196.

Hunter, I. M. L. *Memory.* London: Penguin Books, 1964.

Jarvella, R. J. Syntactic processing of connected speech. *Journal of Verbal Learning and Verbal Behavior,* 1971, **10,** 409–416.

Johnston, W. A., Griffith, D., & Wagstaff, R. R. Information processing analysis of verbal learning. *Journal of Experimental Psychology,* 1972, **96,** 307–314.

Kroll, N. E. A., Parks, T., Parkinson, S. R., Bieber, S. L., & Johnson, A. L. Short-term memory while shadowing: Recall of visually and aurally presented letters. *Journal of Experimental Psychology,* 1970, **85,** 220–224.

Levy, B. A. Role of articulation in auditory and visual short-term memory. *Journal of Verbal Learning and Verbal Behavior,* 1971, **10,** 123–132.

Martin, D. W. Residual processing capacity during verbal organization in memory. *Journal of Verbal Learning and Verbal Behavior,* 1970, **9,** 391–397.

Miller, G. A. The magical number seven plus or minus two: some limits on our capacity for processing information. *Psychological Review,* 1956, **63,** 81–97.

Murdock, B. B., Jr. Effects of a subsidiary task on short-term memory. *British Journal of Psychology,* 1965, **56,** 413–419.

Murray, D. J. The role of speech responses in short-term memory. *Canadian Journal of Psychology,* 1967, **21,** 263–276.

Murray, D. J. Articulation and acoustic confusability in short-term memory. *Journal of Experimental Psychology,* 1968, **78,** 679–684.

Neale, M. D. *Neale Analysis of Reading Ability.* London: Macmillan, 1958.

Norman, D. A. The role of memory in the understanding of language. In J. F. Kavanagh & I. G. Mattingly (Eds.), Cambridge, Mass.: MIT Press, 1972.

Patterson, K. A. Limitations on retrieval from long-term memory. Unpublished doctoral dissertation, University of California, San Diego, 1971.

Peterson, L. R. Concurrent verbal activity. *Psychological Review,* 1969, **76,** 376–386.

Peterson, L. R., & Peterson, M. J. Short-term retention of individual verbal items. *Journal of Experimental Psychology*, 1959, **58**, 193–198.

Posner, M. I., & Rossman, E. Effect of size and location of informational transforms upon short-term retention. *Journal of Experimental Psychology*, 1965, **70**, 496–505.

Rubenstein, H., & Aborn, M. Learning, prediction and readability. *Journal of Applied Psychology*, 1958, **42**, 28–32.

Rumelhart, D. E., Lindsay, P. H., & Norman, D. A. A process model for long-term memory. In E. Tulving & W. Donaldson (Eds.), *Organisation and memory*. New York: Academic Press, 1972.

Sachs, J. D. S. Recognition memory for syntactic and semantic aspects of connected discourse. *Perception & Psychophysics*, 1967, **2**, 437–442.

Shallice, T., & Warrington, E. K. Independent functioning of verbal memory stores: a neuropsychological study. *Quarterly Journal of Experimental Psychology*, 1970, **22**, 261–273.

Silverstein, C., & Glanzer, M. Difficulty of a concurrent task in free recall: differential effects of LTS and STS. *Psychonomic Science*, 1971, **22**, 367–368.

Slak, S. Phonemic recoding of digital information. *Journal of Experimental Psychology*, 1970, **86**, 398–406.

Sperling, G. A model for visual memory tasks. *Human Factors*, 1963, **5**, 19–31.

Taylor, W. L. "Cloze procedure": A new tool for measuring readability. *Journalism Quarterly*, 1953, **30**, 415–433.

Tulving, E. Theoretical issues in free recall. In T. R. Dixon & D. L. Horton (Eds.), *Verbal behaviour and general behaviour theory*. Englewood Cliffs, N.J.: Prentice-Hall, 1968.

Tzeng, O. J. L. Positive recency effect in delayed free recall. *Journal of Verbal Learning and Verbal Behavior*, 1973, **12**, 436–439.

Warrington, E. K., Logue, V., & Pratt, R. T. C. The anatomical localization of selective impairment of auditory verbal short-term memory. *Neuropsychologia*, 1971, **9**, 377–387.

Warrington, E. K., & Shallice, T. The selective impairment of auditory verbal short-term memory. *Brain*, 1969, **92**, 885–896.

Warrington, E. K., & Weiskrantz, L. An analysis of short-term and long-term memory defects in man. In J. A. Deutsch (Ed.), *The physiological basis of memory*. New York: Academic Press, 1973.

Wason, P. C., & Johnson-Laird, P. N. *Psychology of reasoning: Structure and content*. London: Batsford, 1972.

Watkins, M. J. Locus of the modality effect in free recall. *Journal of Verbal Learning and Verbal Behavior*, 1972, **11**, 644–648.

Waugh, N. C., & Norman, D. A. Primary memory. *Psychological Review*, 1965, **72**, 89–104.

Wickelgren, W. A. Short-term memory for phonemically similar lists. *American Journal of Psychology*, 1965, **78**, 567–574.

THE ROLE OF ADAPTATION-LEVEL IN STIMULUS GENERALIZATION[1]

David R. Thomas

UNIVERSITY OF COLORADO, BOULDER, COLORADO

I. Introduction

Although generalization gradients differ markedly in slope and form from one situation to another, their most common attribute is in the locus of maximal response strength at the value of the training stimulus (TS). Pavlov (1927) who performed the first systematic studies of stimulus generalization attributed the empirical gradient to a hypothesized process of irradiation, emanating outward from the cortical site of the CS. Hull (1943) accepted the principle of a gradient of response strength, although silent on its neurological basis, when he wrote, "In general, the more remote on the stimulus continuum the evoking stimulus (S) is from that originally conditioned (S̄), the weaker will be the reaction tendency mobilized by it [p. 184]." Indeed, the principle of generalization is so central to an analysis of learned behavior that it is incorporated into every major theory of learning (cf. Hilgard & Bower, 1966).

[1] The preparation of this chapter and the research reported therein was supported in part by NIH Research Grant HD-03486 and Training Grant MH-10427. The author wishes to thank John A. Hébert, James F. Dickson, Jr., Harry Strub, and Arthur Tomie for their contributions to this research.

There are at least two experimental situations in which maximal response strength commonly does not occur to the training stimulus value. One of these involves the use of prothetic or intensive dimensions, such as loudness, brightness, etc., where a typical result, at least in classical conditioning situations, has been a positive relationship between test stimulus intensity and response strength, regardless of the value of the training stimulus (cf. Hovland, 1937; Razran, 1949). Hull (1943) explained this anomaly by postulating a mechanism of stimulus intensity dynamism. That is, he proposed that more intense stimuli elicit stronger responses through a direct dynamogenic process.

Another case in which maximal responding occurs to a nontraining value involves successive discrimination training employing two stimuli on the same dimension, one associated with reinforcement (S+) and one signaling extinction (S−). In this situation, subjects (Ss) tend to respond most to a value displaced from S+ so as to be farther removed from S− (cf. Hanson, 1959; Thomas, 1962). This finding (called a "peak shift") has been interpreted as supporting Spence's (1937) gradient interaction theory. According to his view, in discrimination training, reinforcement establishes a gradient of excitation around S+, extinction establishes a gradient of inhibition around S−, and the empirically observed postdiscrimination generalization gradient is a consequence of the algebraic summation of excitatory and inhibitory response tendencies at each point on the stimulus continuum. The displacement of maximal responding from the positive stimulus value in the direction away from S− is also consistent with a relational view of discrimination learning (cf. Krechevsky, 1938), although the fact that the gradient is peaked (nonmonotonic) is not.

Both the displacement of maximal generalized responding from S+ measured along intensive dimensions and in postdiscrimination generalization gradients are consistent with the Hull–Spence S-R association view of learning which has long dominated research in this area. In the recent literature, however, are several reports of peak shifts on both extensive (qualitative) and intensive dimensions which follow single stimulus (nondiscriminative) training. The crucial variable in these studies is the asymmetrical spacing of test values around the TS in a within-subject generalization test. Most often in this situation, maximal generalized responding occurs to a stimulus near the center of the test series regardless of the value of the initial TS. Such context effects observed during generalization testing are beyond the purview of S-R associationistic models of generalization and discrimination learning. In interpreting such effects, we have found it fruitful to employ the concept of Adaptation-level, as proposed by Helson (cf. 1959, 1964) and as applied to questions of discrimination learning and stimulus generalization by James (1953), by Zeiler (1963), and by Capehart, Tempone, and Hébert (1969).

The implications of AL theory for stimulus generalization have been investigated in our laboratory in a wide variety of paradigms (including both single-stimulus and discrimination training), involving many different stimulus dimensions and in both human and infrahuman Ss. In this chapter, this program of research will be described in some detail. Related work by others will be discussed only where it is highly relevant to our own efforts. It should be emphasized that we will be concerned only with the implications of AL theory for an analysis of stimulus generalization. Applications of the theory to other aspects of learned behavior have been ignored in this treatment. Furthermore, it should be emphasized that AL theory is not a complete or exhaustive theory of generalization. There are many aspects of generalized behavior which it does not encompass, e.g., differences in the slope of generalization gradients following different training procedures. The theory, in present form, only concerns itself with the location of the point of maximal responding in generalization or with the location of the crossover point between two categories of responding. It is possible that with certain additional assumptions, the theory can be expanded to encompass additional phenomena, but no such expansion has been attempted here. Thus, although for simplicity of exposition reference is made to "the AL theory of generalization," it would be more appropriate to label it "the application of certain AL principles and assumptions to certain aspects of generalized responding." Throughout the chapter, gaps in our knowledge are pointed out, apparent shortcomings or limitations of the theory are treated, and suggestions for further research are made. In a concluding statement, an evaluation of the fruitfulness of the theory is offered.

Procedural Considerations. With few exceptions, the work to be discussed here has been performed with human (college student) subjects and has employed a voluntary generalization task. An early example of such a task, used by Brown, Bilodeau, and Baron (1951), involved instructing Ss to respond only to the center lamp in a semicircular array, but not to be unduly concerned if they were to respond to other test lamps. The Ss were further instructed to react as quickly and accurately as possible. In testing, the Ss tended to respond most to the training lamp but they frequently responded (erroneously) to other lamps as well, in relation to their distance from the training value.

In the present chapter, voluntary generalization experiments will be described which employed such diverse stimulus dimensions as lifted weight, wavelength, brightness, line angle, etc. The essential difference between these studies and those which use conditioning methods is that the response, whether it be a verbal utterance or other motor movement, exists in S's repertoire prior to the start of the experiment. What is learned is the "association" between that response and a particular stimulus value. Through appropriate instructions this association can be formed much more rapidly than is typically the case with conditioning. We make the assumption, however, that the principles which apply to generalization following such training are the same as those which govern the generalization of conditioned responses. We know of no data which challenge the validity of this assumption.

A.   THE CENTRAL TENDENCY EFFECT

In our first study in this area with human Ss (Thomas & Jones, 1962), the apparatus employed was actually a Skinner box for pigeons with a transparent Plexiglas rear wall through which the pecking key could be seen. With the success of this experiment, the key was removed from the box and mounted on a black vertical panel which separated the experimenter and the stimulus source, timers, etc., from the subject. In the early experiments, S responded by removing his finger from a telegraph key as rapidly as possible to signify that the test stimulus was the "same" as the TS. This provided a latency measure in addition to the number of "same" and "different" responses. As a general rule, the latency data were in agreement with the number-of-responses data, with longest latencies to stimuli usually judged the same as the TS and shortest latencies to stimuli most frequently judged as different. Because of this agreement between measures and the substantial variability in latency scores we initially did not report them and subsequently ceased obtaining them. In virtually all of our more recent work, the stimulus has continued to be displayed through a circular aperture the size of a pigeon's pecking key. There is no compelling reason to justify the use of this type of display (unless "tradition" is considered compelling); however, there is also none to warrant dropping it. In one recent experiment (Thomas & Thomas, 1974), we have used a tachistoscope to present the stimuli. In seeking a set of test values sufficiently similar to the TS to permit errors (i.e., generalized responses) to be made, we rediscovered the obvious manipulation of reducing the exposure time. In all of our recent research with human Ss, we have dispensed with the use of a response key in favor of having the S give the verbal response "same" or "different." It is ironic that this research program started with a pigeon Skinner box because in our most recent work we have returned to the use of that apparatus in the manner in which nature intended, i.e., with the pigeon inside.

Our original work on the role of the context created by the generalization test series was suggested by an earlier study by Philip (1952). This investigator required his Ss to rank cards containing varying proportions of green and blue dots along a greenness-blueness scale. The frequency with which a given rank, say Number 3, was attributed to the different cards constituted a gradient of generalization for that value. A separate gradient was thus generated for each rank employed.

Philip systematically varied the length of the generalization test series. With the shortest series employed (six values), there was a tendency for judgments to accumulate near the center of the scale, the "central tendency effect" (Hollingworth, 1909). This effect was reflected in asymmetrical gradients around stimulus values which were noncentrally placed in the series of generalization test stimuli.

Because of the unusual nature of Philip's (1952) procedure, the significance of his finding with regard to generalization as studied by other methods could be questioned. We, therefore, attempted to assess the generality of Philip's results, using a more typical procedure for obtaining generalization gradients. The method used was a modification of the Brown et al. (1951) procedure, first employed by Kalish (1958). With Kalish's procedure, the test stimuli vary in wavelength, rather than in spatial location. The Ss are first exposed to a single stimulus value and are subsequently tested for their ability to select the original from a randomly presented series of test stimuli. This is in contrast to the Philip procedure in which absolute judgments of predominating color are made without previous exposure to some standard stimulus value. It was reasoned that if the central tendency effect were shown to distort measures involving retention and subsequent identification of a TS as well as absolute judgment, its relevance for studies of generalization would be more convincingly demonstrated.

In the Thomas and Jones (1962) study five groups of Ss were exposed to a light of 525 nm for 60 sec with instructions to remember this color and to respond (by lifting a finger from a telegraph key) only to this value in subsequent testing. The groups differed only with regard to the series of stimuli employed in testing for generalization. In Group 1, the test stimuli used were 485 nm through 525 nm in 10-nm steps. For Group 2, the range covered was 495–535 nm, for Group 3, 505–545 nm, for Group 4, 515–555 nm, and for Group 5, 525–565 nm. For each S the five test stimuli were randomized within a series and 12 different series were presented. The number of responses made to the different test stimuli constituted a generalization gradient.

As shown in Fig. 1, the generalization gradients of the five groups of Ss differed strikingly in a manner consistent with the findings of Philip (1952). The tendency to respond to stimuli closer to the center of the test series was so strong that the peak of the generalization gradient was displaced from the value of the TS. Only with Group 3, where the test stimuli were symmetrically distributed around 525 nm, did the peak of the gradient fall clearly at that value.

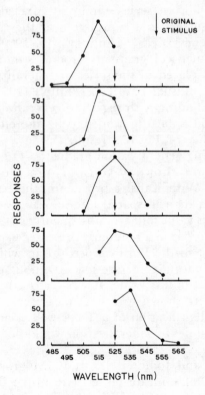

Fig. 1. Generalization gradients of groups of Ss ($n = 10$) which were exposed to a TS of 525 nm and tested with different sets of test values. (From Thomas & Jones, 1962.)

The findings of the Thomas and Jones (1962) experiment was interpreted with reference to Helson's (1947) theory of Adaptation-level (AL) as follows: "It may be argued that the series of test stimuli provides a frame of reference against which the memory trace of the original stimulus is judged. When test stimuli are presented which fall asymmetrically around the original stimulus, a change in the frame of reference may be assumed to result, culminating in a heightened tendency to respond to stimuli nearer to the center of the test series, thereby distorting the resulting generalization gradient [Thomas & Jones, 1962, p. 79]."

In discussion of their findings, Thomas and Jones raised many issues which became the focus of future research in our laboratory. One of these concerned the applicability of Adaptation-level concepts to conditioning situations with infrahuman Ss. Another speculated on the role of amount of training in determining the magnitude of subsequent testing effects. We shall return to these issues later.

In 1967, Helson and Avant reported a replication and extension of the Thomas and Jones (1962) experiment. They used a 3-in. (per side) square as their TS and tested with a series of squares, each $\frac{1}{8}$ in. longer than the next. Five different groups experienced different degrees and directions of asymmetry in their test series. As in the Thomas and Jones study, the Ss tended to respond maximally to the central stimulus in the test series, regardless of the location of the TS in that series.

B. The Adaptation-Level Model

The implicit assumed relationship between AL and the central tendency effect alluded to by Thomas and Jones (1962) and Helson and Avant (1967) was made explicit in an important theoretical paper by Capehart et al. (1969). Capehart et al. view AL as a stored referent against which all experienced stimuli are judged. It is the S's subjective representation of a neutral or average value on the continuum in question. The AL is a dynamic referent, continually subject to change as new stimulus information is processed.

In applying the AL theory to the analysis of the central tendency effect, Capehart et al. assumed that most experimental situations are sufficiently distinctive that the role of residual stimuli from past experience is negligible in determining the Training AL. Thus in single stimulus training, with the initial exposure to the TS, the AL is presumably formed at the value of the TS, the only relevant stimulus experienced in that situation. The instruction to respond on subsequent presentations of the TS presumably establishes the decision rule: "Respond to the Prevailing AL value." During generalization testing, the AL undergoes continual revision with continued exposure to the test stimuli. Thus with an asymmetrical test series, the Prevailing AL would shift toward the central value of the test series, and S's responding would be displaced accordingly.

To further elaborate on Capehart et al.'s position, it may be useful to conceive of three different AL values: Training AL, based on the value of the training stimulus or stimuli; Test AL, i.e., the AL value which would hypothetically be generated by exposure to the test stimuli alone; and Prevailing AL, which is a weighted average of the above two. After training ends and before testing begins, Prevailing AL is equivalent to Training AL. During the course of testing, the Test AL gains in weight relative to the Training AL as the major determinant of Prevailing AL. Thus as testing continues, the Prevailing AL becomes increasingly similar to the Test AL, such that ultimately the two may be indistinguishable.[2]

According to Capehart et al. (1969), in single-stimulus training, the relationship of the TS to Prevailing AL is one of equivalence, since before the start of testing, Training AL and Prevailing AL are necessarily the same. In a situation involving training with two stimulus values from a given dimension, the Training AL is thought to be formed between the two values each of which is then encoded with regard to its relationship to (i.e., distance and/or direction from) the Prevailing AL. In such cases, S may use AL as a crossover point for different classes of behavior, e.g., approach or avoid, go right versus left, etc. In this instance, reward may inform S as to which side of AL appropriate responses belong. It is appropriate to note that this view of the role of AL in discrimination learning was first proposed and developed by James (1953).

Capehart et al. (1969) made explicit certain limiting assumptions of their position which are worthy of note. They restricted their concern to stimuli within a single dimension and even further, to stimuli

[2] Note that in this elaboration of Capehart et al.'s position we have adopted their assumption that residual stimuli from past experience may be ignored in the determination of AL values. In some of our recent work, we have found it useful to reject this assumption and to postulate an additional AL based on preexperimental experience or on an experience to which S is subjected prior to the introduction of the TS. We assume that this "Preexperimental AL" also contributes to Prevailing AL. We further assume that as a consequence of recency and other factors, ultimately the most important contributor to Prevailing AL is Test AL, with Training AL and Preexperimental AL playing a far lesser role.

which are not qualitatively distinct. Thus, for example, within the physical dimension of wavelength there are distinctive color categories such that stimuli from two different categories may not be pooled to form an intermediate AL. Furthermore, stimulus equivalence may be mediated by verbal factors so that AL considerations may not apply in such cases. Capehart *et al.* considered the question of whether the applicability of the theory was restricted to generalization in human Ss and they concluded that no such restriction was necessary at that time. These proposed limiting assumptions have all been the focus of research in our laboratory, and we shall return to a consideration of them later.

A final point made by Capehart *et al.* (1969) is that the value of the application of AL theory to the analysis of stimulus generalization does not depend upon the acceptance of any particular mathematical model for *a priori* prediction of the locus of the AL (e.g., the weighted log mean). That particular model may apply to some stimulus dimensions and not to others. Thus, in some of the work which will be reported here, AL is defined empirically, rather than theoretically, as the average stimulus, as determined in a rating task (cf. Helson, 1964, Ch. 4). In many of the experiments to be described, AL was never directly measured at all. Rather, ordinal predictions were made based on assumptions of changes in AL as a consequence of manipulations known to affect AL in other situations.

In the sections of the chapter which follow, the data will be organized in terms of the independent and dependent variables which have been investigated or the experimental questions which have been raised.

II. Single-Stimulus Training and the Central Tendency Effect

In this section, the most simple paradigm, involving a single training stimulus, will be considered.

A. Changes in Generalized Responding during the Course of Testing

According to the AL theory, as testing progresses, the weight of the Test AL is increased relative to that of the Training AL such that ultimately Test AL and Prevailing AL are indistinguishable. If this is the case, it should be possible to demonstrate that at the beginning of testing, maximal responding occurs to the TS and the point of

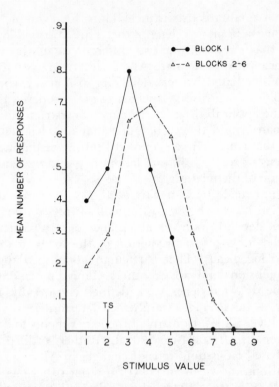

Fig. 2. Generalization gradients for a group of Ss ($n = 10$) obtained during different segments of the test procedure. (Form Thomas *et al.*, 1973.)

maximal responding shifts gradually toward the center of the test series as testing continues. Despite the straightforwardness of this prediction, it has not generally been explicitly tested even though every experiment obtains some data with which a test can be made. Thus, for example, neither the Thomas and Jones (1962) nor the Helson and Avant (1967) studies presented analyses of the data obtained in different portions of the generalization test. One problem in testing the hypothesis is that if the weighing of Test AL is high relative to that of the Training AL, the shift may occur so quickly that it has transpired by the end of the first test series. Thus, it cannot be shown that the gradient peak was initially at the TS value.

A case in point is illustrated by Fig. 2, taken from a study reported by Thomas, Svinicki, and Vogt (1973). In Experiment 3, one group of Ss was presented a dim light and then tested for generalization with test stimuli including the original, one dimmer value, and seven brighter ones. The nine brightness values were equally spaced on a logarithmic scale. In the figure, the mean generalization gradient based upon responding in the first series of test stimuli (Block 1) is compared with that based upon the remainder of the test (Blocks 2–6). The figure shows clearly the shift of generalized responding to values increasingly removed from the TS. Similar evidence for the progressive nature of the central tendency shift has been reported in several recent studies by Giurintano (1972); Hébert et al. (1974); Tomie and Thomas (1974); and Thomas et al. (1973).

The data presented in Fig. 2 are also typical in that the shift in maximal responding from the TS to an adjacent stimulus value had already taken place by the end of the first block of test stimuli. In order to test the assumption that maximal responding initially occurs to the TS value, it may be necessary to obtain a gradient of generalization based upon the very first test trial (i.e., the first test stimulus exposure) for each S. Since each S can contribute only one data point to such a gradient and that data point is based on a single observation, enough Ss must be tested at each stimulus value to generate a reliable index of response strength at that value. To obtain a gradient, groups of Ss must be tested at each of several stimulus values following initial exposure to a given TS. It is understandable that no study has been done specifically for this purpose, since the cost in experimenter and subject time would be excessive. Fortunately, a recent experiment by Thomas, Strub, and Dickson (1974) used enough Ss ($n = 140$) under appropriate conditions to obtain a reliable Trial 1 gradient after a single exposure to a dim light TS. That gradient is presented in Table I and, as predicted, the probability of responding to the TS (#1) was indeed highest, with decreasing response probabilities as a function of increasing distance from the TS

TABLE I

GENERALIZATION GRADIENT OBTAINED ON TRIAL 1[a]

	Test stimulus[b]								
	1	2	3	4	5	6	7	8	9
Probability of "same" response	.793	.560	.478	.167	.210	.125	.125	.000	.000
n	29	25	23	12	19	8	16	4	4

[a] From Thomas et al. (1974).

[b] The TS was equivalent to Test Stimulus Value 1, and the nine numbered test stimuli were equally spaced on a logarithmic scale.

value. This finding is consistent with the view that the TS is encoded as equivalent to the Training (Prevailing) AL value, although, it by no means precludes alternative interpretations. (See Section II, E.)

B.   THE ROLE OF AMOUNT OF TRAINING

Thomas and Jones (1962) speculated that the background or context provided by an asymmetrical test series should have less influence in a conditioning situation than in their voluntary generalization task. As they put it: "In this study, S's experience with the original stimulus was limited to one 60-sec exposure. The resulting limited familiarity with the stimulus makes extensive retroactive interference by the test series which follows more likely. In a conditioning situation, however, S has the opportunity through repeated exposure to become much more familiar with the value of the CS. Greater familiarity with the stimulus should reduce the effect of the test situation which is later employed [Thomas & Jones, 1962, p. 79]."

The prediction cited above is entirely consistent with the AL theory, which assumes that the Prevailing AL at any time in testing is a weighted average of Training and Test ALs. Thus, the more training S is given, the greater the weight of the training stimulus, relative to the test stimuli, in determining Prevailing AL. As a consequence, the more training S is given, the less central tendency shift there should be.

The role of amount of training has been investigated in two different experiments with somewhat conflicting results. Hébert et al. (1972) performed a study in which the Ss lifted the TS weight either once, eleven, or twenty-one times (in different groups) prior to the initiation of an asymmetrical generalization test. This manipulation failed to influence either the shape or slope of the obtained gradients. In each case, the peak of responding was displaced from the TS toward the center of the test series by an equivalent amount.

A related experiment was recently reported by Giurintano (1972). This investigator instructed six groups of Ss to respond to a line oriented 55° (counterclockwise from horizontal) and then tested for generalization with seven different line angles separated by 5°, either symmetrically spaced with regard to the TS (i.e., from 40° to 70°), or asymmetrically spaced (i.e., from 55° to 25°). Under each test condition, there were three different training groups, exposed to the 55° TS for 15, 30, or 60 sec.

The results for the asymmetrical test groups are presented in Fig. 3. As may be seen, the amount of training administered had the pre-

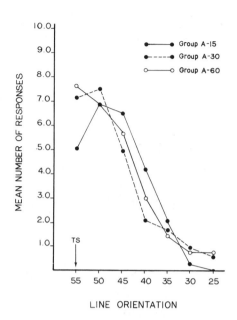

Fig. 3.   Generalization gradients of groups of Ss ($n = 20$) which were exposed to a TS of $55°$ for 15, 30, or 60 sec (Groups A-15, A-30, and A-60, respectively) and were tested with an asymmetrical series from $55°$ to $25°$. (From Giurintano, 1972.)

dicted effect. The 60-sec group shows no central tendency shift at all; the 30-sec group shows maximal responding displaced to the value adjacent to the TS; and for the 15-sec group the displacement is even greater, with responding almost equivalent to $50°$ and $45°$. The three groups tested with a symmetrical series (not shown in the figure) showed no such effect, with maximal responding emitted to the $55°$ TS value under all TS duration conditions.

At present, there are no obvious reasons why the AL prediction was supported in the line angle study and not in its lifted-weights counterpart. In the Giurintano study, amount of exposure was varied by using a single presentation of differing durations in different groups. Intuitively one would think that this would be a less effective manipulation than varying the number of exposure trials, yet the evidence indicated otherwise. It would certainly be appropriate to compare the two procedures for varying amount of training in the same experiment. Hébert (personal communication) has speculated that the contact that S has with the lifted-weight TS may be such that maximal information as to its value may be available after a single exposure, or S may act as if this were the case, being inattentive on subsequent trials. This is, of course, entirely *post hoc*, but it raises a testable possibility. If the contact which S had with the lifted weight were somehow degraded (e.g., by placing the weight upon S's passive hand rather than allowing him to lift it), then the predicted effect of number of training trials might be obtained.

As pointed out previously, the gradual shifting of the point of maximal responding during asymmetrical generalization testing presumably reflects the increasing weight of Test AL relative to Training AL in determining Prevailing AL. Manipulations of amount of training are thought to affect generalized responding in the same way, i.e., by altering the relative weighting of Training and Test ALs. It is interesting to speculate on alternative procedures for producing comparable effects. Perhaps the weighting of Training AL would be enhanced by the use of instructions which more strongly emphasized the need for accuracy, or by providing a reward for accurate judgments and/or a penalty for inaccurate ones. Quite probably the interpolation of a delay period between training and testing would reduce the relative weighting of Training AL. Another method might be to test for generalization in a different context from that present during training, e.g., changed noise level, room illumination, etc. By far, most of the research on the central tendency shift (and on the postdiscrimination peak shift—see Section III) has employed experimental manipulations designed to alter the *values* of the Training and/or Test ALs. More research needs to be done with manipulations designed to alter the relative weighting of these two values.

C. TESTING PARAMETERS

1. The Degree of Asymmetry in the Test Series

One of the variables which has been shown to affect the magnitude of the central tendency effect is the degree of asymmetry in the generalization test series. Typically, the degree of asymmetry has been defined in terms of the relative number of test stimuli on either side of the training value. Thus, for example, Thomas, and Jones (1962) used five equally spaced wavelengths with all of their groups, allowing three different degrees of asymmetry, all four (non S+) test stimuli to one side of S+, three to one side and one to the other, or two to each side (i.e., zero asymmetry). They found, as was illustrated in Fig. 1, that the greater the degree of asymmetry, the greater the magnitude of the central tendency shift. Helson and Avant (1967) in

TABLE II

GENERALIZATION GRADIENTS OF THE SEVEN GROUPS OF Ss IN EXPERIMENT I[a]

Group	Test stimulus									Gradient mean
	1	2	3	4	5	6	7	8	9	
3	.20	.29	.28							2.10
4	.20	.45	.51	.21						2.53
5	.16	.39	.56	.37	.11					2.92
6	.16	.39	.59	.46	.17	.03				3.10
7	.10	.21	.33	.44	.45	.23	.15			4.16
8	.09	.22	.38	.54	.57	.45	.18	.07		4.48
9	.08	.19	.32	.45	.51	.49	.23	.08	.05	4.75

[a] From Thomas et al. (1974).

their experiment with five different sizes of squares found the same relationship.

By far the most extensive investigation of the role of degree of test asymmetry in the central tendency shift was carried out by Thomas et al. (1974). These investigators exposed seven groups of Ss to a dim light TS and then tested with the TS and 2, 3, 4, 5, 6, 7, or 8 values, each .145 log units more intense than the preceding one. To control for total number of test stimuli, the groups were given different numbers of test series, ranging from 16 (in the case of the three-stimulus group) to five (in the nine-stimulus group). The comparison of the gradients of these different groups had to take into account the between-group difference in the number of opportunities to respond to the various test stimuli. This was accomplished by computing for each S the probability of responding to each stimulus when it was presented. The means of these individual probabilities are presented in Table II. The table indicates that the stimulus to which responding is most likely is increasingly displaced from the TS, stimulus value (SV) 1, as longer (more asymmetrical) test series are used. Note, for example, that the three-stimulus group responds maximally to SV 2, the five-stimulus group to SV 3, the nine-stimulus group to SV 5, etc.

In Experiment I of the Thomas et al. study (just described), the total number of test stimuli was matched across groups, thus the remaining group differences were in (1) the range of the test continuum employed, i.e., physical distance between the highest and lowest stimulus values, and (2) the number of different test stimuli within each range. These are alternative ways of defining differences in asymmetry of the test series but they may not be equally valid. To

determine the functional basis of asymmetry, it is necessary to uncon-
found these two variables. This was accomplished in a subsequent experiment by Thomas *et al.* They selected two test series lengths from
Experiment I, those of Groups 5 and 9 (which had five and nine test
values, respectively). Two groups were run under the same test conditions as in Experiment I, while two other groups were run with the
same ranges but fewer (equally spaced) test values within each range.
This constituted a 2×2 factorial design, short versus long range, few
versus many stimuli. Again the groups were matched as well as possible on the basis of total number of test stimuli used by varying the
number of test series to which the different groups were exposed. It
was reasoned that if AL is based upon a simple averaging of the psy-
chophysically equally spaced stimuli in each test series, then the
number of equally spaced stimuli within a given range should be
inconsequential because that number does not affect the average of
the series. On this basis, it was predicted that of the two independent
variables, range and number of stimuli within each range, only the
former would affect the magnitude of central tendency shift which
was obtained. The results clearly supported this prediction.

Several studies have shown that the degree of asymmetry in the
generalization test may have to be substantial before a central tendency shift is obtained. For example, Giurintano (1972) exposed his
Ss to a 55° line for 15 sec and found a reliable central tendency shift
when the test stimuli were the seven values from 55° to 25° in 5°
steps. There was no shift, however, in a group which experienced
those seven stimuli plus the 60° value in testing, despite the fact that
there were still six values to one side of the TS and only one value
to the other side.

Thomas *et al.* (1973, Experiment 3) have reported a study in which
the TS was a dim light and the test stimuli were nine brightness
values equally spaced on a logarithmic scale. When the TS was SV 2
(the second value from the dimmest in the test series), there was a
shift in maximal responding toward brighter values; however, when
the TS was SV 8, there was no shift toward dimmer ones. Thomas
et al. pointed out that this discrepancy is explicable in AL terms
when it is recognized that the shift is toward the psychological center
of the test series (*i.e.*, the Test AL) which is not necessarily coinci-
dent with the physical center. If the occurrence of the central tendency shift requires a substantial discrepancy between the Training
and Test ALs, then the results are explained on the basis of the assumption that with the test series which Thomas *et al.* used, the

Prevailing AL was closer to SV 8 than to SV 2. Thomas *et al.* performed a separate experiment using the category rating method to empirically determine AL (cf. Helson, 1964, Ch. 4) and found that this was indeed the case. The Test AL, based on linear interpolation from the group mean ratings of the various test stimuli, was equivalent to a stimulus value of 6.39.

Perhaps the most striking evidence that the central tendency shift occurs with reference to the AL comes from a recent study by Hébert, Bullock, Levitt, Woodward, and McGuirk (1974). In their Experiment II, a group of *S*s was exposed to a TS weight of 150 grams and then was tested with a symmetrical series including 100-, 125-, 150-, 175-, and 200-gm weights. Maximal responding occurred to the 125-gm weight despite the fact that the 150-gm TS was at the physical center of the test series. However, the *perceived midpoint* or AL of the test series was determined (both by Helson's weighted log mean formula and by a rating procedure) to be very close to the 125-gm test value. This result, in addition to that of Thomas *et al.* (1973) illustrates the value of actually measuring the AL in central tendency studies rather than simply inferring it. This has been done in several recent experiments, which will be described elsewhere in this chapter.

Perhaps it should be noted that in all studies of the central tendency shift which we have described, the degree of asymmetry in the test series was limited by the inclusion of the TS as one of the test values. There is, of course, no logical reason why this need be the case. A study could be performed in which *all* test values fell to one side of the TS. In such a situation, maximal responding to the test value closest to the TS would not constitute a central tendency shift, since greater responding might have accrued to the TS had it been available. If, during the course of testing, the point of maximal responding shifted still farther from the TS, a central tendency shift could then be inferred. Indeed, that shift should be enhanced, relative to that of a group receiving the same test values *plus the TS value* since a greater shift in Prevailing AL should occur under the former condition. It is also possible that the use of the TS as a test stimulus might reduce the degree of shift in a more indirect way, i.e., by "reminding" *S* of the TS value and perhaps thereby increasing its weight, relative to that of other test values, in determining Prevailing AL. This is purely speculative, of course, but the point remains that the effect of omitting the TS value from the test series should be empirically determined.

2. Disproportionate Representation of a Particular Test Value

The expected consequence of overrepresenting any given test value
in the generalization test series is clearly predictable from the AL
theory. Such overrepresentation should increase the weighting of that
test value, relative to all others, in the determination of the Test AL
and, therefore, the Prevailing AL. The effect of this additional
weighting will differ, of course, depending upon the value of the
overrepresented stimulus. If the TS is the overrepresented value, this
will reduce or eliminate the central tendency shift, because the AL
of the test series will remain close to the TS value, and little or no
shift in the Prevailing AL will occur during the course of testing.
This probably accounts for the results of a human voluntary generalization study by White (1965). This investigator used a colored light
TS and five different colors in testing, the TS and four non-TS values
which fell to one side of the TS. White found no central tendency
effect; however, his non-TS test stimuli were interspersed among
presentations of the TS, which was presented more than five times as
often as any other test value.

Hébert and Capehart (1969) explicitly tested the hypothesis that
the finding of a monotonic (rather than peak-shifted or nonmonotonic) gradient in the White (1965) study was due to the overrepresentation of the TS in testing. Hébert and Capehart used a 100-gm
weight as their TS and tested asymmetrically with weights of 100,
110, 120, 130, and 140 gm under one condition and 100, 125, 150,
175, and 200 gm under another. Within each of these conditions, for
one group the test stimuli were presented equally often, whereas for
another group the TS was presented five times as often as any other
test value. Under the equal presentation condition, central tendency
shifts were obtained which were equivalent in relative magnitude
for the two stimulus spacing conditions. Under the TS overrepresentation condition, as in the White study, there was no central tendency
shift at all.

The AL theory leads to the prediction that if the overrepresented
stimulus is farthest removed in the asymmetrical test series from the
TS, the greatest magnitude of central tendency shift should be observed, with the peak of responding possibly displaced beyond the
physical center of the series so as to be closer to the overrepresented
value. That this actually occurs has been shown in a study reported
by Hébert et al. (1974). These investigators used a series of five
weights, ranging in value from 100 to 200 gm in 25-gm steps, following training on a single stimulus, either 100, 150, or 200 gm. They

found that systematically overrepresenting each of the five test stimuli produced an ordered set of generalization gradients. That is, there was a tendency for maximal generalized responding to occur at the value of the overrepresented test stimulus, regardless of which TS value had been employed.

It is, of course, possible to underrepresent a given test stimulus or stimuli as well as to overrepresent it. Recall the discussion (in Section II, c, 1) of a proposed experiment with an asymmetrical test series which did not include the TS value. The omission of a stimulus may be considered as one extreme value on the continuum from under-representation to overrepresentation. The other extreme would be to present one stimulus infinitely more often than any other. The point should be made that the relative frequency of presentation of any one or several test values is manipulable in two directions and such manipulations should affect in predictable ways the value of Prevailing AL and thus the point of maximal generalized respond-ing. As far as we know, however, from this large class of possible manipulations the only one which has been systematically investi-gated is the overrepresentation of a single test value.

3. The Role of Stimulus Labeling and Categorizing

Capehart et al. made explicit certain limiting assumptions of their application of the AL theory. For example, they pointed out that the theory applied only to stimuli within a single dimension, and even further to stimuli (within a dimension) which are not qualitatively distinct. Thus they argued that AL would presumably not operate across color name categories.

It is, therefore, certainly ironic that our first study of the central tendency effect (Thomas & Jones, 1962) employed wavelength stimuli. Nevertheless, the results of that study are not inconsistent with Capehart et al.'s position, since almost all of the test stimuli used fell within the green range of the spectrum, and maximal re-sponding always occurred to a value well within this range.

An explicit test of the categorical specificity of AL effects was car-ried out in a recent study by Tomie and Thomas (1974). In their Experiment I, three groups of Ss viewed a 505-nm (bluish-green) light and then were tested for generalization with a symmetrical series (from 485 to 525 nm) or one of two asymmetrical series (from 505 to 545 nm, or from 505 to 465 nm).

The major results of this study are shown in Fig. 4. Consider first

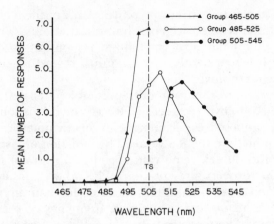

Fig. 4. Generalization gradients of groups of Ss ($n = 20$) which were exposed to a TS of 505 nm (blue-green) and then were tested with a symmetrical series (from 485 to 525 nm) or one of two asymmetrical series (from 505 to 545 nm or from 505 to 465 nm). (From Tomie & Thomas, 1974.)

the gradient of Group 505–545. For these Ss, both the TS and all test stimuli fell within the green category, thus these stimuli should have been pooled to produce a Prevailing AL which shifted toward the center of the test series as generalization testing progressed. As predicted, a substantial displacement of maximal responding from the TS value (i.e., a central tendency effect) occurred with this group. Further analysis indicated that the shift developed progressively during the course of testing.

Given only the marked nominal asymmetry in the generalization test series of Group 465–505, one would expect a central tendency shift toward the center of the series in this group also. However, if all test stimuli in the blue conceptual category (stimuli 465 nm through approximately 490 nm) were nonfunctional in determining the Prevailing AL, then one would expect the AL to be located at a value near the TS. As Thomas *et al.* (1973) have shown, when Test AL and TS value are relatively close, there may be no central tendency shift. Indeed, as shown in the figure, there was none for Group 465–505.

The lack of a central tendency shift in Group 465–505, taken together with the large (and gradually developing) central tendency shift in Group 505–545, argues strongly in support of the hypothesis that AL effects are operative within but not across conceptual categories. If this hypothesis is correct, then it may be argued that for

Group 485–525 the test series is nominally symmetrical but functionally asymmetrical since the "blue" values in the test series are presumably nonfunctional. Note in Fig. 4 that this group does indeed show a peak shift to a longer wavelength value, and further analysis indicated that this shift developed gradually. It is, of course, consistent with AL theory that the shift should be greater for Group 505–545 than for Group 485–525 because the degree of asymmetry is greater, with eight values of longer wavelength than 505 nm rather than four.

The "functional" test series for Group 485–525 may also be less asymmetrical than that of Group 505–545 because *some* test values of shorter wavelength than 505 nm may fall within the conceptual category "green" and thus be operative in determining AL. Figure 4 indicates a high level of generalized responding to 500 nm, suggesting that for this group 500 nm is probably categorized as green, whereas all values of shorter wavelength are probably not. If all wavelength values shorter than 500 nm are nonfunctional for Group 485–525, a comparable gradient might be obtained from a group for which these values are omitted from the test. Tomie and Thomas (1974) ran such a group, using the test values from 500 to 525 nm, and this group revealed the same magnitude of shift as had been observed in the gradient of Group 485–525.

Tomie and Thomas (1974) considered the possibility that their obtained group differences in the locus of maximal responding during generalization testing might have been due to differences in chromatic adaptation. Because each group experienced a different set of (adapting) test stimuli, the differentially altered states of sensitivity of the pigments in the retina might somehow account for the shifts in responding which were observed. Tomie and Thomas proposed that if it were possible to manipulate the category membership of a particular TS so as to produce a central tendency shift or prevent one *with the same set of physical test stimuli,* then a sensory adaptation interpretation of the effect would be precluded. They then performed such an experiment.

Two groups of Ss were exposed to a TS light of 495 nm, an ambiguous blue-green value, and for one group the TS was called "green" (by the experimenter), for the other it was called "blue." Pilot work had suggested that the Ss were approximately equally likely to label this stimulus as blue or green, and it was hypothesized that they would, therefore, be willing to categorize it in the manner suggested by the experimenter.

With regard to the training value of 495 nm, the test series from

465 to 505 nm is nominally asymmetrical, with five test values of shorter wavelength and two of longer wavelength. From the standpoint of AL theory, however, the functional stimuli are those in the same conceptual category as the TS. Logically, if the S categorizes 495 nm as blue, then all five test values of shorter wavelength would also be called blue, and the blue-green boundary would be at a longer wavelength than 495 nm. The values 500 and 505 nm might be called blue and might be called green. In any case, the test series would be functionally asymmetrical with five blues of shorter wavelength than the TS and zero, one, or at most, two blues of longer wavelength. This substantial asymmetry might result in a central tendency shift from 495 nm toward shorter wavelengths.

The situation with the green-label group is very different. If 495 nm is categorized as green, there are only two longer wavelength values which would also be called green. This would not lead to a central tendency shift toward longer wavelengths for two reasons. First, two values to one side of the training stimulus is not a substantial degree of asymmetry. Second, values of 490 and perhaps even 485 nm might also be classified as green, making the functional test series symmetrical or nearly symmetrical for these Ss.

The generalization gradients obtained from the blue-label and green-label groups are presented in Fig. 5. As predicted, the blue-label group gradient shows a peak of responding displaced from 495 nm toward shorter wavelengths, whereas the green-label gradient shows no displacement at all. This difference is not attributable to sensory adaptation, since both groups were exposed to the same physical stimulus values. It is entirely consistent with the view that in the blue-label group the TS and all test stimuli of shorter wavelength fell in the same conceptual category, such that Prevailing AL shifted toward the center of the functional test series and maximal generalized responding shifted accordingly. An analysis of changes during the course of testing revealed that the shift in the blue-label group was indeed gradual, as predicted by the theory.

The two experiments by Tomie and Thomas (1974) suggest that stimulus labeling or categorizing may serve to define the stimulus domain within which AL effects may be manifested. This is a very different conception from that proposed by Capehart et al. (1969) who seemed to assume that when the stimuli were verbally encoded, a process of verbal mediation precluded the operation of an AL mechanism.

The shift in maximal responding from 495 nm to shorter wavelengths in Tomie and Thomas' blue-label group can also be ex-

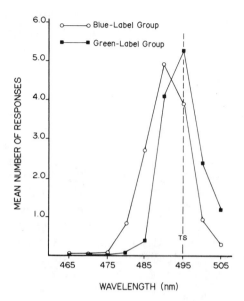

Fig. 5. Generalization gradients of two groups of Ss ($n = 20$) which were exposed to a TS of 495 nm (blue-green) which had been labeled by E as "blue" or as "green," respectively. (From Tomie & Thomas, 1974.)

plained by reference to a single and direct process of verbal mediation. It may be asserted that in training S learns to respond to a particular blue value, thus enhancing the likelihood of responding to any stimulus which would also be labeled blue. As testing progresses and the memory trace of the specific physical value of the TS fades, the S should rely increasingly on the verbal label, with responding shifting toward stimuli to which that label is most appropriate.

This is precisely the interpretation which had been given in several earlier wavelength generalization studies performed in our laboratory. In the first of these, Thomas and Mitchell (1962) replicated a still earlier observation by Kalish (1958) that Ss exposed to a 550-nm TS value (a yellowish-green) and tested with a nominally symmetrical test series extending from 490 to 610 nm showed a gradual shift in maximal responding from 550 nm to 540 nm, a greener value than the TS. Since the Ss were not required to label the TS in the Thomas and Mitchell and the Kalish studies, the verbal mediation interpretation requires the inference that they did so. In a subsequent experiment by Thomas and DeCapito (1966) an ambiguous TS value of 490 nm was used and the Ss were asked to label it. Although the subsequent generalization test was carried out with a nominally symmetrical series, those Ss who had labeled the TS green showed an enhanced tendency to respond to longer wavelength (greener) values and a reduced tendency to respond to shorter (bluer) ones, in comparison with the blue-label group. This finding was later replicated in a study by Thomas, Caronite, LaMonica, and Hoving (1968) in which the blue (or green) label for the 490-nm TS was suggested by the experimenter, rather than volunteered by the subject.

Each of these earlier studies may be reinterpreted as evidence for the AL theory applied to stimulus generalization. In every case the label attached to the TS may have functioned to define the conceptual category in which the TS *and only some* of the test stimuli fell. That TS and the test values in the same category would constitute a functionally asymmetrical generalization test series, despite the fact that in each of the studies described, the test series was nominally a symmetrical one. A gradual shift in Prevailing AL toward the center of the functional test series would indeed have resulted in the shifts which were interpreted as evidence of a "direct" process of verbal mediation. The adjective "direct" is used to emphasize that Tomie and Thomas (1974) did not deny the importance of verbal labeling or categorizing. They proposed, however, that these activities determine the domain within which AL effects then take place, rather than directly affecting the probability of a generalized response.

It is reasonable to ask whether the postulation of two processes or mechanisms (i.e., AL shift and verbal mediation) is appropriate if one of these will suffice. Parsimony favors the acceptance of the simpler interpretation in such a case. The results of the Tomie and Thomas (1974) study, however, indicate the inadequacy of the direct verbal mediation interpretation. In their Experiment II, the gradient of the blue-label group shifted toward shorter wavelengths. However, the gradient of the green-label group showed no comparable tendency to shift toward longer wavelengths (greener values) despite the fact that there were two wavelength values above 495 nm to which maximal response strength might have shifted. The failure to find comparable shifts in the two groups is consistent with the differences in the degree of test asymmetry for blue values versus green ones and therefore consistent with the hypothesized shift in AL (specifically in the blue-label group) during the course of testing.

Further evidence of the need for an AL mechanism is the greater magnitude of central tendency shift observed in Experiment I for Group 505–545 in comparison with both the 485–525 and the 500–

525 groups. Presumably all three groups would have labeled the 505-nm TS in the same way, thus they would be expected to show the same magnitude of shift. According to the AL interpretation, the magnitude of shift varies directly with the amount of asymmetry in the functional test series, thus the obtained results are entirely consistent with that view.

Stimulus labels such as green or blue define a rather broad class of stimuli within which many different values may be distinguished. Other classes of stimuli may be so narrowly defined as to consist of only one member, thus no shift of AL would be possible within such a class. An example would be the class of vertical lines. If the S encoded the TS as vertical, no central tendency effect would be expected, regardless of the nominal asymmetry of the test series, because the functional test series would consist of only the TS value. Such a demonstration would not be very convincing evidence for the role of AL, however, since it is well known that people, and even animals who cannot verbally encode the stimulus, find it easy to discriminate vertical from oblique angles.

In order to pinpoint the role of a narrowly defined TS category in precluding the development of a central tendency effect, it is appropriate to use a given TS value and either apply the label to it or not, in different groups. Such an experiment was performed by Thomas and Thomas (1974). The TS used was a black line oriented 60° counterclockwise from horizontal, tachistoscopically presented for 1.0 sec. For 20 Ss, the test series used was symmetrical, extending from 40 to 80° in 5° steps. For 40 other Ss, an asymmetrical series from 60° to 40° in 5° steps was used. For one symmetrical test group and one asymmetrical test group ($n = 20$ in each) quite standard instructions were given, asking Ss to attend to the line angle because they would have to identify it later. For the other asymmetrical test group ($n = 20$), in addition to standard instructions, the Ss were told: "Some people find it helpful, in trying to remember the line angle, to think of it as a hand or hands on a clockface. Try this yourself. What time would it be if the hand or hands were pointed in that way?"

Most Ss run under this condition labeled the TS as "one o'clock," "seven o'clock," or "five minutes after seven." The major results of this experiment are the generalization gradients presented in Fig. 6. Note first that the standard-instruction (i.e., control) asymmetrical test group showed a clear central tendency shift in their gradient with maximal responding made to the 50° line. In contrast to this group, the Ss who received the clockface instructions showed sharp decremental gradients with no sign of a central tendency shift. Indeed, of

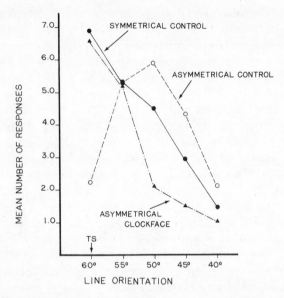

Fig. 6. Generalization gradients of groups of Ss ($n = 20$) which were exposed to a TS of 60° following standard (control) or "clockface" instructions and then were tested with either an asymmetrical series (from 60° to 40°) or a symmetrical series (from 40° to 80°). Responses of the symmetrical control group to stimulus values 65°, 70°, 75°, and 80° are not shown in the figure. (From Thomas & Thomas, 1974.)

the 20 Ss run under this condition, not one responded more to 55° than to the 60° TS. The data reported for the standard-instruction symmetrical (control) group indicates a decremental gradient, revealing that the asymmetrical test condition is a necessary prerequisite to obtaining a central tendency shift. Test asymmetry is not a sufficient condition, however, since the asymmetrical clockface group did not show it. These results are consistent with the interpretation that for the clockface group the TS class was so narrowly defined that the functional test series consisted of only the TS value. Thus, there was no averaging of test stimulus values to form a new Prevailing AL and thus no central tendency shift. The very sharp gradient of the clockface group is further evidence of the narrowness of the TS class.

D. THE EXTENSION OF THE AL THEORY TO INFRAHUMAN Ss

Capehart *et al.* (1969) considered restricting the application of their theory to research with human Ss but decided against it. Without referring to any evidence obtained in animal studies, they proposed that the assumptions of the theory apply equally to humans and infrahumans. They suggested that animal studies which test for generalization over many blocks of test trials would provide an arena suitable for the evaluation of the AL theory.

Actually, at least two studies investigating the effect of testing pigeons for generalization with asymmetrical test series had been reported prior to the publication of the Capehart *et al.* paper. In the first of these, Guttman (1956) tested two pigeons with three stimuli of shorter wavelength than the 550-nm TS value and six longer wavelength values, and concluded that the shape of the generalization gradient is independent of such context effects. Guttman employed the generalization test procedure he had earlier developed in collaboration with Kalish (Guttman & Kalish, 1956). In this procedure, the birds are given extensive training, with variable interval (VI) reinforcement, to peck a light of a given wavelength. They are then tested (in extinction) for response rate to a random sequence of successively presented wavelengths, with the test wavelengths organized into many blocks of trials with each stimulus appearing once in each block.

A more extensive study, using the same test procedure, was reported by Thomas and Barker (1964). These investigators trained two groups of ten pigeons each to respond to a TS of 550 nm and then tested one group asymmetrically, with values from 550 to 490 nm, and one group symmetrically, with values extending from 490 to 610 nm. Thomas and Barker found no evidence even suggesting a central tendency effect; the asymmetrical group's gradient was monotonic and no flatter than the symmetrical group's gradient.

Upon reflection, the failure of these early pigeon studies to produce a central tendency effect is *not* inconsistent with the AL theory. The theory clearly predicts, and Giurintano (1972) has shown with human *Ss*, that the magnitude of the shift is a negative function of amount of training (or exposure) to the TS. Presumably extensive training weights the Training AL so heavily relative to the Test AL that Prevailing AL changes very little during the course of generalization testing. Because the Guttman–Kalish test procedure is carried out in extinction, substantial training is required to generate adequate resistance to extinction so that responding can be sustained through the duration of testing. The obvious alternative of continuing to reinforce responding during generalization testing is unacceptable for several reasons. If only responses to the TS are reinforced, this constitutes discrimination training, which quickly sharpens the gradient. If responses to all stimuli are reinforced, this constitutes equivalence training which quickly flattens the gradient. Testing in extinction seems more appropriate, but for present purposes the requirement of substantial training prior to the administration of the test precludes the procedure from providing a critical test of the AL theory.

What is required is a procedure whereby substantial resistance to extinction and thus a gradient of generalization can be obtained following minimal exposure to the (dimensional) TS. Such a procedure was developed in a study reported by Schadler and Thomas (1972). These investigators speculated that the acquisition by a TS of dimensional stimulus control (defined as a sharp decremental gradient) might be separable from the acquisition of response strength by giving the S substantial pretraining on a stimulus orthogonal to the test dimension subsequently explored. Presumably a strong tendency to respond would quickly transfer to a TS on the test dimension, such that this TS might be demonstrated to have gained dimensional control over responding in a very short time.

Under one of their conditions, Schadler and Thomas gave their Ss 10 days of VI training with a white key light and then gave them 0, 5, 10, or 20 min of VI training with a white 30° line on a dark surround. In general, the greater the amount of training with the 30° line, the greater the tendency to respond maximally to it in the subsequent generalization test. The gradient after 20 min of training, however, was not reliably sharper than that after 10 min, suggesting that asymptote had been reached. In an earlier study, Hearst and Koresko (1968) had reported the progressive sharpening of angularity generalization gradients for training durations up to 14 50-min sessions. This was 35 times as much training as was required to approach asymptote under the conditions of the Schadler and Thomas (1972) experiment. On the basis of their results, Schadler and Thomas concluded that the acquisition of response strength and the acquisition of dimensional stimulus control over responding may be viewed as conceptually and empirically distinct processes, with the latter occurring far more rapidly than had previously been supposed.

For present purposes, the value of the Schadler and Thomas study was in providing a procedure permitting the testing of implications of the AL theory with infrahuman Ss. That procedure involves extensive pretraining with an orthogonal TS, brief training with a dimensional TS, and then testing in extinction with an asymmetrical generalization test series.

A further refinement of the Schadler and Thomas procedure was suggested by the observation in their study that stimuli which are logically orthogonal to the angularity dimension may not be functionally orthogonal. Without any training experience with a line angle, their Ss responded most to 90°, less to 60°, and least to the 30° test stimulus which they used. In a subsequent experiment reported by Giurintano, Schadler, and Thomas (1972), different groups of Ss were tested for generalization with the same three line angles following pretraining with a white light, a very dim white light, a green light, and a white dot on a dark surround. The "preference" for the 90° line was replicated in the white light group and was also found in the dim white light group. Subjects pretrained with the dot, however, reliably preferred the 30° line. Only the green pretraining stimulus proved to be functionally orthogonal to the angularity dimension in this experiment. It was, therefore, this value which was used by Giurintano (1972) in his investigation of the central tendency effect in pigeons.

Giurintano gave his pigeons 10 30-min sessions of variable interval training with a 538-nm light and then gave three groups of Ss 15, 30, or 60 min of VI training with a 57.26° (counterclockwise from horizontal) white line on a dark surround. These groups were then tested, in extinction, for generalization with an asymmetrical series ranging from the 57.26° TS to 0° in 8.18° steps. Three other groups, with comparable training, were tested with a symmetrical series from 81.80° to 32.72°.

The gradients obtained from the three asymmetrical test groups are presented in Fig. 7. Note in the figure that while the 60-min group gave a monotonic decreasing gradient, the two groups given less training with the 57.26° TS emitted clear central tendency shifts. There was no comparable shift in the gradients of groups tested with the symmetrical series, each of which peaked, as expected, at the TS value. Thus, this experiment not only demonstrated a central tendency effect in pigeons; it indicated that in accordance with the AL theory, the magnitude of the shift is a negative function of the amount of training (with the dimensional TS). This doubtlessly accounts for the failure of the earlier studies to show the effect.

Consistent with his parallel experiment with human Ss, Giurintano found that reducing the asymmetry of the test series by including a test value of 65.44° essentially eliminated the central tendency shift. Giurintano's work provides convincing evidence of the applicability of the AL model to generalization in infrahumans.

One problem with Giurintano's procedure was that the gradients obtained tended to be quite flat. Although giving the birds additional

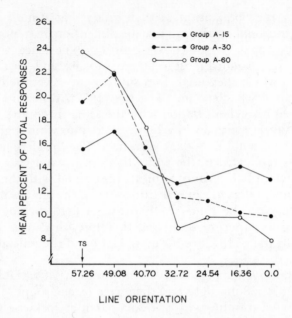

Fig. 7. Generalization gradients of groups of pigeons ($n = 10$) which were trained with a TS of 57.26° for 15, 30, or 60 min (Groups A-15, A-30, and A-60, respectively) and were tested with an asymmetrical series from 57.26° to 0°. (From Giurintano, 1972.)

training with the oblique line TS sharpened the gradients, this procedure presumably worked against finding a central tendency shift by weighting the Training AL so heavily relative to the Test AL that Prevailing AL could change but little during the course of generalization testing. In a series of recent experiments with pigeons, it has been shown that Ss which have been trained on one successive discrimination problem show positive transfer to the acquisition of a second discrimination along an orthogonal dimension (cf. Eck, Noel, and Thomas, 1969; Eck and Thomas, 1970; Keilitz and Frieman, 1971). Thomas (1970) has interpreted these results as indicating that discrimination training makes Ss more attentive to all stimulus change. An implication of this position is that if Giurintano (1972) had given his Ss discrimination training between, say, green and blue stimuli in the first stage of his experiment, control by the oblique line TS would have been more quickly established in the second stage. If this were to occur, it might be possible to test for generalization after perhaps five or ten minutes of training with the line stimulus and thereby to obtain a central tendency shift of far greater magnitude than Giurintano reported. Additional proposed future studies testing applications of the AL model to stimulus generalization in pigeons will be discussed in Section III of this chapter.

E. The Central Tendency Effect and Direct Concurrent Measurement of Adaptation-Level

By far the majority of the studies performed on the central tendency effect have inferred changes in AL on the grounds that the theory predicts such changes and/or the changes have been observed in other test situations. Two experiments have been described in which AL was actually measured in the context of the central tendency study. In one of these (Hébert *et al.*, 1973, Experiment II), the peak of generalized responding shifted from the TS, which was at the physical center of the test series, to a lower (lifted weight) value. Both a rating-scale method and Helson's (1964) weighted log mean formula for lifted weights affirmed that the Test AL was very near the stimulus value to which maximal responding had shifted.

Thomas *et al.* (1973) used an AL value which was empirically determined by the rating-scale method to help explain an apparent anomaly in their data. In a test series of nine equally spaced brightness values they observed that if the TS were SV 2 (the second value from the dimmest), there was a central tendency shift toward brighter values, whereas when the TS was SV 8, there was no corresponding shift toward dimmer stimuli. They suggested that the shift required a large initial discrepancy between Training and Test AL values, and hypothesized that the Test AL might be too close to the SV 8 training value to produce a central tendency shift. A separate experiment revealed a mean AL corresponding to a test value of 6.39, far closer to SV 8 than to SV 2 and thus consistent with Thomas *et al.*'s interpretation.

If changes in AL underlie shifts in generalized responding, then it should be possible to observe this relationship directly by structuring an experimental task such that individual Ss provide both AL and generalization test data throughout the course of generalization testing. This was accomplished in the third experiment of the study by Hébert *et al.* (1974). The procedure used was as follows:

"Upon entering the experimental room, Ss were informed they were participating in a weight perception experiment. Each S was instructed to lift a 150-gm weight five times and was told to identify it in a subsequent series of test weights. They were instructed to push a 'same' key if they thought a stimulus was the same as S+, or to push a 'different' key if they thought it was different. Again, Ss were urged to respond as quickly and accurately as possible. After each response in the test series, Ss were asked to rate the stimulus they had just lifted on a seven-point scale (1 = very light, 2 = light, 3 = fairly light, 4 = neither light nor heavy, 5 = fairly heavy, 6 = heavy, 7 = very heavy) and to call out the number appropriate to their judgment. For S's convenience, the verbal and numerical equivalents of this scale were displayed at eye level on the housing. The training stimulus, 150 gm, was not identified at any place on the rating scale by E, and no instructions to do so were given to S."

The test stimuli used by Hébert *et al.* (1974) included the values from 100 to 200 gm in 25-gm steps. Hébert *et al.* found, in agreement with several other experiments, that maximal responding occurred to the 125-gm test weight although the 150-gm TS was at the physical center of the test series. Using a linear interpolation procedure, they determined that the stimulus which would have received a neutral 4.00 rating was 131 gm, which can be taken as an average AL for the experiment. Thus the peak of the gradient had shifted to the test stimulus value closest to the Prevailing AL.

The most convincing evidence that AL and "same" responses were linked was the finding that 50 of the 54 "same" responses made by the nine Ss in the experiment were made to stimuli which were subsequently rated "4," regardless of their value on the physical dimension, but none of the 171 "different" responses was made to a stimulus subsequently rated "4." Additionally, the four "same" responses not associated with a "4" rating were rated either "3" or "5." This is direct evidence that the Ss in the Hébert *et al.* (1973) experiment associated the TS with the AL or neutral rating, even though they had not been instructed to do so.

The Hébert *et al.* (1974) procedure was modified in a recent study by Thomas *et al.* (1974). The TS was a dim light and the test stimuli consisted of the TS and several brighter values. The Ss were instructed to remember the brightness of the original light because they would be asked to identify it later. In subsequent generalization testing the Ss had two judgments to make. The first was to determine whether the test stimulus was the "same" as or "different" from the original and to make the corresponding verbal response. The second was to rate the brightness of the test stimulus and assign a number from 1 to 9, with 1 being very dim and 9 being very bright.

The independent variable in the Thomas *et al.* (1974) experiment was the number (and range) of logarithmically equally spaced test values, from three to nine in seven independent groups. As reported earlier in this chapter, the magnitude of the central tendency shift varied positively with the number of test values in the series, a measure of the asymmetry of the test series. Thus the stimulus to which maximal responding occurred was farther removed from the TS value with the longer test series. Table III presents the mean ratings of the different test values to which the *S*s in each group were exposed. The AL may be defined as that stimulus to which the neutral rating of "5" would have been given. It is clear from the table that the AL value is farther removed from the TS with the longer test series. Note, for example, that the group mean AL in Group 4 is less than SV 4, that of Group 6 is almost exactly at SV 5, and that of Group 8 is almost exactly at SV 6. For statistical purposes, Thomas *et al.* actually computed an AL score for each subject, based on linear interpolation or extrapolation with the least squares method. The effect of the length of the test series on group mean AL scores was highly significant.

The AL interpretation of the central tendency shift demands that AL and the location of maximal generalized responding be similarly affected by the manipulation of length of test series. A comparison of the matrices in Tables III and II (see p. 105) indicates that this was indeed the case. At a more molecular level, however, a necessary correspondence between the two measures of performance is lacking. If *S*s perceived their task as that of responding to the stimulus at their Prevailing AL level, then, aside from measurement error, maximal responding should have occurred to the stimulus value closest to the measured AL. A comparison of Tables III and II indicates, however,

TABLE III

MEAN STIMULUS RATINGS BY THE SEVEN GROUPS OF *S*s IN EXPERIMENT I[a]

	Test stimulus								
	1	2	3	4	5	6	7	8	9
3	3.18	4.07	5.17						
4	2.63	3.57	4.38	5.24					
5	2.35	3.23	3.95	4.81	5.74				
6	1.82	2.39	3.03	3.72	4.63	5.69			
7	2.00	2.47	3.19	3.80	4.38	5.20	6.07		
8	2.18	2.78	3.42	3.76	4.19	4.82	5.73	6.68	
9	1.78	2.27	2.55	3.13	3.44	3.95	4.92	5.61	6.08

[a] From Thomas *et al.* (1974).

that in each of the seven groups maximal responding occurred to a stimulus of lower intensity than the group's mean AL. This finding can also be demonstrated on an individual basis. For 77 of the 140 Ss in the experiment, the stimulus rating which most frequently accompanied the judgment of "same" as the TS was "3" or "4," not "5." Indeed, the majority of the Ss in each group responded maximally to a value rated lower than "5."

Thomas et al. (1974) reported a second experiment (previously described) in which they also concurrently measured AL and generalized responding. They found in that experiment that the magnitude of the central tendency shift varies with the stimulus range covered by the generalization test series and not with the number of equally spaced stimuli within that range. This finding was based on the assumption that AL would also vary only with the range, an assumption confirmed by the direct measurement of AL in the same experiment. It was further determined in that experiment, as in Experiment I, that Ss tended to respond maximally to stimuli which they subsequently rated as "4" or "3," not "5."

Thomas et al. (1974) concluded on the basis of these two experiments that a direct relationship clearly exists between Prevailing AL and the point of maximal generalized responding, but that the relationship is not that of a one-to-one equivalence, as proposed by Capehart et al. Rather, the data suggested that their Ss encoded the TS as, say, X log units below the "preexperimental AL" value. During the course of testing the weighting of preexperimental (residual) factors decreased such that eventually Prevailing AL was almost entirely determined by the range of *test* stimuli experienced. The Ss continued to respond in accordance with the decision rule: $TS = AL - X$ units, resulting in the group differences in generalization gradients which were obtained.

This interpretation accepts the major tenet of the Capehart et al. (1969) position, which is that stimulus equivalence is defined with reference to the AL value. It differs with the Capehart et al. position insofar as they assume that the effect of residual stimuli will be negligible, such that in single-stimulus training the AL will initially take the value of the TS. If so, Ss should continue to respond maximally to the stimulus at the Prevailing AL value at any point in time. Where the TS is not encoded as the AL (as in the Thomas et al., 1974 study), presumably the value perceived as the TS (i.e., responded to maximally) bears the same relationship to the Prevailing AL as the actual TS had to the initial ("preexperimental") AL.

It is not clear at this time why an equivalence relationship was observed between the measured AL and the point of maximal responding in the Hébert *et al.* (1974) study but not in the Thomas *et al.* (1974) experiment. There are many procedural differences, including the use of brightnesses rather than lifted weights, the use of a nine-point rating scale without the midpoint ("5") labeled as neutral by *E* rather than a seven-point scale with a verbal equivalent of each point continuously displayed to the *S*, etc. Thomas *et al.* proposed that the crucial difference was a greater familiarity with their test stimuli (brightnesses of light) than Hébert *et al.*'s *S*s would have had with the lifted weights. Presumably, the lifted weights were such novel stimuli that the *S*s entered the experiment with no preconception of what constitutes an "average" or "medium" weight. They would, therefore, readily accept the TS, whatever it was, as "average." However, the TS light in the Thomas *et al.* study was so dim, in comparison with all the lights with which the *S*s would be familiar that the *S*s could not accept it as "average" and, therefore, they encoded it as some value lower than their "preexperimental AL."

There are several ways in which this interpretation is subject to empirical test. Presumably, if the TS value selected by Thomas *et al.* (1974) had been bright enough for the *S*s to view it as "average," then a one-to-one correspondence between measured AL and the point of maximal responding would have been revealed. If the Thomas *et al.* study were repeated with SV 9 used as the TS and dimmer values as test stimuli, a closer correspondence between AL and generalized response measures would be expected. Such an experiment needs to be done.

The logic of the proposed experiment is to select a TS more in keeping with the preexperimental experience (i.e., the "preexperimental AL") of the *S*s. An alternative plan would be to control the "preexperimental" experience of the *S*s such that the subsequently used TS would have a known relationship to the "preexperimental AL." Note that "preexperimental AL" in this case is not preexperimental at all, but only pre-TS presentation. It is necessary to assume that because of recency and presumed relevance to the experiment, the overriding determinant of "preexperimental AL" would be the pre-TS stimuli presented in the experimental situation. By creating a "preexperimental AL" higher or lower than the TS it should be possible to obtain a central tendency shift with maximal responding displaced to one or the other side of the measured Prevailing AL.

Such an experiment was performed by Dickson and Strub (1974). In their study, 11 different brightnesses of light equally spaced on a logarithmic scale were used as stimuli. The *S*s in two experimental

groups were initially exposed to one of two conditions: five series of
three (relatively) bright lights (SV 9, 10, 11) or five series of three
(relatively) dim ones (SV 1, 2, 3). They were then presented a TS of
intermediate brightness (SV 4) and asked to remember that value
because they would have to identify it later. For both the "preexposed bright" and "preexposed dim" groups, the generalization
test included the TS and four brighter values, i.e., SV 4, 5, 6, 7, and
8. It was anticipated that this asymmetrical test would produce a
central tendency shift from the TS to a brighter value. It was assumed, however, that the shift would be greater in the preexposed
dim group because they would have encoded the TS as brighter than
their "preexperimental AL." They should, therefore, respond maximally to a test value brighter than their Prevailing AL. On the other
hand, the preexposed bright groups should encode the TS as dimmer
than their "preexperimental" AL and they should respond maximally to a test value dimmer than their Prevailing AL.

All stimuli experienced by S were also rated on an 11-point brightness scale, making it possible to compute an AL value for each condition. The group mean AL value for the preexposed bright group obtained during the generalization test procedure was equal to a scale
value of 7.80 compared to 6.31 for the preexposed dim group. Thus
stimuli experienced prior to the introduction of the TS had a lasting
effect, as far as ratings of subsequently experienced stimuli (which
were the same for both groups) were concerned. Note in Fig. 8 that,
in agreement with prediction, the gradient of the preexposed dim
group peaked at a value higher than their Prevailing AL and the
gradient of the preexposed bright group peaked at a value lower
than their's. Even the relative extent of the deviation of the peak
value from the measured AL is consistent with the theory. The TS
value used was much closer to the "dim" preexposure stimuli than to
the "bright" ones. Thus, the rule adopted by Ss should have taken
the form: "respond to a value *slightly greater than* the Prevailing
AL" in the preexposed dim condition, and "respond to a value
much dimmer than the prevailing AL" in the preexposed bright
condition. Note that the obtained gradients are entirely consistent
with the application of such a rule.

III. The Application of the AL Model to Discrimination
Learning Situations

Capehart *et al.* (1969), in agreement with James (1953), proposed
that in discrimination training, the two training stimuli, whether pre-

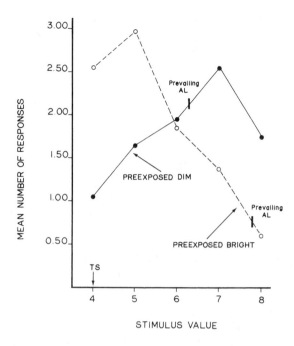

Fig. 8. Generalization gradients and Prevailing AL values of groups of Ss ($n = 20$) which were preexposed to lights much brighter (preexposed bright group) or slightly dimmer (preexposed dim group) than the TS later presented. Both groups were tested with an asymmetrical series consisting of the TS and four brighter values. (From Dickson & Strub, 1974.)

sented simultaneously or successively, are encoded with regard to their relationship to the Training AL, which would fall somewhere between them. The S may use the AL as a crossover point for different classes of behavior, e.g., approach or avoid, go right versus left, etc. Presumably, reward, punishment, etc., do not affect Training AL but rather these conditions may inform S as to which side of the AL appropriate responses belong.

An example of this use of AL is provided by a study reported by Capehart and Pease (1968). These investigators trained their Ss to respond on a "left" key on presentation of a 100-gm weight and on a "right" key with a 200-gm weight. After meeting a discrimination criterion, the Ss were tested for generalization with an asymmetrical series of weights, including 150-, 200-, 250-, 300-, 350-, 400-, and 450-gm values. It was presumed that after training, the AL fell between the 100- and 200-gm values and the Ss had adopted the strategy: "respond 'right' to a value above (or 'left' to a value below) Prevailing AL." During the course of generalization testing, Prevailing AL presumably converged on the Test AL, calculated to be 248 gm. Theoretically, this should produce a transposition of responding, with Ss now responding "left" to values of 200 and 150 gm, despite the fact that the 200-gm value had been the TS for a "right" response. The results revealed a clear confirmation of this prediction.

The findings of the Capehart and Pease (1968) study were replicated and extended in an experiment reported by Hébert (1970). This investigator employed the same paradigm as used by Capehart and Pease, but used a brightness dimension, rather than lifted weights. Hébert employed two different asymmetrical test conditions, one with mostly brighter values than the training stimuli and one with mostly dimmer ones. In each case, he observed transposition, i.e., a shift in the response tendency associated with a given TS (from left to right or vice versa) as a consequence of asymmetrical generalization testing.

Hébert also presented an analysis of changes in the pattern of responding as they developed during the course of generalization testing. He observed a gradual shift in the tendencies to respond "left" or "right" to the test values, such that initially Ss responded "correctly," i.e., in accordance with their training. As testing progressed, they were increasingly likely to show the transposition effect. These results are entirely consistent with Capehart et al.'s proposal that AL may serve as a crossover point to direct responding in a choice situation.

On the basis of their studies using single-stimulus training and testing on a brightness dimension, Thomas et al. (1974) and Dickson and Strub (1974) proposed that the TS may be encoded not just in terms of its direction from AL but also its distance. Thus, they would suggest that in the Capehart and Pease (1968) study the Ss may have learned to respond "right" to the value $AL - X$ grams and "left" to the value $AL + Y$ grams, or more probably "right" to the ratio X gm/AL and "left" to the ratio Y gm/AL. Regardless of the specific form of the encoding of the TS, according to this general conception, there would theoretically be a single test value to which maximal "right" responding and another single test value to which maximal "left" responding would occur. Neither the data from the Capehart and Pease study nor the Hébert studies support this view. In both cases, the gradients obtained are monotonic (sigmoid) and not peaked. Furthermore, sigmoid generalization curves are commonly obtained in choice situations, for reasons that are not well understood (cf.

Ernst, Engberg, & Thomas, 1971; Heinemann & Avin, 1973). Thus, to test predictions about points of maximal response strength a discrimination paradigm must be employed which produces nonmonotonic (peaked) generalization gradients. The go/no-go successive discrimination paradigm satisfies this requirement.

Suppose that with such a procedure an S is trained to respond to a 200-gm weight (S+) and not to respond to a 100-gm weight (S−), and subsequently he is tested for generalization to a wide range of weight values. Presumably, equal experience with the two training stimuli will establish an AL somewhere between them, e.g., at the midway point (150 gm). The S may then learn to respond to a value 50 gm greater than AL. During generalization testing in which the 200-gm S+ is the central stimulus, as is typical practice in studies of this sort, Prevailing AL should drift toward the 200-gm value. If S continues to respond to a value 50 gm heavier than AL, maximal responding should gradually shift from the previous S+ toward a value 50 gm heavier. This explains the postdiscrimination "peak shift" in AL terms, and it leads to an intriguing additional prediction. Suppose that in original training the S+ had been 200 gm, the S−, 180 gm, and the AL had been halfway between at 190 gm. If, in testing, 200 gm were again the central value, a shift in peak responding of only 10 gm would be expected. Thus, this application of AL principles leads to the predictions that: (a) the greater the separation of S+ and S−, the *greater* the resulting peak shift, and (b) the peak of responding should shift gradually during generalization testing as AL changes with experience with the test stimuli. Prediction (a) is additionally dictated by another postulated determinant of AL, the amount of training required. If, as expected, groups with the more closely spaced S+ and S− values take longer to achieve criterion, their AL should be more firmly anchored at the end of training and thus less subject to change during subsequent generalization testing.[3]

These predictions are particularly noteworthy because they are directly contradictory to typical results obtained with animal Ss (cf. Hanson, 1959; Thomas, 1962). Furthermore, they are in opposition to predictions based upon Spence's (1937) theory of discrimination learning in animals.

An experiment performed by Doll and Thomas (1967) provided

[3] In order to simplify the exposition, the decision rule used in the above example was the simple one $S+ = AL + X$ gm. It should be obvious that if the S+ were encoded as a ratio of S+ to AL values, the predicted positive relationship between S+ to S− distance and magnitude of peak shift would still attain.

data relevant to the above predictions but unfortunately the results were somewhat equivocal. In that study, three groups of Ss were given wavelength discrimination training to respond to the S+ (530 nm) but not to the S— (540 nm, 550 nm, and 590 nm, respectively). A control group received instructions to respond only to S+ but received no discrimination training. All Ss were then tested for generalization to wavelengths ranging from 510 to 550 nm symmetrically spaced around the 530 nm S+. Relative to the control gradient, both the 540-nm S— and 550-nm S— groups showed displacement of the mode of responding from S+ in the direction opposite to S—, i.e., the peak shift. Contrary to the animal literature but consistent with AL prediction, the 550-nm S— group with the greater S+ to S— distance showed the greater displacement. The 590-nm S— group showed no displacement at all, however, with maximal responding to the 530-nm S+. This result appears inconsistent with the AL theory, but in fact it is not. It should be remembered that only stimuli which fall in the same conceptual category as the TS should contribute to Prevailing AL, and the 590-nm S— is orange and not green. Thus the failure to find a peak shift under this condition is to be expected, and success, rather than failure, would have constituted an embarrassment to the theory.

In a more recent study, Thomas *et al.* (1973) investigated the role of both amount and direction of S+ to S— difference in determining the magnitude of the peak shift. Seventy Ss served in seven different groups in this experiment. For all groups the S+ value was an intermediate brightness of white light, SV 5 in a series of nine logarithmically equally spaced brightnesses which were later used in generalization testing. The Ss in all seven groups in the experiment were shown the central scale value, SV 5, and were instructed that whenever they saw this value, and only this value, they were to respond by lifting their finger from the response key as quickly as possible. Then Ss in the single-stimulus group (Group 5) were shown this stimulus four additional times. After each response by S, E said "right."

After *their* first exposure to the S+, Ss in the other six groups were shown an S— and were told not to respond to this stimulus or to any stimulus value other than the S+. The discrimination training was then initiated. The S+ and S— values were randomly alternated, with the restriction that neither occurred more than three times in succession. When S responded to the S+, E said "right"; when S responded to the S—, E said "wrong." Failure to respond by S produced no feedback from E.

The Ss in the six discrimination groups were run to a criterion of 10 successive correct trials. The six groups differed in the value of the S— stimulus used (and thus the S+ to S— distance) and also in the direction of the S+ to S— difference, i.e., with the S— dimmer for three groups and brighter for three. The discrimination groups were designated according to the code value of S+ and S—, i.e., Groups 5-2 (S+ at SV 5; S— at SV 2, dimmest S—), 5-3, 5-4, 5-6, 5-7, and 5-8 (S+ at SV 5; S— at SV 8, brightest S—).

Immediately following the completion of training, and with no instructional indication to S that the experimental conditions had changed, generalization testing was initiated. Six randomly permuted blocks of all nine test stimuli were presented with no further feedback given to S.

As expected, the S+ to S— difference was negatively related to the number of trials required to meet the discrimination criterion. Thus, the differences in amount of training could summate with a "direct" effect of S+ to S— distance to produce the predicted differences in amount of shift. The role of amount of training in this paradigm should be investigated independently of differences in S+ to S— distance, although to our knowledge this has not yet been done.

The principal results of this experiment are shown in Fig. 9, in which the mean generalization gradients of Groups 5, 5-2, 5-3, and 5-4 are presented. The generalization function for the single-stimulus group (Group 5) is decremental, with a clearly defined peak at the S+ (SV 5), and it is approximately symmetrical. The three discrimination groups, however, all show substantial displacement of the gradient with the peak shifted from S+ so as to be farther removed from S—. In the case of Groups 5-3 and 5-4, the mode of responding falls at SV 6; for Group 5-2 it falls at SV 7.

Where generalization gradients are not very sharp, the *point* of maximal responding (i.e., the mode) may not be unequivocally determinable. In such cases, it is often useful to derive another measure indicating the location of maximal responding along the test dimension. One such measure is the mean of the generalization gradient which may be obtained by treating each S's gradient as a grouped frequency distribution. The higher the mean, the greater the proportion of that S's responses which were made to the brightest test stimuli.

For present purposes, the gradient mean was based only upon responding emitted to SVs 5 and above, so as not to be confounded by the different locations of S— in the three discrimination groups. The group mean values thus obtained were: Group 5, 5.76; Group 5-4,

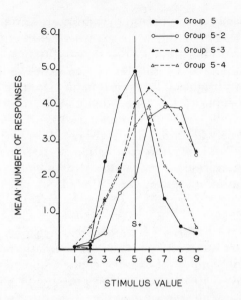

Fig. 9. Generalization gradients of groups of Ss ($n = 20$) trained to respond to a light of moderate brightness (SV 5) and (in discrimination groups) trained not to respond to a dimmer value. The group label indicates the training condition; thus Group 5 received no discrimination training, for Group 5–4, the S− was a light slightly dimmer than S+, etc. (From Thomas *et al.*, 1972.)

5.98; Group 5–3, 6.79; and Group 5–2, 7.04. These scores were ordered in accordance with AL prediction, and the differences were significant. Further analysis revealed that whereas the gradient of Group 5 peaked at the S+ value throughout testing, the gradients of Groups 5–2, 5–3, and 5–4 showed an increasing displacement from S+ as testing progressed.

Unexpectedly, the results of Groups 5–6, 5–7, and 5–8 were not as clearcut as those of the groups just reported. Only Group 5–8, with the largest S+ to S− difference, showed a peak of responding displaced from S+ to a dimmer value (SV 4). A statistical analysis of area shift, parallel to that reported for Groups 5–2, 5–3, and 5–4, was carried out and the group differences failed to achieve significance.

Thus, striking confirmations of AL predictions were obtained in this experiment when S− was dimmer than S+ but not when it was brighter. This effect of S+ to S− direction was not predicted, but Thomas *et al.* (1973) suggested an interpretation consistent with the theory. They pointed out that the AL prediction of peak shift is based upon the simple assumption that AL will fall at approximately the central or mean value of the logarithmically spaced test stimulus series, i.e., SV 5. With some stimulus dimensions, e.g., lifted weights (cf. Hébert *et al.*, 1974), the AL may be systematically displaced from the mean—in that case to a lower value. Assume that the actual AL in the present experiment was at a value greater than SV 5. Then Groups 5–2, 5–3, and 5–4 would show very large shifts, because they had learned to respond to an S+ brighter than AL, and in subsequent generalization testing AL increased—not only to SV 5, but to some value still greater. For Ss in Groups 5–6, 5–7, and 5–8, on the other hand, an AL at a value greater than SV 5 would attenuate or cancel out a peak shift. These Ss would have learned to respond to a stimulus dimmer than AL. If in testing, the AL increased to a value substantially brighter than SV 5, responding maximally to SV 5 remains consistent with S's response strategy in that S is preferring a stimulus dimmer than the (higher) AL level established by the test series. Only in the case of Group 5–8, with the largest S+ to S— difference, might there be a large enough shift of responding from AL to displace the peak to a value below the SV 5 training value.

These speculations led to the hypothesis that the AL produced by the test series used in Experiment I was, in fact, at a value greater than SV 5. Thomas *et al.* (1973) performed a second experiment designed to provide an empirical determination of AL in their experimental situation. For this purpose, AL was designated as the physical value of the stimulus rated as "5," the central value in the rating test series (cf. Helson, 1964, Ch. 4). The obtained AL, based on linear interpolation from the mean ratings of 10 Ss, was equivalent to a scale value of 6.39. This result supported the interpretation that Groups 5–6 and 5–7 failed to show a peak shift in Experiment I because of the increase in AL when the test series was introduced. Presumably a shift in peak responding to values dimmer than S+ would have occurred if the Test AL were dimmer than the AL established in training.

This hypothesis was tested in a third experiment reported by Thomas *et al.* (1973). One of the groups in this experiment received discrimination training in which S+ was SV 8 and S— was SV 9. In agreement with prediction, this group showed a substantial peak shift toward dimmer values. Thus, taken as a whole, the results of this series of three experiments provides strong support for the AL theory as applied to successive discrimination learning in human Ss.

In the introduction to their study, Thomas *et al.* (1973) proposed that the use of the S+ as the central stimulus in the generalization test series would result in a shift in Prevailing AL from its training to its testing value. It was this AL shift which presumably underlay the peak shift in the postdiscrimination generalization gradients. Thomas *et al.* assumed that the Test AL would be at the physical center of the test series, an assumption which was subsequently refuted. Nevertheless, the peak shifts in the 5–2, 5–3, and 5–4 groups were in the predicted direction (i.e., toward brighter values) because the Test AL *was* at a higher value than the Training AL. According to the theory, a peak shift will be obtained when this situation attains, i.e., whenever there is a change in Prevailing AL, for whatever reason.

In several experiments with logarithmically equally spaced brightness values, empirically determined AL values have been substantially above the physical center of the test series. Thus, the predicted peak shifts in the three groups of the Thomas *et al.* (1973) experiment listed above would probably have occurred even if S+ had not been the central test value. Indeed, in that experiment if the Test AL *had* been at the physical center of the test series, it is quite possible that the predicted peak shifts would not have been observed because the Training AL and Test AL values were not sufficiently discrepant. Perhaps this study more than any other demonstrates the necessity of obtaining actual AL measures in testing hypotheses based on presumed changes in AL during an experiment.

The logic of the AL interpretation of the Thomas *et al.* (1973) experiment implies that there is one condition under which maximal responding in the generalization test should accrue to the stimulus value which had been the S—, i.e., the signal for nonresponding, in training. That condition is the one in which the S— stimulus value bears the same relationship to Test AL as the S+ stimulus value did to Training AL. Suppose, for example, that in a lifted-weights experiment the S+ were 20 gm heavier than the S—. Presumably, the S+ would be encoded as, say, AL + 10 gm and S— as AL − 10 gm. If the test series were designed in such a way that Prevailing AL shifted to a value 20 gm below its training level, then Ss should respond maximally to the previous S—. Such a finding would be particularly significant because the *direction* of the peak shift would be opposite that encompassed by Spence's theory and obtained in so many animal experiments.[4]

---

[4] Again for illustrative purposes, the decision rule used was S+ = AL + X gm. Several alternative rules would work as well.

It would be of great interest to determine whether a positive relationship between S+ to S— distance and amount of peak shift could also be shown in infrahuman Ss. Spence's (1937) theory of discrimination learning which predicts an inverse relationship between these variables was intended to apply to animals, and several experiments have supported his prediction with pigeons. For example, Hanson (1959) trained his Ss to respond to a light of 550 nm (S+) and not to respond to a S—, which was 555 nm, 560 nm, 570 nm, or 590 nm for different groups. He found that the smaller the S+ to S— difference, the greater the resulting displacement of the postdiscrimination generalization gradient. This result has since been replicated with wavelength stimuli by Thomas (1962) and with line angle stimuli by Hearst and Koresko (1968).

The success of Giurintano's (1972) investigation of a central tendency shift in pigeons suggests, however, that if an appropriately brief training procedure were developed, a positive relationship between S+ to S— distance and amount of peak shift might result. Terrace (1963) has reported an experiment which suggests one possible technique. He showed that the acquisition of a horizontal-vertical discrimination in pigeons could be greatly accelerated by first training a red-green discrimination and then gradually fading in the line angles superimposed upon the colors. Terrace then faded the colors out in order to show that the line angles had gained control over responding. For present purposes, this probably would not be necessary. If it is assumed that the line angles have gained some control during the superimposition phase of the experiment, a peak shift along the line angle dimension might result, since Thomas (1962) has shown that a peak shift occurs prior to the attainment of a high level of discrimination performance. Recent research has also indicated that the use of a correction procedure, in which responses to S— postpone the onset of S+, may also substantially hasten the acquisition of the discrimination. It remains to be determined whether a combination of superimposition and correction methods will establish a discrimination rapidly enough to permit a test of the AL hypothesis of a positive relationship between S+ to S— distance and amount of peak shift.

There is an alternative procedure for the rapid acquisition of a discrimination which might also be applied to the problem in question. This procedure was developed by Thomas and Caronite (1964) in order to study the stimulus generalization of conditioned reinforcement. In their experiment, two groups of pigeons were trained in a Skinner box to peck at an unlighted key for a periodic 2-sec exposures of 550 nm, the conditioned reinforcer, which was immediately followed by food reward. For the discrimination group, 2-sec exposures of 570 nm (never followed by food) were alternately presented. Both groups were tested for generalization in extinction with a procedure which allowed each S equal opportunity to respond to the blank key to produce the stimuli of 510, 530, 550, 570, and 590 nm. The control group showed a stable decremental gradient with decreased responding on either side of 550 nm. The post-discrimination gradient of the other group showed the peak shift typically found following successive discrimination training along a single dimension.

Thomas and Caronite also measured "superstitious" responding which occurred during the 2-sec presentations of the monochromatic stimuli. The gradients of superstitious responding, said to reflect the discriminative function rather than the reinforcing function of the stimuli, also showed the peak-shift phenomenon. For present purposes, the most significant point is that the discrimination between the 550- and 570-nm values was based upon a total of less than 30 min of exposure to the S+ and only 10 min of exposure to the S−.

As was the case in the Giurintano (1972) study, substantial resistance to extinction for testing purposes was created by reinforcement for responding to an orthogonal stimulus. The relevant difference is that in the Giurintano study, that training preceded introduction to the dimensional stimulus whereas in the Thomas and Caronite (1964) study the orthogonal training was concurrent with the dimensional training. The rapidity with which the discrimination was formed in the latter study is probably due to both the large number of alternations or comparisons of the two stimuli and to their informativeness. The onset of the 550-nm value signified that reinforcement was imminent. In the more typical operant free response paradigm, the stimulus correlated with VI 1-min reinforcement provides far less information. It seems likely that an adequate discrimination could be produced, in the Thomas and Caronite (1964) paradigm, in far less time than they used, by shortening the stimulus exposure durations from 2 sec to 1.5 or 1 sec. The procedure used in their discrimination group can be used to test the role of the S+ to S− difference in the peak shift. The procedure used in their control group can be used in studies of the central tendency effect following "single-stimulus training." Research is now planned with several procedures in an effort to test a variety of AL hypotheses with pigeon subjects.

IV. Summary and Conclusions

A. SUCCESSES OF THE AL THEORY

It is our intention in this section of the chapter to sum up the successes and failures of the AL theory of stimulus generalization and thereby to provide an evaluation of its fruitfulness. In general, the theory has been extremely successful in predicting or interpreting the results of stimulus generalization experiments. With regard to the Central Tendency Effect, the following conclusions can be made with some certainty.

1. The point of maximal responding in an asymmetrical generalization test is initially at the value of the TS and it shifts gradually from the TS value as testing progresses. The shift may occur so rapidly that it may be complete after several exposures to the generalization test series.

2. The central tendency shift occurs with reference to the psychological center (AL) of the generalization test series, which may not coincide with the physical center. In such cases, a shift of maximal responding from the TS value may occur even when the test series is nominally symmetrical, i.e., the TS is at the physical center of the series.

3. The amount of central tendency shift obtained varies inversely with the amount of training or exposure to the TS and may be absent altogether in those situations (e.g., typical conditioning paradigms) in which extensive training is given. Presumably, such training weights the Training AL so heavily in the determination of Prevailing AL that Test AL has very little effect.

4. The amount of shift obtained varies directly with the degree of asymmetry in the generalization test series. Furthermore, substantial asymmetry may be required before any central tendency shift is obtained.

5. Overrepresentation of a particular test value results in a heightened tendency to respond to the overrepresented value. This may attenuate or accentuate the central tendency shift, depending on the relationship of the overrepresented value to the TS.

6. Central tendency shifts occur within but not across conceptual categories. Where the TS falls in an extremely narrow category, there may be no central tendency shift at all. Where the category member-

ship of the TS is manipulable by the experimenter, central tendency shifts appropriate to that categorization may be produced. This is presumed to occur because the categorization of the TS defines the functional test series within which stimuli are averaged to provide a Test AL.

7. Central tendency shifts can be obtained in infrahuman Ss when a sufficiently brief period of exposure to the dimensional TS is provided. Even a small amount of dimensional training (e.g., one hour) may preclude the development of a central tendency shift, which doubtlessly accounts for the failure of the previous experiments to find one.

8. In studies in which an AL for the generalization test series has been measured or calculated, maximal generalized responding typically occurs to the stimulus value closest to the Test AL.

9. In studies in which both AL and generalization measures have been obtained from the same Ss during the course of testing, a direct relationship between AL and the point of maximal generalized responding has been observed. In one reported case, that relationship was one of equivalence, i.e., Ss responded most to their AL value at the time. In several other cases, the Ss responded most to that stimulus which had a given relationship to prevailing AL throughout testing, e.g., one scale value below AL or one-half scale value above it.

Capehart *et al.* (1969) had proposed that Ss encode and judge all stimuli with regard to their relationship to the Prevailing AL. They presumed that in single-stimulus training, the TS would generally be encoded as equivalent to the Prevailing AL value. Thus, as Prevailing AL shifted toward the center of the asymmetrical test series during continued testing, the point of maximal responding would be displaced accordingly. The major findings listed from 1 to 8 above are all consistent with this interpretation. The finding in Point 9 is not inconsistent with the notion that the TS is encoded with regard to its relationship to the Prevailing AL value but only with the specification that the relationship need be one of equivalence. Apparently there are situations in which S enters the experiment with a strong preexperimental AL and the TS is encoded with regard to its relationship to it. Subsequent responding then reflects this relationship. As the Prevailing AL changes during testing the point of maximal responding changes accordingly, so as to maintain the same relationship with Prevailing AL as the TS had to the preexperimental AL.

With regard to postdiscrimination generalization gradients, two important additional findings can be listed.

10. In a choice discrimination situation in which different re-

sponses (e.g., "go right" or "go left") are trained to two stimuli on a single dimension, transposition can be produced by testing for generalization with an asymmetrical test series. That is, Ss appear to use the AL as the dividing point between responding "right" or "left" such that by the end of testing, they may be consistently responding "left" to the training value with which a response of "right" was originally associated.

11. In a go/no-go discrimination situation with two stimuli on the same dimension, followed by a generalization test in which S+ is the central test value, a peak shift is observed with maximal responding displaced from S+ in the direction opposite from S—. The magnitude of this displacement may be shown to vary *positively* with the difference between the two training stimuli.

Both of these findings are consistent with the view that in discrimination situations, S encodes the two training stimuli with regard to their relationship to the Prevailing AL. In the choice paradigm, AL seems to serve as the crossover point, such that stimuli above AL are to be responded to in one fashion and stimuli below AL are to be responded to in another. In the go/no-go situation, it appears that the training stimuli are encoded not just with regard to their direction from, but also their distance from, the Prevailing AL. This finding is, of course, parallel to the postulated use of AL following single-stimulus training in those situations where a strong preexperimental AL must be considered.

B. Limitations of the AL Theory

Although the ordinal predictions made in accordance with AL theory have withstood empirical examination quite well, there are some puzzling inconsistencies. An example is the failure of Hébert *et al.* (1972) to find any difference in the magnitude of the central tendency effect following 1, 11, or 22 exposures to the lifted-weight TS. It was speculated that S may learn all there is to know about the value of the TS in one exposure. If this were so, we might reasonably expect no central tendency effect at any level of training, rather than an equal effect at all three levels. To encompass the obtained results, there must be a low ceiling on the weight of the Training AL relative to the Test AL in determining Prevailing AL. Why such a situation should attain with lifted-weight stimuli and not with line angles (cf. Giurintano, 1972) is certainly unclear at this time, and the theory in its current state is unequipped to handle it. Nevertheless, the parallel evidence obtained by Giurintano in both his human and his pigeon studies suggests that, under some conditions at least, amount of training has its predicted negative relationship with the magnitude of the central tendency shift. It should be apparent that far more work has been carried out on testing than on training parameters of the central tendency effect and it is time for this imbalance to be remedied.

Another problem for the theory is that the magnitude of the predicted effect for a given experimental manipulation may be far greater than that observed. Three studies, Thomas and Jones (1962), Helson and Avant (1967), and Thomas et al. (1974) found a graded systematic relationship between degree of test asymmetry and magnitude of central tendency shift. Giurintano (1972) found reliable central tendency shifts in both humans and pigeons with a line angle TS and six test angles to one side of it. He found, however, that the addition of but one test stimulus on the other side of the TS eliminated the shift altogether, although the degree of test asymmetry was still very substantial. Thomas et al. (1973) reported a central tendency shift when the TS was SV 2 (second from the dimmest) in a series of nine equally spaced brightness values, but not when it was SV 8. They later determined that the Test AL was much closer to SV 8 than to SV 2 and postulated that a "substantial" discrepancy must exist between the TS and Test AL values before a central tendency shift is evidenced. This is a reasonable supposition, but no such stipulation was made by Capehart et al. (1969). There does seem to be an inconsistency across dimensions with minor asymmetry leading to a shift along wavelength and size-area dimensions, but greater asymmetry required along brightness and angularity dimensions. It seems unlikely that this discrepancy will be resolved by a quantitative formulation of the required initial discrepancy between the TS and Test AL values to produce a central tendency shift, but the effort should be made.

A clear limitation of the theory is the fact that although ordinal predictions based upon it may fare rather well, absolute quantitative predictions do not. As argued earlier, the go/no-go discrimination paradigm has the advantage of determining a point of maximal responding. Thus, for example, in the Thomas et al. (1973) experiment, it could be predicted that the gradient of Group 5–4 would peak at SV 7, approximately one-half log unit brighter than the empirically determined AL of 6.39. It did not. Indeed, although the magnitude of the peak shifts in the 5–4, 5–3, and 5–2 groups had the predicted relationships to each other, none of the gradients peaked at the absolute value which a strict quantitative application of the theory would demand. This problem is not unlike that described earlier, in that some experimental manipulations have a far greater effect than that predicted by the theory whereas others have unexpectedly little influence.

A similar problem exists in the interpretation of the results of the Dickson and Strub (1974) experiment. In that study, preexposure to the bright lights (SV 9, 10, and 11), training with SV 4, and then testing with SV 4, 5, 6, 7, and 8 led to maximal generalized responding to a test value substantially below the measured Prevailing AL. On the other hand, Ss preexposed to the dim lights (SV 1, 2, and 3) and otherwise trained and tested like the first group showed maximal responding to a value slightly above their Prevailing AL. Both the direction and *relative* magnitude of these displacements from Prevailing AL were in accord with the hypotheses that S encoded the TS as $AL - X$ log units in the former case and as $AL + Y$ log units in the latter, with $X > Y$. In absolute physical terms, however, the locations of the peaks of generalized responding were not in accordance with prediction. If the preexperimental AL of the preexposed bright group were approximately equivalent to SV 10, the TS value (SV 4) should have been encoded as dimmer than Prevailing AL by a distance equivalent to six scale units. Their generalization test data, however, revealed a substantial level of responding and maximal response strength to a value approximately three scale units below their measured Prevailing AL (see Fig. 8). One view of the obtained discrepancy is to argue that the decision rule: $TS = AL - X$ is surely an oversimplification, but a useful first approximation to a more complex relational rule which Ss apparently use. Alternatively it might be proposed that it is an overcomplication, and that Ss may encode the TS in even simpler terms, e.g., $TS = AL -$ a large brightness difference. If this were the level of processing employed, we would never expect to be able to predict the precise location of maximal responding in a generalization test but only its location relative to some other training or testing condition. Clearly, research should be directed at determining the nature of the decision rule actually employed in various experimental situations. The recognition of this need, however, should not preclude an appreciation of the considerable predictive success which the theory, in its current inexact form, has had.

A final point which must be reemphasized is that the AL theory is not a complete or exhaustive theory of stimulus generalization. Thus, for example, there is nothing in the theory to account for differences in the slopes of generalization gradients obtained following various experimental manipulations. The theory only concerns itself with the location of the point of maximal responding or the location of the crossover point between two categories of responding. Furthermore, the theory does not deny that other mechanisms may produce changes in the same measures, as revealed in such phenomena as the peak shift observed with animals following extended training. On the other hand, the AL theory has been fruitfully applied to a wide range of training and testing situations. For example, its application to situations in which stimuli are classified or labeled by S has led to a significantly altered conception of the way in which verbal mediation affects generalized responding.

It may be of value to speculate on possible extensions of the AL theory which would enable it to encompass additional generalization phenomena. Consider, for example, the finding by Hansen, Tomie, Thomas, and Thomas (1974) that the greater the range of stimuli used in a symmetrical generalization test, the flatter the resulting gradient. Since the *location* of the AL is presumably unaffected by this manipulation, the theory in its present form is unequipped to handle this finding. On the other hand, the greater the range of test stimuli used, the greater the trial-by-trial fluctuation (variance) of Prevailing AL. As S compares each test stimulus with his AL, the greater the AL variance, the greater should be S's uncertainty about whether or not the test stimulus is the same as the AL value. Given the assumption that S has a set to respond when in doubt, enhanced uncertainty would result in a flattened generalization gradient. This assumption seems reasonable but a great deal of additional research needs to be done to determine whether this extension of the AL theory is a valid one. This is but one example of a possible direction which an extension of the AL theory might take.

The data summarized in this chapter indicate that both humans and animals encode training stimuli in a relative rather than an absolute manner, and that they do so not only in explicit discrimination training situations but in "single-stimulus training" as well. Indeed, we would argue that single-stimulus training is a misnomer, since even a single stimulus is encoded with regard to its relationship to an internal referent which we, following Helson (1947, 1964), have called Adaptation level. It remains to be seen what new insights into the analysis of learned behavior will result from the further application of AL principles to situations in which an S-R analysis has already been shown to be inadequate. Clearly, however, such situations constitute the rule, rather than the exceptions thereto.

REFERENCES

Brown, J. B., Bilodeau, E. A., & Baron, M. R. Bidirectional gradients in the strength of a generalized voluntary response to stimuli on a visual-spatial dimension. *Journal of Experimental Psychology*, 1951, **41**, 52–61.

Capehart, J., & Pease, V. An application of adaptation-level theory to transposition responses in a conditional discrimination. *Psychonomic Science*, 1968, **10**, 147–148.

Capehart, J., Tempone, V. J., & Hébert, J. A. A theory of stimulus equivalence. *Psychological Review*, 1969, **76**, 405–418.

Dickson, J. F., Jr., & Strub, H. The central tendency effect in stimulus generalization: Effects of establishing a preexperimental frame of reference. Unpublished manuscript, University of Colorado, 1973.

Doll, T. J., & Thomas, D. R. Effects of discrimination training on stimulus generalization for human subjects. *Journal of Experimental Psychology*, 1967, **75**, 508–512.

Eck, K. O., Noel, R. C., & Thomas, D. R. Discrimination learning as a function of prior discrimination and nondifferential training. *Journal of Experimental Psychology*, 1969, **82**, 156–162.

Eck, K. O., & Thomas, D. R. Discrimination learning as a function of prior discrimination and nondifferential training: A replication. *Journal of Experimental Psychology*, 1970, **83**, 511–513.

Ernst, A. J., Engberg, L. A., & Thomas, D. R. On the form of stimulus generalization curves for visual intensity. *Journal of the Experimental Analysis of Behavior*, 1971, **16**, 177–180.

Giurintano, L. P. Stimulus generalization in humans and pigeons as a function of training and test stimulus parameters. Unpublished doctoral dissertation, University of Colorado, 1972.

Giurintano, L. P., Schadler, M., & Thomas, D. R. Angularity preferences and stimulus orthogonality in pigeons. *Psychonomic Science*, 1972, **26**, 273–275.

Guttman, N. The pigeon and the spectrum and other perplexities. *Psychological Reports*, 1956, **2**, 449–460.

Guttman, N., & Kalish, H. I. Discriminability and stimulus generalization. *Journal of Experimental Psychology*, 1956, **51**, 79–88.

Hansen, G., Tomie, A., Thomas, D. R., & Thomas, D. H. The effect of the range of test stimuli on stimulus generalization in human subjects. *Journal of Experimental Psychology*, 1974, **102**, 634–639.

Hanson, H. M. Effects of discrimination training on stimulus generalization. *Journal of Experimental Psychology*, 1959, **58**, 321–334.

Hearst, E., & Koresko, M. B. Stimulus generalization and amount of prior training on variable-interval reinforcement. *Journal of Comparative and Physiological Psychology*, 1968, **66**, 133–158.

Hébert, J. A. Context effects in the generalization of a successive conditional discrimination in human subjects. *Canadian Journal of Psychology*, 1970, **24**, 271–275.

Hébert, J. A., Bullock, M., Levitt, L., Woodward, K. G., & McGuirk, F. D., III. Context and frequency effects in the generalization of a human voluntary response. *Journal of Experimental Psychology*, 1974, **102**, 456–462.

Hébert, J., & Capehart, J. Generalization of a voluntary response as a function of presentation frequency of the training stimulus in testing. *Psychonomic Science*, 1969, **16**, 315–316.

Hébert, J. A., Origlio, D. P., & McGuirk, F. D., III. Training and testing effects in the generalization of a voluntary response. *Psychonomic Science,* 1972, **26,** 209–210.

Heinemann, E. G., & Avin, E. On the development of stimulus control. *Journal of the Experimental Analysis of Behavior,* 1973, **20,** 183–196.

Helson, H. Adaptation-level as a frame of reference for prediction of psychophysical data. *American Journal of Psychology,* 1947, **60,** 1–29.

Helson, H. *Adaptation-level theory.* New York: Harper, 1964.

Helson, H., & Avant, L. L. Stimulus generalization as a function of contextual stimuli. *Journal of Experimental Psychology,* 1967, **73,** 565–567.

Hilgard, E. R., & Bower, G. H. *Theories of learning.* New York: Appleton, 1966.

Hollingworth, H. L. The inaccuracy of movement. *Archives of Psychology,* 1909, 2 (Whole No. 13).

Hovland, C. I. The generalization of conditioned responses. II. The sensory generalization of conditioned responses with varying intensities of tone. *Journal of Genetic Psychology,* 1937, **51,** 279–291.

Hull, C. L. *Principles of behavior.* New York: Appleton, 1943.

James, H. An application of Helson's theory of adaptation level to the problem of transposition. *Psychological Review,* 1953, **46,** 345–351.

Kalish, H. I. The relationship between discriminability and generalization: A reevaluation. *Journal of Experimental Psychology,* 1958, **55,** 637–644.

Keilitz, I., & Frieman, J. Transfer following discrimination learning with and without errors. *Journal of Experimental Psychology,* 1970, **85,** 293–299.

Krechevsky, I. A study of the continuity of the problem-solving process. *Psychological Review,* 1938, **45,** 107–133.

Pavlov, I. P. *Conditioned reflexes.* London: Oxford University Press, 1927.

Philip, B. R. Effect of length of series upon generalization and central tendency in the discrimination of a series of stimuli. *Canadian Journal of Psychology,* 1952, **6,** 173–178.

Razran, G. Stimulus generalization of conditioned responses. *Psychological Bulletin,* 1949, **46,** 337–365.

Schadler, M., & Thomas, D. R. On the acquisition of dimensional stimulus control in pigeons. *Journal of Comparative and Physiological Psychology,* 1972, **79,** 82–89.

Spence, K. W. The differential response in animals to stimuli varying within a single dimension. *Psychological Review,* 1937, **44,** 430–444.

Terrace, H. S. Errorless transfer of a discrimination across two continua. *Journal of the Experimental Analysis of Behavior,* 1963, **6,** 1–27.

Thomas, D. R. The effects of drive and discrimination training on stimulus generalization. *Journal of Experimental Psychology,* 1962, **64,** 24–28.

Thomas, D. R. Stimulus selection, attention, and related matters. In J. H. Reynierse (Ed.), *Current issues in animal learning.* Lincoln: University of Nebraska Press, 1970.

Thomas, D. R., & Barker, E. G. The effects of extinction and central tendency on stimulus generalization in pigeons. *Psychonomic Science,* 1964, **1,** 119–120.

Thomas, D. R., & Caronite, S. C. Stimulus generalization of a positive conditioned reinforcer: II. Effects of discrimination training. *Journal of Experimental Psychology,* 1964, **68,** 402–406.

Thomas, D. R., Caronite, A. D., LaMonica, G. L., & Hoving, K. L. Mediated generalization via stimulus labeling: A replication and extension. *Journal of Experimental Psychology,* 1968, **78,** 531–533.

Thomas, D. R., & DeCapito, A. Role of stimulus labeling in stimulus generalization. *Journal of Experimental Psychology,* 1966, **71,** 913–915.

Thomas, D. R., & Jones, C. G. Stimulus generalization as a function of the frame of reference. *Journal of Experimental Psychology,* 1962, **64,** 77–80.

Thomas, D. R., & Mitchell, K. Instructions and stimulus categorizing in a measure of stimulus generalization. *Journal of the Experimental Analysis of Behavior,* 1962, **5,** 375–381.

Thomas, D. R., Strub, H., & Dickson, J. F., Jr. Adaptation level and the central tendency effect in stimulus generalization. *Journal of Experimental Psychology,* 1974.

Thomas, D. R., Svinicki, M. D., & Vogt, J. Adaptation level as a factor in human discrimination learning and stimulus generalization. *Journal of Experimental Psychology,* 1973, **97,** 210–219.

Thomas, D. R., & Thomas, D. H. Stimulus labeling, adaptation-level, and the central tendency shift. *Journal of Experimental Psychology,* 1974.

Tomie, A. & Thomas, D. R. Adaptation level as a factor in human wavelength generalization. *Journal of Experimental Psychology,* 1974.

White, S. H. Training and timing in the generalization of a voluntry response. *Journal of Experimental Psychology,* 1965, **69,** 269, 273.

Zeiler, M. D. The ratio theory of intermediate size discrimination. *Psychological Review,* 1963, **70,** 516–533.

RECENT DEVELOPMENTS IN CHOICE[1]

Edmund Fantino and Douglas Navarick

UNIVERSITY OF CALIFORNIA, SAN DIEGO, LA JOLLA, CALIFORNIA

AND

CALIFORNIA STATE UNIVERSITY, FULLERTON, CALIFORNIA

I. Introduction

Much recent work in choice has been carried out with pigeons and a two-response-key version of the conventional operant chamber (Ferster & Skinner, 1957). Out of this research has come several plausible accounts specifying a quantitative relationship between choice behavior and schedules of reinforcement (e.g., Baum, 1973; Fantino, 1969a; Herrnstein, 1961, 1970; Killeen, 1968; Premack, 1965; Rachlin, 1973; Squires & Fantino, 1971). While each account adequately describes much of the relevant data, none accurately describes choice proportions across a variety of reinforcement schedules. One of the main points to be made in the present paper is that no such general quantitative theory of choice is likely to be forthcoming. Models adequate to describe choice proportions with precision will be restricted to particular procedures and schedules of reinforcement. Before we document these assertions we should add that we are far from pessimistic about recent developments in choice. Indeed, several exciting generalizations have emerged from the re-

[1] The research reported herein was supported by National Institutes of Health Grant MH20752 to the University of California, San Diego.

147

search program we are about to describe. If the promise of an adequate quantitative theory of choice behavior having broad generality is a casualty of our work, we feel it is more than compensated for by some of the empirical generalizations about choice and conditioned reinforcement that this work is uncovering.

Obviously, a theory which provides an adequate quantitative description of choice is preferable to one that does not. The accounts cited above make precise quantitative predictions about choice rather than ordinal predictions. For example, Herrnstein (1961) and others have shown that the pigeon will not only prefer a variable-interval 1-min (VI 1) schedule to a VI 3 but will—to a close approximation —match its choice responses to the proportions of reinforcement available in each schedule (here, 3:1). We shall see below, however, that theories of choice which make precise quantitative predictions assume that choice behavior meets the rigid criterion of strong stochastic transitivity (e.g., Navarick & Fantino, 1972b) which we shall elaborate on later. Unfortunately, this assumption has rarely been tested. Suppose that the same pigeon which generated a choice proportion of .75 for a VI 1 over a VI 3 schedule emitted the same choice proportion when the VI 1-min schedule was compared with a fixed-ratio 30 (FR 30). Would the FR 30 and the VI 3-min schedules be equally preferred when presented for choice? If not, choice behavior would be intransitive across comparisons involving VI and FR schedules. It can be shown that such intransitivities do occur and that they impose serious limitations on theories of choice.

Where choice is a function of more than one dimension—for example, when subjects are not sensitive exclusively to the reinforcement variable specified by the theory—additional problems arise. In the first place, choice is likely to be intransitive when it is under multidimensional control (Navarick, 1973; Tversky, 1969). Indeed, the organism may reliably choose one stimulus of a pair in one test and the other in another test (Rachlin & Green, 1972). For example, consider a reluctant dieter faced with the choice of a delectable hot-fudge sundae, a scoop of orange sherbet, or no dessert at all. His choice is based on taste and caloric content. If he is asked to order his dessert 24 hours before the meal is to be served he may well choose neither since the caloric dimension may be more important to him at this time. As the meal approaches, however, taste becomes more important and preference may shift from omitting dessert to ordering the sherbet. When the sundae and sherbet are physically presented for choice, at the actual meal, however, selection of the sundae becomes more likely since the taste dimension should be most important at this time. The opposite sort of effect is also possible: the shy adolescent or the fantasizing husband may choose an orgy to an evening of television, if asked in advance, but may get "cold feet" when the moment of decision arrives. When the basis for choice is multidimensional, our account of choice must necessarily be more complex. Indeed, especially where quantitative models are concerned it may be well to limit our scope to choice that exhibits both transitivity and unidimensional control. When we have succeeded at this level, we may be in a stronger position to tackle more complex instances of choice.

A. A Procedure for Studying Choice

Assume we are interested in evaluating a person's preference for hot-fudge sundaes, peanuts, and hot onion soup. One obvious way to proceed would be to give the person experience with each of the three foods, deprive him for some time, and then present all three in a simple choice test. Leaving aside the problem that amount of deprivation is likely to interact with the food chosen, this simple choice procedure is fine for providing a crude measure of choice. For a more continuous quantitative measure of choice, however, we need to know how much more reinforcing the chosen food is than the others. The answer we obtain will depend, of course, upon our method. An obvious measure, rate of eating, is fraught with problems. Hot onion soup, for example, may be the preferred food, but the person may eat it more slowly than the others. Similarly, the amount of time spent engaged in eating the food may also be misleading: peanuts may be munched into the night whereas the person is likely to satiate quickly on hot-fudge sundaes. One way around this problem is to study the rate of responding the person emits in order to obtain access to each of the three foods. This kind of simple concurrent schedule, in which relative response rates are used as a measure of choice, has become the standard operant choice procedure over the past 15 years (e.g., Catania, 1966; Findley, 1958; Herrnstein, 1958, 1961).

The research to be discussed and described in the present paper involves not preferences for different reinforcers, but preferences for different schedules of the same reinforcers. Many studies of choice for schedules of reinforcement have utilized simple concurrent schedules. While these appear to provide reasonable measures of choice for many pairs of schedules, the method is flawed by a confounding feature that becomes apparent when two widely discrepant schedules are utilized: *the measure of choice is confounded with the rates of responding generated by the schedules themselves.* Thus, if a fixed-interval (FI) and a variable-ratio (VR) schedule were compared for choice in a simple concurrent design it would be impossible to determine to what extent responding represented choice for one schedule over another and to what extent the behavior is controlled by the nature of FI and VR schedules. For example, response rates on VR schedules tend to be much higher than on typical FI schedules. If we take the relative rates of responding on a simple concurrent schedule as our measure of choice, therefore, we are stacking the deck in favor of the VR schedule. Such a choice procedure would be more obviously inappropriate if we were comparing choice between a ratio schedule and a schedule which *required* low rates of responding. Perhaps to avoid such confounding of choice with the response rates generated by the schedules being chosen, Autor (1960) developed the concurrent-chains procedure, diagrammed in Fig. 1. In this procedure, the organism responds on two concurrently available keys, each of which is illuminated by the stimulus of the initial link of one chain. Responses on each key occasionally produce a stimulus of the terminal link of the chain on that key. Responses in the presence of either of the (nonconcurrent) terminal-link stimuli are reinforced with food. The independent variable has generally involved some difference in the conditions arranged during the two terminal links. The dependent variable is the measure of choice: the distribution of responses in the initial, concurrently presented links of the chain. The figure legend provides a detailed description of the general procedure that has been used in these experiments.

The concurrent-chains procedure has several advantages in the study of choice. In the first place, the procedure keeps the number of reinforcements for responding on each key close to the number intended by the experimenter over a wide range of preference for pecking one key or the other. If a subject responded exclusively on one key, for example, all reinforcements would be delivered for those responses. Due to the nature of concurrently available VI schedules, however, the subject produces a higher rate of reinforcement if it responds on both keys.[2] In practice, this assures that the terminal link of each key will be entered equally often. Thus, the effects of number of reinforcements are not confounded with those of the intended independent variable. In the second place, choice responding (i.e., responding in the initial links) is separated from the particular response rates and patterns of responding generated by the schedule of primary reinforcement in the terminal links. As

2 We shall see that there are instructive exceptions to this rule (pp. 155–156).

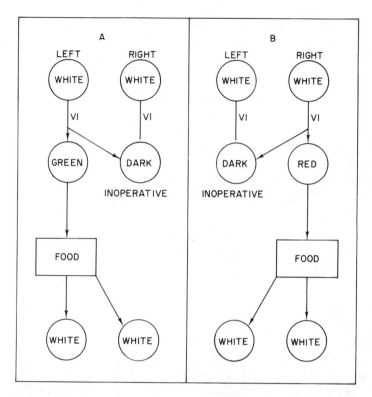

Fig. 1. Pictorial representation of the concurrent-chains procedure. Figure 1A in-dicates the sequence of events when responses on the left key are reinforced. Figure 1B represents the analogous sequence on the right key. Identical, but independently operated, VI schedules arrange access to the stimuli of the terminal links. When access to the stimulus of a terminal link is scheduled by either VI programer, it stops operating, but the other VI programer continues to operate. The next response on the appropriate key produces the terminal-link stimulus associated with that key and two additional events: (1) the VI programer associated with the other key stops operating; (2) illumination is removed from the other key which becomes inoperative. Pecks in the presence of the terminal-link stimuli produce food according to different schedules. Following reinforcement, the initial links are reinstated. Because of the nature of concurrent VI schedules, the pigeon, on the average, generally receives an equal number of food presentations on each key.

pointed out above, this is not the case when choice is studied with simple concurrent schedules. Finally, in studying choice with the concurrent-chains procedure, the experimenter obtains a dividend in that the results are also relevant to the topic of conditioned re-inforcement, a point to which we will return at the end of this paper.

B.   Models for Choice in the Concurrent-Chains Procedure

In the first experiment utilizing concurrent-chains schedules, Autor (1960) employed VI, VR, and response-independent schedules in the terminal links and found that the relative rates of choice responding (the number of choice responses on one key divided by the total number of choice responses on the two keys) matched the relative rates of reinforcement (the rate of reinforcement on one key divided by the sum of the two rates of reinforcement) in the two terminal links. In a follow-up experiment utilizing VI and VR terminal-link schedules, Herrnstein (1964b) obtained similar results. The Autor–Herrnstein relationship may be summarized by the equation

$$\frac{R_L}{R_L + R_R} = \frac{1/t_{2L}}{1/t_{2L} + 1/t_{2R}}, \tag{1}$$

where R_L is the number of responses in the left initial link, R_R is the number of responses in the right initial link, t_{2L} is the mean interreinforcement interval in the left terminal link, and t_{2R} is the mean length of the right terminal link.

While Eq. (1) appeared to offer a good quantitative description of choice in the concurrent-chains procedure, there was at least one sense in which it was counterintuitive. An implication of Eq. (1) is that the organism's preference for one schedule over another should be invariant regardless of how accessible the two schedules are. In particular, if t_{2L} and t_{2R} were equal to 30 and 90 sec, respectively, Eq. (1) requires a choice proportion of .75 for the VI 30-sec schedule regardless of the value of the initial-link schedules. Fantino (1969b) reasoned that if the terminal links were highly accessible (as with short initial-link schedules approaching continuous reinforcement), preference for the preferred alternative should increase. Why should the organism ever enter the VI 90-sec terminal link if it could obtain almost immediate access to the VI 30-sec terminal link? At the other extreme, when the two terminal-link schedules were relatively inaccessible (as with unusually long VI's such as VI 10-min), the organism should be more indifferent between the two schedules than required by the matching formulation. With long initial links, entrance into either terminal link should be highly reinforcing. Fantino speculated that with sufficiently long initial links organisms should be indifferent between the terminal links and that with sufficiently short initial links the organism should respond exclusively on the side leading to the short terminal link. If so, then only for a particular band of intermediate values should the distribution of choice responses match the distribution of reinforcements obtained in the terminal links.

Fantino (1969a) incorporated these intuitive predictions into an alternative formulation and found that the data of Autor (1960) and of Herrnstein (1964b) were as consistent with this alternative formulation as was formulation 1. This newer formulation states that

$$P_L = \frac{R_L}{R_L + R_R} = \frac{T - t_{2L}}{(T - t_{2L}) + (T - t_{2R})} \qquad \text{(when } t_{2L} < T, t_{2R} < T\text{)}$$

$$= 1 \qquad \text{(when } t_{2L} < T, t_{2R} > T\text{)} \qquad (2)$$

$$= 0 \qquad \text{(when } t_{2L} > T, t_{2R} < T\text{)},$$

where T represents the average time to primary reinforcement from the onset of the initial links.[3] Note that when entry into either terminal link produces an *increase* in the average time to primary reinforcement (either $t_{2L} > T$ or $t_{2R} > T$), Eq. (2) requires the organism to emit all of its choice responses to the other key. In other words, Eq. (2) specifies when the organism should respond exclusively on one key. Of course, the case in which both t_{2L} and t_{2R} are greater than T is impossible. This formulation implies that the relative rate of responding in the initial links matches "the amount of reduction in the expected time to primary reward signified by

---

[3] The value of T is computed in the following manner. In the first place, the expected time to reach a terminal link from the onset of the initial links is

$$(1/t_{1L} + 1/t_{1R})-1,$$

where t_{1L} and t_{1R} are the average durations of the left and right initial links, respectively. The average time to reinforcement after the onset of a terminal link is

$$pt_{2L} + (1 - p)t_{2R},$$

where p and $(1 - p)$ represent the probability of entering the left and right terminal links, respectively, and where $p = t_{1R}/(t_{1L} + t_{1R})$. Therefore,

$$T = (1/t_{1L} + 1/t_{1R})-1 + pt_{2L} + (1 - p)t_{2R}.$$

For example, in the schedule Chain VI 120-sec VI 30-sec versus Chain VI 120-sec VI 90-sec, the average time spent in the initial links is 60 sec and the average time spent in the terminal links is also 60 sec, which is $[.50 \times 30 \text{ sec}] + [.50 \times 90 \text{ sec}]$, since each terminal link is entered one-half of the time. Therefore, $T = 60 \text{ sec} + 60 \text{ sec} = 120$ sec and the predicted choice proportion is

$$\frac{(120 - 30)}{(120 - 30) + (120 - 90)} = .75.$$

entry into one terminal link relative to the reduction in expected time to reward signified by entry into the other terminal link" (Fantino, 1969a). This prediction was tested by using three different pairs of identical VI schedules to arrange entry into the two terminal links; the rate of reinforcement in the presence of one terminal link was always three times the rate of reinforcement in the other terminal link. When the pair of initial-link schedules of intermediate interreinforcement duration was in effect, the choice proportions in the initial links matched the relative rate of reinforcement in the terminal links (Eq. 1), a result consistent with both formulations. When the initial links of shorter or longer average interreinforcement duration were in effect, however, the distribution of choice responses no longer matched the relative rates of reinforcement, but continued to be well described by Eq. (2).

In addition, Fantino (1969a) utilized two schedules in which both the initial and terminal links were unequal: chain VI 90-sec VI 30-sec versus Chain VI 30-sec VI 90-sec. The data from this procedure were also consistent with Eq. (2), raising the possibility that Eq. (2) might apply to cases in which the initial links are unequal as well as to the more typical case of equal initial links.

C. Strengths of Choice Eq. (2)

In addition to its intuitive appeal, Eq. (2) provides reasonably accurate predictions of choice behavior as measured in several experiments with the concurrent-chains procedure. Not only does the formulation describe choice over the ranges of VI values generally in effect in experiments utilizing concurrent-chains schedules, but it also has proved adequate with values outside that range. Moreover, it predicts the circumstances under which the organism should respond with exclusive preference for the shorter VI: *when entry into one terminal link fails to bring the organism closer in time to primary reinforcement, that terminal link will not be entered.* In other words, the organism should respond on both initial-link schedules only when the onset of both terminal links produces a reduction in the average-time-to-reinforcement. Thus $P_L = 0$, when $T = t_{2L}$; and $P_L = 1$, when $T = t_{2R}$. In either case exclusive preference is predicted since entry into one terminal link does not advance the organism in time toward primary reinforcement. When either t is greater than T, of course, entrance into the longer terminal link actually moves the organism further from reinforcement (as when the initial links are VI 60-sec and the left and right terminal links are VI 20-sec and VI 180-sec, respectively; in this case, $T = 130$ sec, $t_{2L} = 20$ sec, and $t_{2R} = 180$ sec). The results from Fantino (1969a) showed that exclusive preferences are indeed approximated under these conditions.

Earlier we noted that the organism maximizes its rate of primary reinforcement by responding on each of two concurrent VI schedules. Equation (2) thus specifies when this is *not* the case: when either t_{2L} or t_{2R} is greater than T, rate of reinforcement is maximized by responding in only the right and left initial links, respectively. In other words, Eq. (2) requires the organism to shun one key as soon as responses on that key no longer increase the rate of primary reinforcement. Thus, concurrent VI's generally maintain responding on both schedules because responding on each alternative schedule increases the overall rate of primary reinforcement. On concurrent FR schedules the subject maximizes its rate of reinforcement by responding only on the lower FR (or on either FR if they are equal). According to the present analysis responding should be largely restricted to one key in concurrent FR's, an outcome supported by some data (Herrnstein, 1958).

Hursh and Fantino (1974) confirmed one of the implications of Eq. (2), namely that the magnitude of preference in concurrent-chain schedules depends critically on the value of the initial-link schedules, a conclusion that has also received support from several recent studies including Wardlaw and Davison (1974). These results also indicate that caution should be exercised when interpreting the results of different studies utilizing concurrent-chain schedules with different initial-link values.

Hursh and Fantino (1974) evaluated some earlier findings (Bower, McLean, & Meacham, 1966; Hendry, 1969) bearing on the reinforcing value of discriminative stimuli. In particular, Bower *et al.* and Hendry had compared pigeons' preferences for multiple and mixed schedules of reinforcement. Multiple schedules arrange reinforcements according to several requirements each of which is correlated with a distinct exteroceptive stimulus. Mixed schedules also arrange reinforcements for responses according to several requirements; these different requirements are not correlated with different stimuli, however. In the Bower *et al.* and Hendry studies two interval or ratio requirements alternated unpredictably. Only during the multiple schedule were the schedule requirements correlated with different key colors. When both the multiple and mixed schedules were freely available, the pigeons chose the multiple schedule about 90% of the time. In other words, these subjects preferred the schedule providing distinct cues correlated with the component requirements. Bower *et al.* used a choice procedure which was a combination of forced-choice trials and free-choice trials in which both alternatives were available according to concurrent FR 1 schedules. This procedure and the similar one employed by Hendry produced uniformly large preferences for the multiple schedules which might be expected to arise because of the short initial links. Hursh and Fantino (1974) evaluated this hypothesis by utilizing a concurrent-chains procedure with two different initial-link schedules: either VI 60-sec or VI 15-sec. They found that multiple schedules are preferred to comparable mixed schedules, but that preferences were small (i.e., close to .50) when the initial-link schedules were concurrent VI 60-sec. With VI 15-sec initial links, however, large preferences, comparable to those found by Hendry and Bower *et al.*, were obtained. The size of the initial-link schedules was thus shown to be a major factor controlling the magnitude of the obtained preferences, suggesting that the large preferences reported by Bower *et al.* and by Hendry depended upon their use of short FR initial-link schedules.

According to Eq. (2) manipulating the size of the terminal-link schedules relative to the initial-link schedules should also affect preference. For example, it can be shown that if the initial links were held constant, increasing the absolute size of the terminal links should increase preference, provided that the ratios of the terminal-link schedules are held constant. This prediction may be evaluated by considering data collected by MacEwen (1972). He varied terminal-link values from VI 5-sec versus VI 10-sec, through VI 20-sec versus VI 40-sec. For each of four pigeons, choice proportions for the shorter VI schedule increased monotonically as the absolute size of the terminal links increased. MacEwen found analogous results when the size of terminal link fixed-interval pairs was manipulated.

More generally, the present formulation suggests that a reduction in the size of the initial links (relative to the size of the terminal links) will result in larger preferences for the more preferred of two terminal links, even when the average-times-to-reinforcement are equivalent as in the Hursh and Fantino (1974) experiment. The following related prediction is also consistent with the spirit of this formulation: *any* manipulation which results in preference for one of two terminal-link schedules (e.g., increasing the duration of primary reinforcement in one terminal link or introducing punishment for responding in the other) should be more effective the smaller the size of the initial-link schedules. For example, Duncan and Fantino (1970, pp. 83–84) discuss some data suggesting that a change in the value of initial-link VI schedules will have a predictable effect upon choice that is independent of the type of schedules associated with the terminal links.

D. LIMITATIONS OF CHOICE EQ. (2)

There is a prediction of Eq. (2) that seemed doubtful, however. Whenever $t_{2L} = t_{2R}$, a choice proportion of 0.50, i.e., indifference is required no matter what the initial-link values are because the two terminal-link stimuli represent the same degree of improvement in average-time-to-reinforcement. Instead, one might expect that preference would vary with the relative values of the initial links because the rates of both primary reinforcement ($1/[t_{1L} + t_{2L}]$ and $1/[t_{1R} + t_{2R}]$) and conditioned reinforcement ($1/t_{1L}$ and $1/t_{1R}$) are different for the two keys when the initial-link VI schedules differ. Therefore, a critical test of the generality of this equation is to see whether indifference occurs when the initial links are different for the two keys with $t_{2L} = t_{2R}$.

A study by Squires and Fantino (1971) supplied that test and suggested that an additional variable, which takes into account the rate of primary reinforcement on each key separately, should be incorporated into Eq. (2):

$$\frac{R_L}{R_L + R_R} = \frac{r_L(T - t_{2L})}{r_L(T - t_{2L}) + r_R(T - t_{2R})} \quad \text{(when } t_{2L} < T, t_{2R} < T\text{)}$$

$$= 1 \quad \text{(when } t_{2L} < T, t_{2R} > T\text{)} \quad (3)$$

$$= 0 \quad \text{(when } t_{2L} > T, t_{2R} < T\text{)},$$

where $r_L = n_L/(t_{1L} + n_L t_{2L})$, the rate of primary reinforcement on the left key (n_L is the number of primary reinforcements obtained during one entry into the terminal link of the chain on the left key), and $r_R = n_R/(t_{1R} + n_R t_{2R})$, the rate of primary reinforcement on the right key. This formulation for choice behavior has the important additional advantage that when $t_{2L} = t_{2R} = 0$, which is the (simple) concurrent VI situation, matching of response rates to rates of primary reinforcement is predicted. Neither Eqs. (1) nor (2) can accurately predict simple (concurrent) choice behavior [i.e., when $t_{2L} = t_{2R} = 0$ in either Eqs. (1) or (2); however, these formulations have not been held to apply outside the realm of concurrent-chains schedules]. Although the results of the Squires and Fantino (1971) experiment unequivocally supported the modification of Eq. (2) represented by Eq. (3), for sake of clarity we shall discuss the simpler, unmodified, version in this paper. This is acceptable since Eqs. (2) and (3) make equivalent predictions in most situations.

A more serious drawback of Eq. (2) is its limited generality. Up to now we have been primarily discussing choice for VI schedules of reinforcement. It turns out that the quantitative predictions made by Eq. (2) may be inappropriate when other schedules are presented for choice. For example, Duncan and Fantino (1970), Killeen (1970), and others have shown that Eq. (2) fails to make accurate quantitative choice predictions when periodic schedules of reinforcement constitute the terminal links of concurrent chains. Duncan and Fantino (1970) and others have felt that once a principle for transforming periodic schedules into their aperiodic equivalents (and vice versa) were developed, Eq. (2) could be shown to have general applicability. Choice between any two schedules could be described then by first converting the schedules into their VI equivalents and then by applying Eq. (2). The search for a principle of transformation (or of "averaging"), spanned a dozen studies with concurrent-chains schedules beginning with Herrnstein (1964a) and continuing at least through Hursh and Fantino (1973).

We shall see that the problem is considerably more complex than first thought and that the applicability of Eq. (2) must be restricted largely to VI schedules where precise quantitative descriptions of choice are required. The formulation is still useful in making ordinal predictions about choice (i.e., whether one schedule will be preferred to another) when schedules other than VI's are involved. It may also provide some handsome theoretical dividends in the area of conditioned reinforcement as we shall see at the end of this paper. We should first explain why the problem of schedule transformation —or "the averaging problem"—looms more intractable today.

II. The Averaging Problem

The impetus for discovering a transformation rule arose from an observation by Herrnstein (1964a) that pigeons strongly preferred a VI schedule with an average interreinforcement interval of 15 sec to an FI schedule of the same duration. This finding was at odds with the prevalent assumption that choice behavior in the initial links of concurrent chains was a function of the relative rate of reinforcement in the terminal links [Eq. (1)]. Here, the relative rate of reinforcement provided by the VI schedule was .50 and the pigeon should have shown indifference between the two schedules. The marked preference for the VI schedule could have meant that something more than rate of reinforcement was operating in this situation—that, for example, the variability of intervals on the VI schedule made VI and FI schedules qualitatively different—or that the method of measuring rate of reinforcement was incorrect. Herrnstein (1964a) chose the latter, more parsimonious, alternative. He suggested that ". . . the pigeon's method of averaging tends to weight the shorter intervals of the variable interval more than the longer [p. 181]." The customary measure of reinforcement frequency was an arithmetic average of the intervals, which gives equal weight to each interval. Herrnstein was suggesting, instead, that a weighted average be used which allowed for the greater importance of short intervals as compared with long. This is a parsimonious conception because it seeks to represent VI and FI schedules in the same terms, as points on a single dimension of "rate of reinforcement." The significance of such a "unidimensional" interpretation is perhaps best appreciated by considering some of its empirical implications. Let us call the VI schedule that Herrnstein used—VI 15-sec— Schedule A, and the FI 15-sec schedule, Schedule B. We know that A would be preferred to B, and if the unidimensional account is correct, then A would lie at a higher point on this dimension than B. Now suppose that we offered the pigeon a choice between Schedule B (FI 15-sec) and some new schedule, say, FI 30-sec, which we shall label Schedule C. There is little doubt that the pigeon would choose B over C, and in terms of the unidimensional theory, B would lie at a higher point on the dimension than C. Now, A is preferred to B and B is preferred to C. If we gave the pigeon a choice between A and C, could we predict which schedule the pigeon would prefer? The unidimensional theory makes a very clear prediction, which is quite consistent with intuition. Since A lies at a higher point on the dimension than B, and B lies at a higher point than C, then A must lie at a higher point than C, and the pigeon should choose A over C. This fundamental relationship is known as "transitivity" and it is a major implication of any unidimensional theory of choice (Luce & Suppes, 1965).

But in the present case there is a more exacting test of the unidimensional idea, which can be understood as a special form of transitivity. Suppose that we offered the pigeon a choice between

VI 15-sec (Schedule A) and a new Schedule B, which was valued as much as Schedule A. If Schedule B were an FI schedule, its duration would have to be considerably less than 15 sec, since if the duration were 15 sec or higher, we know (from Herrnstein's study) that the VI schedule would be preferred. Let us assume that the pigeon shows indifference between VI 15-sec (A) and FI 5-sec (B). Herrnstein's averaging idea now suggests that, from the pigeon's standpoint, the rates of reinforcement on the two schedules would be equal. Killeen (1968) has made this implication of the averaging hypothesis more explicit: ". . . whenever an organism is indifferent between different schedules of reinforcement, appropriate measures of reinforcement frequency for these schedules will be equal [pp. 263–264]." In other words, on this basis, we should expect the pigeon to treat the VI and FI schedules in precisely the same way despite the fact that they differ in two salient respects: (1) the intervals on the VI vary randomly while the interval on the FI is fixed; (2) the arithmetic average of the intervals on the VI schedule exceeds the interval on the FI schedule. In order to test this we can first present Schedule A (VI 15-sec) for choice with our old Schedule C (FI 30-sec) and record the proportion of choice responses for A, and then present Schedule B for choice with C and record the choice proportion for B. If the averaging hypothesis is correct, these choice proportions should be equal. Navarick and Fantino (1972b) have suggested that this sort of test would constitute the best evidence that VI and FI schedules are "functionally equivalent," the basic assertion of the averaging hypothesis.

The possible functional equivalence of VI and FI schedules carries broad theoretical implications. Should VI and FI schedules prove functionally equivalent, then any choice model that held for VI schedules (such as Fantino's, Eq. 2), should also hold for FI schedules. It would probably prove necessary to transform schedule values in some way to take account of the pigeon's tendency to give greater weight to shorter interreinforcement intervals, but once this transformation was performed, the model should be applicable. Insofar as Fantino's model is concerned, if functional equivalence held but Eq. (2) did not, there would be reason to suspect that his model was fundamentally wrong, even if it did hold for VI schedules. Under such conditions, the model would show some predictive utility, but we could be confident that another, more general model, would quite likely replace it, a model that held for both VI and FI schedules. On the other hand, if VI and FI schedules were not functionally equivalent, it would be unlikely that any single model would ex-

TABLE I

HYPOTHETICAL DATA ILLUSTRATING A TEST OF FUNCTIONAL
EQUIVALENCE FOR VI VERSUS FI SCHEDULES

Condition	Terminal-link schedules		Choice proportion
	Left	Right	
1	VI 30″ (A)	FI 30″ (C)	.80 (A)
2	FI X″ (B)	FI 30″ (C)	.78 (B)
3	VI 30″ (A)	FI X″ (B)	.80 (A)
4	FI X″ (B)	VI 30″ (A)	.70 (A)
5	VI 30″ (A)	FI 30″ (C)	.85 (A)
6	FI X″ (B)	FI 30″ (C)	.84 (B)

hibit generality, at least any model that sought to represent choice in unidimensional terms, and attempted to make precise quantitative predictions (e.g., Baum, 1973; Herrnstein, 1970).

Despite the simplicity of this logic, an empirical test of "functional equivalence" is fraught with complications. One must take into account, for example, the possibility of position preferences. If a position preference existed and an inappropriate procedure were used, a failure to demonstrate functional equivalence might result from the position preference alone. One procedure which seems to control for position preference reasonably well is illustrated in Table I. The data are hypothetical. The basic question addressed by this paradigm is actually the converse of one stated earlier. The earlier problem was the following: if indifference prevails between two schedules, will they be equally preferred to a third schedule? Here, the question is: if two schedules are equally preferred to a third schedule, will indifference prevail between the first two? The schedules shown in Table I are presented for choice in the terminal links of a concurrent-chains schedule. In the first condition, the pigeon chooses between VI 30-sec (Schedule A) and FI 30-sec (Schedule C) and gives a choice proportion for A of .80. In Condition 2, the VI 30-sec schedule (A) is removed and an FI schedule is substituted for it on the same side (Schedule B). The duration of this FI schedule is adjusted up and down on successive sessions until the stable choice proportion for B over C approximately equals the choice proportion for A over C. Table I shows a choice proportion for B of .78, as compared with a choice proportion for A of .80. Any choice proportion for B in the range of .75–.85 would have been acceptable. By employing this criterion, we assume that a difference between choice proportions of .05 or less represents incidental variation rather than a difference in schedule values. Obviously, however, the lower the difference between the choice proportions, the greater would be our confidence that they were indeed "equal."

Now, VI 30-sec (A) and FI X (B) sec are "equally" preferred to FI 30-sec (C). Will the pigeon be indifferent between A and B? Herrnstein's (1964a) averaging hypothesis implies that indifference would prevail, since from the pigeon's standpoint, the rates of re-inforcement on A and B would be equal. Conditions 3 and 4 consti-tute the test of functional equivalence. Schedules A and B are pre-sented for choice with one another, with A first on one side and then on the other. If A and B were indeed functionally equivalent, the average choice proportion for A in Conditions 3 and 4 would be .50. Table I shows an average choice proportion for A of .75, so that the "deviation from transitivity" in this case would be $(.75 - .50) = .25$.

Could a possible position preference produce such a result? That would be unlikely, since in Conditions 1 and 2, when A and B are chosen equally over C, A and B are presented on the same side. Any bias that is constant over the two conditions should affect the two choice proportions equally. Similarly, if a key bias is present and constant over both Conditions 3 and 4, the bias should have an equal effect on both A and B, since they are each presented on both sides and the average choice proportion is taken. A more likely complication is random variation. Suppose that Conditions 1 and 2 were replicated after the transitivity test and that the replicated choice proportions differed substantially from the original ones. Then it would be possible to argue that the substantial deviation from transitivity observed earlier simply represented a tendency for preferences to drift over time.

Two types of replication error could arise. One type relates to the difference between the choice proportions for A and B in the A versus C and B versus C choices. It is important to know, given a substantial deviation from transitivity, whether A and B are still equally preferred to C. Table I shows that in Conditions 5 and 6, the preferences for A and B over C are .85 and .84, respectively. Originally, in Conditions 1 and 2, the choice proportions were .80 and .78. Therefore, replication error based on the difference between choice proportions would be $(.80 - .78) - (.85 - .84) = .01$, a negligible change. Another type of replication error takes into ac-count possible changes in the absolute values of choice proportions. In the A versus C choices, the absolute change in choice proportions was $|(.80 - .85)| = .05$; in the B versus C choices, the absolute change was $|\,(.78 - .84)\,| = .06$. The average change in values would be $(.05 + .06)/2 = .06$. One may compare each of these estimates of replication error—the one based on differences and the one based on absolute values—with the deviation from transitivity. If the deviation from transitivity exceeded both estimates of error, one could say that Schedules A (VI) and B (FI) indeed failed to exhibit functional equivalence. Confidence in this judgment would depend on two factors: (1) the size of the difference between the deviation from transitivity and the estimates of error; (2) the extent to which the cases of transitivity and intransitivity exhibited a pattern or appeared to be predictable from some rule or principle. The latter criterion is particularly important. If the deviation from transitivity simply reflected random variation, then there should be no evidence of predictability.

Navarick and Fantino (1972b) have performed several functional equivalence tests such as the one described above. Their data indicate that aperiodic (VI and VR) and periodic schedules (FI and FR) are frequently not functionally equivalent in their effects upon choice. Moreover, the results are consistent with a rule, derived from previous studies, that enables prediction of intransitivities. Figure 2 illustrates the results of a subsequent experiment (Navarick, 1973)

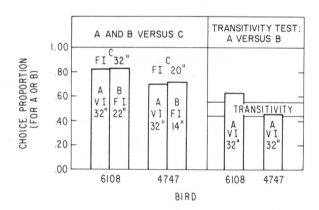

Fig. 2. Outcome of tests for "functional equivalence" of VI and FI schedules of reinforcement. The left portion of the figure illustrates results from the preliminary phase of the procedure, in which Schedule A (VI) and B (FI) are equally preferred to Schedule C (FI). The right portion of the figure illustrates the results of the actual transitivity test, in which A and B are presented for a direct choice. If A and B are "functionally equivalent" in their effects upon choice, as the averaging hypothesis assumes, then the choice proportion for A over B should approximate .50. Acceptable outcomes ranged from .45 to .55, as indicated by the band labeled "transitivity."

explicitly designed to test that rule. Schedule A for each pigeon was a VI schedule, Schedule B an FI schedule, and Schedule C an FI schedule. The rule pertains to the intervals of the VI and FI schedules. One compares the shortest interval obtainable in the A versus C choice with the shortest interval obtainable in the B versus C choice. If there is a substantial difference between these intervals, then Schedules A and B should fail to exhibit functional equivalence in the subsequent transitivity test. The theoretical basis for this rule is discussed in Navarick and Fantino (1972b). In the present experiment, the schedules were arranged in such a manner that the shortest obtainable intervals differed substantially. For example, the shortest interval on the VI 32-sec schedule used as Schedule A was 2 sec. Thus, in the A versus C choice, the shortest interval was 2 sec, since Schedule C (FI) had a value of 20 (Bird 4747) or 32 sec (Bird 6108). Schedule B was FI 22-sec for Bird 6108 and FI 14-sec for Bird 4747, so that the shortest obtainable interval for Bird 6108 exceeded that for Bird 4747 (22 sec versus 14 sec). Intransitivity, according to our rule, should thus be more likely to occur with Bird 6108.

The left portion of Fig. 2 shows the choice proportions for A and B in the A versus C and B versus C choices. The right portion of the graph shows the choice proportion for A in the A versus B choice. Schedules A and B would be considered "functionally equivalent" if the choice proportion for A over B fell within the zone labeled "Transitivity": .45 − .55. The choice proportion for Bird 6108 fell outside the transitive zone, but the choice proportion for 4747 did not (in each case, the deviations from transitivity exceeded the estimates of error, not shown). For the intransitive bird, the difference between the shortest intervals obtainable in the A versus C and B versus C choices was 20 sec (22–2), while for the transitive bird, the difference was 12 sec (14–2). These results suggest that a difference between intervals of as much as 20 sec may be necessary before choice becomes consistently intransitive. Nevertheless, the lack of functional equivalence in this and the previous experiment (Navarick & Fantino, 1972b) suggests that the averaging hypothesis is not generally valid. From a theoretical standpoint, it would be unsafe to assume that any model that held for aperiodic schedules should necessarily hold for periodic schedules. The potential significance of research and theory on functional equivalence is sufficiently great to justify a fuller treatment of the topic and its applications to several theories of behavior. Following this, we will return to a consideration of Eq. (2) and its implications for conditioned reinforcement.

III. Functional Equivalence and "Simple Scalability"

Our concept of "functional equivalence" has broad applications. Many theories of choice share with the averaging hypothesis a set of assumptions that imply functional equivalence, and to the extent that functional equivalence was violated, major changes in these theories would be required.

In formal terms, we would consider two conditions, A and B, "functionally equivalent" if either of the following relationships held:

$$P(a, b) = .50 \text{ implies } P(a, c) = P(b, c), \qquad (4)$$

or

$$P(a, c) = P(b, c) \text{ implies } P(a, b) = .50, \qquad (5)$$

where $P(a, b)$ represents the probability of choosing A over B. These implications, which were introduced by Krantz (1964) and labeled "substitutability," follow from a set of widely held theoretical assumptions about choice behavior that Krantz (1964) has called "simple scalability." The basic idea of simple scalability is that when a subject makes a choice, he evaluates his alternatives on a common basis. The most general term for that basis of judgment is "utility," or "subjective value," but in practice, choice could be a function of directly observable parameters as well as theoretical ones. Stated formally

$$P(a, b) = F[u(a), u(b)], \qquad (6)$$

where $u(a)$ represents the utility of Alternative A and F represents a monotonic function relating utility to choice probability. With $u(b)$ held constant, $P(a, b)$ increases with $u(a)$. With $u(a)$ held constant, $P(a, b)$ decreases with $u(b)$. The averaging hypothesis considered earlier is actually a special case of simple scalability. Instead of utility, rate of reinforcement is said to be the basis of choice, so that Eq. (6) could be rewritten as follows:

$$P(a, b) = F[r(a), r(b)], \qquad (7)$$

where $r(a)$ represents the rate of reinforcement provided by Schedule A, and Schedule A is a VI schedule and Schedule B an FI schedule.

The relationship between our transitivity paradigm (Table I) and simple scalability is straightforward. Imagine a vertical line corresponding to some dimension of value to the subject, such as rate of reinforcement. The pigeon first chooses between Schedules A and C and gives some choice proportion, X, for A. If the pigeon is choosing between A and C on the basis of rate of reinforcement, this should place A higher than C on the vertical line, and at a distance proportional to X. Next, the pigeon chooses between B and C and gives a choice proportion for B equal to X. This should place B at the same distance from C on the vertical line as A; that is, A and B should lie at the same point. Finally, the pigeon chooses between A and B. If our conception of choice in terms of the vertical line is correct, A and B should have equal values, and the pigeon should be indifferent between them (satisfying functional equivalence).

A violation of functional equivalence would not necessarily mean that choice was a function of more than one dimension. Simple scalability makes the additional assumption that the function relating choice probability to utility is monotonic, and it is quite possible that a nonmonotonic function could prevail even when choice was unidimensional. Thus, if we held the utility of Condition B constant and increased the utility of A over a substantial range, choice probability for A may fail to increase over part of the range or even decrease. This factor, rather than multidimensionality, could lead to a violation of functional equivalence. How is the theorist to decide between these two possibilities? In general, a unidimensional representation is tenable only if some minimal degree of transitivity is present (Tversky, 1969): if A is preferred to B ($P > .50$), and B is preferred to C, then A must be preferred to C. If intransitivity prevails, even at this minimal level, then choice is probably multidimensional in nature. The problem becomes more complex, however, when this kind of "weak" transitivity is satisfied, as multidimensional choices could, in principle, lead to transitive choices under some conditions. A more detailed consideration of the problem beyond this point is outside the scope of the present paper. It is sufficient for our purposes to recognize that when functional equivalence fails to hold, one or both assumptions of simple scalability are probably incorrect.

The formula for simple scalability (6) does not specify the nature of the function, F, relating choice probability to utility. However, many theorists concerned with schedule preference have posited a function that is characteristic of a "strict utility" model (Luce & Suppes, 1965). Stated formally,

$$P(a, b) = u(a)/[u(a) + u(b)]. \tag{8}$$

This strict utility function is extremely pervasive; theories as divergent as Fantino's (1969a) and Herrnstein's (1964a) have adopted it. In Herrnstein's model, for example, u is replaced by rate of reinforcement and the probability of choosing A over B equals the relative rate of reinforcement. In Fantino's model, u is replaced by the reduction in average time to reinforcement, and $P(a, b)$ equals the relative reduction in time to reinforcement. Tests of these theories are usually tantamount to tests of Eq. (8), a practice that could lead to erroneous conclusions if Eq. (8) were violated. There are actually three major assumptions implicit in Eq. (8): (1) unidimensional control of choice (by rate of reinforcement, the reduction in average time to reinforcement, etc.); (2) a monotonic function relating values on this dimension to choice probability; and (3) the strict utility function. A model might well be correct in adopting the first two assumptions but incorrect in adopting the third. Often, the theorist himself fails to make these distinctions explicit and may be prepared to reject all of the assumptions if the test of Eq. (8) fails. A safer experimental strategy would be one which enabled separate tests of simple scalability (6) (which embodies the first two assumptions), and strict utility (8) (which constitutes the third assumption). If strict utility were violated, while simple scalability held, a search for a different function, F, in Eq. (6) might be appropriate.

An experimental strategy which permits separate tests is the transitivity paradigm outlined in Table I. To show how this paradigm would apply, we shall consider a theory of choice proposed by Premack (1965) and adopted also by Neuringer (1967), Rachlin and Baum (1969), Rachlin (1971), Ten Eyck (1970), and others. According to Premack, the time to reinforcement and the duration of reinforcement are functionally equivalent parameters. They are reducible to a single dimension—the rate of "reinforcement-time"—which is the product of rate and duration of reinforcement. For example, suppose that the terminal link of a concurrent-chains schedule consisted of an FI 30-sec schedule that provided 6 sec of hopper time per reinforcement. Then, the reinforcement-time per minute would be 2 reinforcements/min $\times$ 6 sec per reinforcement $= 12$ sec/min. In terms of the simple scalability equation

$$P(a, b) = F[s(a), s(b)], \tag{9}$$

where $s(a)$ represents the rate of reinforcement-time provided by Schedule A and $s(b)$ represents the rate of reinforcement-time provided by Schedule B. This alone would be a very strong theoretical assumption; rate and duration are objectively independent parameters and a demonstration of functional equivalence would be important and provocative. But Premack has gone beyond this assumption to assert that choice probability is a function of the relative frequency of reinforcement-times—a strict utility model:

$$P(a, b) = s(a)/[s(a) + s(b)]. \tag{10}$$

Thus, if the rate of reinforcement-time provided by Schedule A were 12 sec/min, and the rate of reinforcement-time provided by Schedule B were 24 sec/min, the choice proportion for A should be $12/(12 + 24) = .33$.

The strict utility aspect of the theory is also a very strong assumption for, in principle, there are innumerable functions that relate choice to reinforcement-time. It would be unfortunate if the central assumption of the theory—the functional equivalence of rate and duration of reinforcement—were rejected when only the strict utility aspect was incorrect. Moreover, there are additional complications. Suppose that Premack's method of calculating reinforcement-times were inappropriate. One of the parameters—rate or duration—could be more effective for the organism than the other. A pigeon might "weight" this parameter more heavily before integrating the two—a kind of weighted average. If differential weighting took place, then our predictions in an experiment might well prove incorrect. It is important to recognize that the simple scalability equation (6) actually contains two unknowns—the function, F, and the scale value, u. Before one can make a prediction, assumptions must be made both about the method for calculating schedule values and the function relating these values to choice. Either assumption could be incorrect and lead erroneously to rejection of the entire theory. A test of functional equivalence can help the theorist decide: (1) whether his method of calculating schedule values is correct; (2) whether a strict utility function holds (given that the schedule values are appropriate). Figure 3 illustrates these features of functional equivalence tests.

Each panel of the graph represents a different functional equivalence test. The left half of each panel shows the part of the procedure in which Schedules A and B are chosen equally over Schedule C. The right half shows the preference for A over B; if A and B were functionally equivalent, then the preference for A over B would be .50. The open bars in Fig. 3 represent choice proportions, the

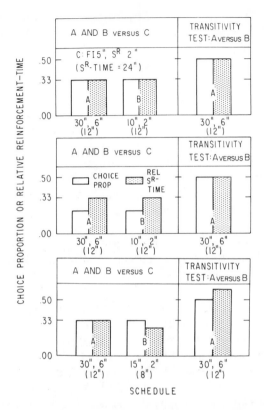

Fig. 3. Three hypothetical functional equivalence tests for rate versus duration of reinforcement. Open bars represent choice proportions; filled bars, the relative rates of reinforcement-time. Conditions A, B, and C consist of FI schedules of various durations combined with various durations of reinforcement (hopper times). The FI value is given first beneath the relevant bars, followed by the reinforcement duration. In parentheses, beneath these values are the reinforcement-times, the number of seconds per minute during which the organism engages in the reinforcing activity (here, eating). The relative reinforcement-times are calculated by dividing the reinforcement-time for one condition by the sum of the reinforcement-times for both conditions. All three panels—top, middle, and bottom—show results supporting simple scalability, the essential assumption of the reinforcement-time hypothesis. In each case, Conditions A and B are equally preferred to Condition C (left portion of panels) and are also equally preferred to each other (right portion). The top panel supports, in addition, a "strict utility" model (choice proportions equal relative reinforcement-times). The middle panel does not support a strict utility model, but indicates that reinforcement-times were the basis of choice and were calculated in an appropriate manner (since reinforcement-times of A and B are equal). In the bottom panel, the reinforcement-times of A and B are not equal despite the fact that A and B are equally preferred to C. Such results would suggest either that reinforcement-times were calculated in an inappropriate manner or that reinforcement-time was not the basis of choice.

stippled bars, the relative rates of reinforcement-time. The schedule values on the abscissa indicate, first, the FI duration and second, the reinforcement duration. In parentheses under these values is the amount of reinforcement-time per min provided by the schedule.

All three transitivity tests in Fig. 3 indicate that Schedules A and B are functionally equivalent, a result that supports simple scalability. The difference between the three tests lies in the relationship between choice proportions and reinforcement-times. In the upper panel, choice proportions in the A versus C and B versus C choices equal relative reinforcement-times, supporting the strict utility assumption of Premack's theory. In the middle panel, choice proportions do not equal relative reinforcement-times, violating the strict utility assumption. If the results of a functional equivalence test resembled those of the middle panel, we would conclude that the central assumptions of the theory—unidimensional control of choice, a monotonic function relating choice to values on this dimension—were supported, despite the negative evidence on the strict utility assumption.

One could not evaluate the strict utility assumption without evidence that (1) reinforcement-time was the basis of choice, and (2) the method of calculating reinforcement-times was correct. What aspects of the data provide this evidence? The relevant data are the relationships between the relative reinforcement-times. If reinforcement-time is the basis of choice, and the method of calculating reinforcement-times is correct, then the reinforcement-times of two schedules should be equal whenever the preferences for these schedules are equal. The left halves of the upper and middle panels of Fig. 3 are consistent with this principle—the stippled bars are equal. Similarly, the right halves of the upper and middle panels show that the relative reinforcement-times are .50, just as we would expect if Schedules A and B lay at the same point on a common dimension. The lower panel in Fig. 3 illustrates the outcome of a test in which reinforcement-times of A and B are unequal, and such results could mean one of two things: (1) choice was a function of some other dimension than reinforcement-time; or (2) the method of calculating reinforcement-times requires modification. In either case, simple scalability is upheld and the central assumptions of the reinforcement-time hypothesis are supported. Table II summarizes the empirical relationships that are generated by a functional equivalence test and their theoretical implications.

In summary, outcomes of functional equivalence tests which sat-

TABLE II

Empirical relationship	Theoretical implication
1a. $P(a, c) = P(b, c)$, $P(a, b) = .50$	1a. Simple scalability holds, evidence for unidimensional control and a monotonic choice function
1b. $P(a, c) = P(b, c)$, $P(a, b) \neq .50$	1b. Simple scalability violated; choice was multidimensional and/or the choice function was not monotonic
[If 1a holds]	
2a. Schedule values of A and B are equal	2a. The method of calculating schedule values is supported
2b. Schedule values of A and B are unequal	2b. The method of calculating schedule values is inappropriate or choice was a function of another dimension
[If 2a holds]	
3a. Choice proportions equal relative schedule values	3a. A strict utility model is supported
3b. Choice proportions do not equal relative schedule values	3b. A strict utility model does not hold; a search for a different function, F, in Eq. (6) would be appropriate

isfy the conditions illustrated in the top panel of Fig. 3, and Conditions 1a, 2a, and 3a of Table II, support certain kinds of theories, namely, strict utility models. Despite the very strong assumptions made by strict utility models, they are the most prevalent kinds of theories that have been advanced to account for schedule preference. Violations of any one of the three conditions in Table II would indicate that the theory required some form of modification. Whatever the outcome of such functional equivalence tests, they should prove useful in evaluating a broad range of theories, some examples of which will be discussed in the next section.

IV. New Directions

The present research program is presently pointing in two main directions. In the first place, our work on transitivity has demonstrated that functional equivalence—an implicit property of several theories of choice—does not generally hold across different schedules of reinforcement. Our present work is aimed at further evaluating under what conditions functional equivalence may be expected to characterize choice and to use functional equivalence tests to evaluate theories of behavior as diverse as the single-process theory of punishment and Young's hedonic theory of motivation. Following this, we will return to a discussion of our basic choice model—represented by Eq. (2)—and to its potential value in describing choice behavior in procedures not involving concurrent-chains schedules, for example, in choosing between two stimuli that have had different temporal associations with primary reinforcement.

A. TRANSITIVITY

Functional equivalence tests should prove valuable in evaluating several fundamental assertions about behavior. In particular, any conception of choice behavior which assumes unidimensionality, explicitly or implicitly, should be scrutinized with functional equivalence tests. Indeed, the concept of unidimensionality in choice behavior has appealed to numerous theorists. Parsimony is perhaps the basis of this appeal, a desire to reduce a multiplicity of variables to a more manageable number. For example, Premack (1965) assumes that rate and duration of reinforcement are reducible to a single dimension, reinforcement-time. If this assumption is correct, it will not be necessary to measure rate and duration of reinforcement separately. Rather, to calculate schedule value, we will simply need to measure the amount of time during which an organism engages in a reinforcing activity over a given unit of time.

The prevalence of unidimensional theories makes advisable a closer examination of the unidimensionality assumption. The approach which we have emphasized requires a decision as to whether a theory constitutes a special case of simple scalability (Krantz, 1964). If it does, choice behavior should exhibit the property of transitivity, and in particular, functional equivalence. Although we have emphasized this functional equivalence condition, other forms of transitivity may also be fruitfully studied. Coombs (1964), for example, describes three forms of stochastic transitivity varying in their degrees of "strength." Where $P(a, b)$ and $P(b, c) \geq .50$, an outcome, $P(a, c)$ satisfies

Weak transitivity if $P(a, c) \geq .50,$ (11)

Moderate transitivity of $P(a, c) \geq$ minimum $[P(a, b), P(b, c)],$ (12)

Strong transitivity if $P(a, c) \geq$ maximum $[P(a, b), P(b, c)].$ (13)

For example, if $P(a, b) = .60$ and $P(b, c) = .80$, strong transitivity would be satisfied if $P(a, c) = .90$, moderate transitivity if $P(a, c) = .70$, and weak transitivity if $P(a, c) = .55$. Other relationships, all implications of simple scalability, have been set forth by Tversky and Russo (1969).

When is it appropriate to test these forms of transitivity and when should a test of functional equivalence be conducted? The decision on how best to proceed must take into account a number of factors, the most significant being the relative difficulty of conducting each type of test. Functional equivalence is the most difficult property to test because it requires the experimenter to establish an equality— $P(a, c) = P(b, c)$. Not only must this equality be achieved, but it must be replicable if the results of the transitivity test are to be decisive. In contrast, tests of weak, moderate, and strong transitivity require only the establishment of inequalities—$P(a, b)$ must exceed $P(b, c)$— and these inequalities are likely not only to be easier to establish, but easier to replicate. Therefore, the experimenter would do well to establish some kind of screening procedure before conducting a particular transitivity test. He should ascertain, either experimentally or by conjecture, whether weak, moderate, or strong transitivity is likely to be satisfied. If so, then a test should be conducted with more stringent requirements. Thus, in our tests of the averaging hypothesis, it was our feeling that choice would probably satisfy strong transitivity: if VI 15 was preferred to FI 15 by .80, and FI 15 to FI 30 by .70, then VI 15 would probably have been preferred to FI 30 by more than .80. For this reason we examined a relationship which imposed additional constraints upon acceptable outcomes. If the experimenter lacked confidence that, say, weak transitivity was going to be satisfied, then weak transitivity would best be tested before functional equivalence.

A second consideration relates to the objective of theories. If a theory aspires to the prediction of exact choice probabilities, every effort should be made to conduct a functional equivalence test. But if a theory lays no claim to such precision, if only the direction of preference is of interest, then a test of weak or moderate transitivity may be sufficient.

B. Uses of Functional Equivalence Tests

We feel that functional equivalence tests can serve a useful purpose in at least establishing the domain successfully addressed by choice theories. We now turn to a brief description of some of these theories.

1. The Single-Process Theory of Punishment

Reinforcement increases the probability of a response; punishment decreases the probability of a response. According to some theorists (e.g., Azrin & Holz, 1966; Fantino, 1973; Herrnstein, 1969; Premack, 1971; Rachlin, 1966, 1967), reinforcement and punishment are two sides of the same process: whatever the mechanism by which reinforcement increases response probability, that mechanism, working in reverse, determines the effect of punishment. The clear implication of this notion is that reinforcement and punishment are reducible to a common dimension of reinforcement magnitude, with reinforcement representing positive values, punishment negative values, and extinction a zero point. In terms of simple scalability:

$$P(a, b) = F[m(a), m(b)], \tag{14}$$

where $m(a)$ represents the magnitude of reinforcement provided by Schedule A. A possible paradigm for testing the functional equivalence of reinforcement and punishment would include schedules that terminated in hopper presentations or shocks. Preference for a schedule could possibly be adjusted by manipulating the intensity of shock, the duration of the hopper presentation, or the percentage of trials in which food or shock was administered. Then one would ask the standard question: if two combinations of reinforcement and punishment were equally preferred to a third combination, would indifference hold between the first two?

For example, consider the following experimental paradigm. Identical but independently operated VI 1-min schedules are correlated with the initial links of concurrent-chains schedules. In addition, all responses in the presence of one of the terminal-link stimuli are followed by an electric shock. The shock intensity is varied until a value is obtained which produces a preference of .75 for the unpunished terminal link. Next, shock is discontinued and a VI value is found which will also produce a preference of .75 for entry into the terminal link with the VI 15-sec. Assume this VI value is VI 45-sec (a value consistent with the results of Fantino, 1969a). In this comparison, then, the VI 45-sec schedule is equivalent to a VI 15-sec schedule with a particular value of superimposed electric shock.

The test involves a direct comparison between the VI 45-sec schedule and the VI 15-sec schedule with punishment. If indifference occurs (choice proportions around .50) in this and in other, similar comparisons, the functional equivalence of reinforcement and punishment would be supported.

2. Young's Hedonic Theory of Motivation

Young (1961, 1973) has for many years interpreted the results of food preference experiments in unidimensional terms. Fluids varying in the concentration of a solute, or combining different solutes, are offered for a choice. The subject (usually a rat) samples the fluid only briefly, allowing for stimulation of the head receptors but minimizing postingestive factors. Stimulation of the head receptors (taste, temperature, etc.) is said to be the basis of "palatability," or the hedonic response to foods, and diverse fluids may be represented in terms of their location on the "hedonic continuum." For example, if an organism is indifferent between two fluids, then the fluids are said to be "hedonically equivalent." This suggests that Young's hedonic theory is interpretable as a special case of simple scalability:

$$P(a, b) = F[h(a), h(b)], \qquad (15)$$

where $h(a)$ represents the hedonic value of Stimulus A. A test of this theory would perhaps most appropriately use rats as subjects, as much is already known about their response to different fluids. Adaptation of the concurrent-chains procedure for rats should be relatively straightforward and would be of interest in its own right. Most concurrent-chains work has employed pigeons as subjects and it would be useful to extend the generality of present formulations. In a test of Young's theory, the terminal links might consist of FI schedules terminating in brief access to solutions of various sorts. Solution A might consist of $X\%$ sucrose; Solution C, $Y\%$. Solution B might consist of $Z\%$ quinine (bitter and aversive) plus a sufficient concentration of sucrose to offset the effects of the quinine and make A and B equally preferred to C. If the hedonic theory is correct, indifference should hold between A and B.

3. The Delay-of-Reinforcement Hypothesis

It is known that organisms prefer short delays of reinforcement to long delays (Chung & Herrnstein, 1967). During the delay period an organism may work hard, emitting many unreinforced responses, or may not work at all. According to the delay hypothesis (e.g., Neuringer, 1969), the work factor has no influence upon choice; choice is a function of the time to reinforcement alone. In terms of simple scalability

$$P(a, b) = F[d(a), d(b)], \tag{16}$$

where $d(a)$ represents the delay of reinforcement on Schedule A. Neuringer (1969) found that pigeons were indifferent between FI schedules and "blackout" schedules (providing reinforcement independently of responding) of equal duration. Since the pigeons responded rapidly on the FI schedule and rarely responded on the blackout schedule, the factor of response rate appeared to be functionally irrelevant. A test of functional equivalence would employ a different paradigm. If an FI and a blackout schedule were equally preferred to a third schedule (e.g., FI or blackout), would indifference hold between the first two?

C. MOLECULAR ANALYSIS OF CHOICE

Only one aspect of choice behavior has thus far been considered —the choice proportion. The choice proportion is a gross measure and there is obviously much more going on during the initial links of concurrent-chains than the choice proportion indicates. Consequently, closer looks at the molecular structure of choice behavior in concurrent-chains schedules may prove valuable, as the results of Fantino and Duncan (1972) and Navarick and Fantino (1972a) have already suggested. A molecular analysis of choice is often tantamount to an analysis of conditional probabilities (e.g., Reynolds, 1963; Shimp, 1966). The overall choice proportion for an alternative might be .75, but the probability of choosing this alternative could vary dramatically as a function of the preceding sequence of choices. For example, Shimp (1966), using a discrete-trials procedure, showed that the probability of choosing an alternative sometimes increased as a function of the number of preceding consecutive responses for that alternative, a finding suggesting the presence of a "perseveration" factor. Working with concurrent-chains schedules, Navarick and Fantino (1972a) found that the probability of choosing an alternative often varied with the time since the last choice response.

One pigeon in that study had an overall choice proportion for the left key of .57. If a choice response occurred within .5 sec of the last response (a "quick" choice), the probability of a peck on the left was approximately .35. If more than .5 sec elapsed since the previous response (a "delayed" choice), the probability of a response on the left rose as high as .91. These changes in choice probabilities occurred irrespective of the location of the previous peck: there was simply an increased tendency to peck the left key when the choice response occurred after a "delay." Such data suggest that at least in some cases, choice responses terminating long and short inter-response times may not be "functionally equivalent," or quantitatively interchangeable, in concurrent-chains studies.

The presence of sequential and temporal patterns of choice responding should be dealt with in any account of choice that lays claim to completeness. The current emphasis on choice proportions may leave the false impression that order does not exist on other levels. The extent to which conditional probabilities exist in choice behavior, their controlling variables, and their significance for theory, are areas ripe for research and discussion. While Shimp and his colleagues (e.g., Menlove, 1974; Shimp, 1966, 1973) and others (e.g., Nevin, 1969; Silberberg & Fantino, 1970; Silberberg & Williams, 1974) have begun the molecular analysis where simple concurrent schedules are involved, the study of choice in concurrent-chains schedules should also profit from further molecular analysis.

V.   Equation (2) and Conditioned Reinforcement

Our work on transitivity has demonstrated that quantitative models of choice which aspire to apply to different types of reinforcement schedules (Baum, 1973; Herrnstein, 1970) can at best make ordinal predictions. Thus the model of choice represented by Eqs. (2) and (3) (Fantino, 1969a; Squires & Fantino, 1971) which applies admirably to data from choice between VI schedules should not be expected to make accurate quantitative predictions when other schedules are being chosen. Nonetheless its fundamental assertion and implications appear to apply to other schedules in terms of making accurate ordinal predictions. Thus, for example, the effects of decreasing the size of the initial links in the concurrent-chains procedure has been shown to increase preference as required by Eqs. (2) and (3) with a variety of terminal-link schedules and in a variety of recent experiments cited earlier. These equations also suggest a viable theory of conditioned reinforcement which we propose to test. Briefly, we believe that the greater the reduction in average time to primary reinforcement signified by the onset of a stimulus, the more effective that stimulus will be as a conditioned reinforcer. In the context of the concurrent-chains procedure, the stimuli associated with the terminal links are conditioned reinforcers while choice responding in the initial links is taken as a measure of the strength of these conditioned reinforcers (Autor, 1960; Fantino, 1969b; Herrnstein, 1964b). Equation (2) suggests that the strength of each conditioned reinforcer is a function of the relative reduction in the average time to primary reinforcement signified by its onset. The relevance of the concurrent-chains procedure for conditioned reinforcement has been discussed elsewhere (Fantino, 1969b; Nevin, 1973) and need not be reviewed here. Nor does the usefulness of Eq. (2) in providing an account of conditioned reinforcement rest on its adequacy in the concurrent-chains procedure. Instead, we propose to test Eq. (2) with additional procedures. These tests will simultaneously enable us to assess the utility of Eq. (2) in describing choice behavior in other procedures, for example, in choice for two stimuli that have had different temporal associations with primary reinforcement. Some widely cited experimentation (Egger & Miller, 1962, 1963), taken in conjunction with our work, suggests a productive area of further research. Egger and Miller (1962) concluded that "a necessary condition for establishing any stimulus as a secondary reinforcer is that the stimulus provide information about the occurrence of primary reinforcement; a redundant predictor of primary reinforcement should not acquire secondary reinforcement strength [p. 97]." In the first of their experiments, Egger and Miller presented two stimuli (S_1 and S_2) that had different onsets and whose mutual offset was paired with food. In one condition, S_1 was a reliable predictor of S_2, and hence, of food, and was shown to be a more effective secondary reinforcer than the redundant stimulus, S_2. For a second group, S_1 was occasionally presented alone and, therefore, was no longer an informative and reliable predictor of food reinforcement. In this condition, S_2 was a reliable predictor of food. As predicted by Egger and Miller, S_2 was now an effective secondary reinforcer. In the second experiment (Egger & Miller, 1963), the redundant condition consisted of a single pellet of food followed by a stimulus which remained in effect until three additional food pellets were presented. Egger and Miller reasoned that in this condition the stimulus was redundant since the single food pellet was a reliable and informative predictor of the following three pellets. When a single pellet, *not* followed by three pellets, was occasionally presented to the organism, however, the stimulus (but not the single pellet) was now an informative and reliable predictor of the three pellets. Again, as in their previous study, the stimulus was an effective conditioned reinforcer only in the informative condition.

The Egger and Miller findings have been widely cited by students of conditioned reinforcement (e.g., in Hendry, 1969; see also Nevin, 1973; Wike, 1966). As Gollub (1970) has noted, however, "while many articles contained discussions that centered on the information hypothesis, that concept was most frequently used as a metaphor [p. 370]." Proponents of the hypothesis often invoke information as an explanatory principle without specifying it in physical (or even psychological) terms and without varying it parametrically.

We believe that conditioned reinforcement may be specified more precisely in terms of our notion of reduction in average time to reinforcement. In particular, we feel that reduction in average time to reinforcement and not uncertainty reduction—in terms of traditional information theory—will prove to be a fruitful way of reducing "information" to psychologically meaningful, i.e., controlling variables. This variable has the advantage of being defined quantitatively, of accounting for choice behavior in the concurrent-chains procedure, and of being consistent with the Egger and Miller results. By utilizing the general Egger and Miller paradigm, we feel that we can more readily evaluate a theory of conditioned reinforcement in terms of reduction in average time to primary reinforcement. At the same time, this general procedural approach looks like a good one with which to test our model of choice behavior outside the concurrent-chains framework wherein its success has been demonstrated.

Egger and Miller's results, while interesting, are useful only in assessing the value of the (informative) conditioned reinforcer in a qualitative fashion. Our hypothesis is that their findings are a special case of a more general quantitative rule that the strength or value of a conditioned reinforcer is a function of the reduction in average time to reinforcement signaled by its onset. Of course, tests of Eq. (2) with the concurrent-chains procedure have shown that it provides a precise quantitative description of choice only when VI schedules are utilized. This work—and the studies of transitivity—suggest that any quantitative account of conditioned reinforcement may be restricted in scope. At the same time, however, it may still prove valuable, in terms of ordinal predictions (such as one stimulus will be

more or less reinforcing than the second) for a much broader range
of situations. At this time these speculations are premature and will
not be considered further. The information hypothesis is not only
nonquantitative, but it is restricted: Egger and Miller held their
hypothesis to apply only when the two stimuli were paired closely in
time. Our general hypothesis, however, need not have this restriction.
It predicts when S_1 should be more or less reinforcing than S_2. Let T
represent the intertrial interval, I (for "informative") the interval
between S_1 and the primary reinforcement, and R (for "redundant")
the interval between S_2 and the primary reinforcement. Then
$(T - I)/T$ signifies the reduction in time to reward (relative to T)
signaled by the occurrence of S_1 and $(I - R)/I$ signifies the reduction
in time to reward (relative to the remaining time I) signaled by the
occurrence of S_2. We propose the following formula to describe the
relative conditioned-reinforcing value of S_1 to S_2:

$$\frac{V_1}{V_1 + V_2} = \frac{(T - I)/T}{(T - I)/T + (I - R)/I}, \tag{17}$$

where V_1 and V_2 represent some measure of the value (strength) of
the stimuli as conditioned reinforcers. For example, if T, the intertrial, interval, is 100 sec, $I = 20$ sec, and $R = 4$ sec (see Fig. 4A), then
the two stimuli should be equally reinforcing. In this case, S_1 signals
that 4/5 of the intertrial interval has elapsed, while S_2 signifies that
4/5 of the remaining time has elapsed. Figures 4B and 4C illustrate
cases in which the informative and redundant stimuli are more reinforcing, respectively. In the second example (Fig. 4B), the parameter
values are more analogous to those used by Egger and Miller:
$T = 100$ sec, $I = 6$ sec, and $R = 4$ sec. In this case, the informative
stimulus should be about three times as reinforcing as the redundant
stimulus. Finally, the situation pictured in Fig. 4C makes the opposite prediction: when $T = 100$ sec, $I = 60$ sec, and $R = 4$ sec, Eq. (15)
requires a value of about .30, indicating that the "redundant" stimulus should be more than twice as reinforcing as the informative one.
Of course, this in no way is inconsistent with the Egger–Miller hypothesis. As indicated above, they restricted the hypothesis to cases
similar to that described in Fig. 4B. Moreover, they would presumably say that in Fig. 4C, for example, the second stimulus is more
"informative" about the forthcoming reward even though it occurs
after the first stimulus. We maintain that if Eq. (17) is consistent with
the data from the procedures outlined in Fig. 4 there will no longer
be any necessity to utilize words like "informative" or "redundant";

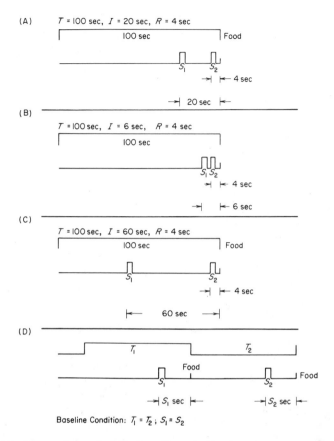

Fig. 4. Procedures for evaluating Eqs. (17) and (18). According to Eq. (17), the conditioned reinforcing strength of S_1 and S_2 should be equal in A, S_1 should be the stronger of the two in B, and S_2 should be the stronger in C. A procedure to evaluate Eq. (18) is shown in D.

but at least, when they are utilized, they can be specified in terms of more concrete temporal variables.

An additional test of whether the notion of reduction in average time to reinforcement has value in describing the strength of the conditioned reinforcer outside of the concurrent-chains procedure, will come from a procedure similar to that shown in Fig. 4D, but in which only one stimulus change is presented during a given intertrial interval. This procedure, no longer comparable to Egger and Miller's, permits an assessment of the relative conditioned-reinforcing value of two stimuli when they do not have a fixed ordering with relation to primary reinforcement, i.e., when the procedure does not have a chain-like quality in which the first stimulus is always an extra stimulus away from reward. In this procedure, unlike the first, the stimulus more contiguous with food should always be the stronger conditioned-reinforcer (provided that the intertrial intervals are equal) and the relative reinforcing value of the two stimuli is described by

$$\frac{V_1}{V_1 + V_2} = \frac{(T_1 - S_1)/T_1}{(T_1 - S_1)/T_1 + (T_2 - S_2)/T_2}, \tag{18}$$

where T_1 and T_2 refer to the duration of the two intertrial intervals and where S_1 and S_2 refer to the corresponding intervals between the onset of the stimulus and the onset of primary reinforcement.

Tests of Eqs. (17) and (18) will assess our notion that the strength of a stimulus (whether or not it is conceptualized as a conditioned reinforcer) as measured in a choice situation depends upon the relative reduction in the average time to primary reinforcement signified by its onset. If these results prove useful in developing an adequate theory of choice and/or conditioned reinforcement our story will indeed have a happy ending. For although Eqs. (2) and (3) cannot describe choice for different types of reinforcement schedules with the same degree of precision as for VI schedules (since the different reinforcement schedules are not functionally equivalent), they will have nourished a conception of choice with promising generality.

REFERENCES

Autor, S. M. The strength of conditioned reinforcers as a function of frequency and probability of reinforcement. Doctoral dissertation, Harvard University, 1960. [Reprinted in D. P. Hendry (Ed.), *Conditioned reinforcement.* Homewood, Ill.: Dorsey Press, 1969. Pp. 127–162.]

Azrin, N. H., & Holz, W. C. Punishment. In W. K. Honig (Ed.), *Operant behavior: Areas of research and application.* New York: Appleton, 1966. Pp. 380–447.

Baum, W. M. The correlation-based law of effect. *Journal of the Experimental Analysis of Behavior,* 1973, **20,** 137–153.

Bower, G., McLean, J., & Meacham, J. Value of knowing when reinforcement is due. *Journal of Comparative and Physiological Psychology,* 1966, **62,** 184–192.

Catania, A. C. Concurrent operants. In W. K. Honig (Ed.). *Operant behavior: Areas of research and application.* New York: Appleton, 1966. Pp. 213–270.

Chung, S. H., & Herrnstein, R. J. Choice and delay of reinforcement. *Journal of the Experimental Analysis of Behavior,* 1967, **10,** 67–74.

Coombs, C. H. *A theory of data.* New York: Wiley, 1964.

Duncan, B., & Fantino, E. Choice for periodic schedules of reinforcement. *Journal of the Experimental Analysis of Behavior*, 1970, **13**, 73–86.

Egger, M. D., & Miller, N. E. Secondary reinforcement in rats as a function of information value and reliability of the stimulus. *Journal of the Experimental Analysis of Behavior*, 1962, **64**, 97–104.

Egger, M. D., & Miller, N. E. When is a reward reinforcing?: an experimental study of the information hypothesis. *Journal of Comparative and Physiological Psychology*, 1963, **56**, 132–137.

Fantino, E. Choice and rate of reinforcement. *Journal of the Experimental Analysis of Behavior*, 1969, **12**, 723–730. (a)

Fantino, E. Conditioned reinforcement, choice and the psychological distance to reward. In D. Hendry (Ed.), *Conditioned reinforcement*. Homewood, Ill.: Dorsey Press, 1969. Pp. 163–191. (b)

Fantino, E. Aversive Control. In J. A. Nevin & G. S. Reynolds (Eds.), *The study of behavior*. Glenview, Ill.: Scott, Foresman, 1973. Pp. 238–279.

Fantino, E., & Duncan, B. Some effects of interreinforcement time upon choice. *Journal of the Experimental Analysis of Behavior*, 1972, **17**, 3–14.

Ferster, C. B., & Skinner, B. F. *Schedules of reinforcement*. New York: Appleton, 1957.

Findley, J. D. Preference and switching under concurrent scheduling. *Journal of the Experimental Analysis of Behavior*, 1958, **1**, 123–144.

Gollub, L. R. Information on conditioned reinforcement. *Journal of the Experimental Analysis of Behavior*, 1970, **14**, 361–372.

Hendry, D. P. Reinforcing value of information: fixed-ratio schedules. In D. P. Hendry (Ed.), *Conditioned reinforcement*. Homewood, Ill.: Dorsey Press, 1969. Pp. 300–341.

Herrnstein, R. J. Some factors influencing behavior in a two-response situation. *Transactions of the New York Academy of Sciences*, 1958, **21**, 35–45.

Herrnstein, R. J. Relative and absolute strength of response as a function of frequency of reinforcement. *Journal of the Experimental Analysis of Behavior*, 1961, **4**, 267–273.

Herrnstein, R. J. Aperiodicity as a factor in choice. *Journal of the Experimental Analysis of Behavior*, 1964, **7**, 179–182. (a)

Herrnstein, R. J. Secondary reinforcement and rate of primary reinforcement. *Journal of the Experimental Analysis of Behavior*, 1964, **7**, 27–36. (b)

Herrnstein, R. J. Method and theory in the study of avoidance. *Psychological Review*, 1969, **76**, 49–69.

Herrnstein, R. J. On the law of effect. *Journal of the Experimental Analysis of Behavior*, 1970, **13**, 243–266.

Hursh, S., & Fantino, E. Relative delay of reinforcement and choice. *Journal of the Experimental Analysis of Behavior*, 1973, **19**, 437–450.

Hursh, S., & Fantino, E. An appraisal of preference for multiple *vs* mixed schedules. *Journal of the Experimental Analysis of Behavior*, 1974, in press.

Killeen, P. On the measurement of reinforcement frequency in the study of preference. *Journal of the Experimental Analysis of Behavior*, 1968, **11**, 263–269.

Killeen, P. Preference for fixed-interval schedules of reinforcement. *Journal of the Experimental Analysis of Behavior*, 1970, **14**, 127–131.

Krantz, D. H. The scaling of small and large color differences. Unpublished doctoral dissertation, University of Pennsylvania, 1964.

Luce, R. D., & Suppes, P. Preference, utility, and subjective probability. In R. D.

Luce, R. R. Bush, & E. Galanter (Eds.), *Handbook of mathematical psychology.* Vol. 3. New York: Wiley, 1965.

MacEwen, D. The effects of terminal-link fixed-interval and variable-interval schedules on responding under concurrent chained schedules. *Journal of the Experimental Analysis of Behavior,* 1972, **18,** 253–261.

Menlove, R. L. Local patterns of responding maintained by concurrent and multiple schedules. *Journal of the Experimental Analysis of Behavior,* 1974, in press.

Navarick, D. J. Stochastic transitivity and the unidimensional control of choice. Unpublished doctoral dissertation, University of California, San Diego, 1973.

Navarick, D. J., & Fantino, E. Interresponse time as a factor in choice. *Psychonomic Science,* 1972, **27,** 4–6. (a)

Navarick, D. J., & Fantino, E. Transitivity as a property of choice. *Journal of the Experimental Analysis of Behavior,* 1972, **18,** 389–401. (b)

Neuringer, A. J. Effects of reinforcement magnitude on choice and rate of responding. *Journal of the Experimental Analysis of Behavior,* 1967, **10,** 417–424.

Neuringer, A. J. Delayed reinforcement *versus* reinforcement after a fixed interval. *Journal of the Experimental Analysis of Behavior,* 1969, **12,** 375–383.

Nevin, J. A. Interval reinforcement of choice behavior in discrete trials. *Journal of the Experimental Analysis of Behavior,* 1969, **12,** 875–885.

Nevin, J. A. Conditioned reinforcement. In J. A. Nevin & G. S. Reynolds (Eds.), *The study of behavior.* Glenview, Ill.: Scott, Foresman, 1973. Pp. 154–198.

Premack, D. Reinforcement theory. In D. Levine (Ed.), *Nebraska symposium on motivation.* Lincoln: University of Nebraska Press, 1965. Pp. 123–180.

Premack, D. Catching up with common sense or two sides of a generalization: reinforcement and punishment. In R. Glaser (Ed.), *The nature of reinforcement.* New York: Academic Press, 1971. Pp. 121–150.

Rachlin, H. Recovery of responses during mild punishment. *Journal of the Experimental Analysis of Behavior,* 1966, **9,** 251–263.

Rachlin, H. The effect of shock intensity on concurrent and single-key responding in concurrent-chain schedules. *Journal of the Experimental Analysis of Behavior,* 1967, **10,** 87–93.

Rachlin, H. On the tautology of the matching law. *Journal of the Experimental Analysis of Behavior,* 1971, **15,** 249–251.

Rachlin, H. Contrast and matching. *Psychological Review,* 1973, **80,** 217–234.

Rachlin, H., & Baum, W. M. Response rate as a function of amount of reinforcement for a signalled concurrent response. *Journal of the Experimental Analysis of Behavior,* 1969, **12,** 11–16.

Rachlin, H., & Green, L. Commitment, choice and self-control. *Journal of the Experimental Analysis of Behavior,* 1972, **17,** 15–22.

Reynolds, G. S. On some determinants of choice in pigeons. *Journal of the Experimental Analysis of Behavior,* 1963, **6,** 53–59.

Shimp, C. P. Probabilistically reinforced choice behavior in pigeons. *Journal of the Experimental Analysis of Behavior,* 1966, **9,** 443–455.

Shimp, C. P. Sequential dependencies in free-responding. *Journal of the Experimental Analysis of Behavior,* 1973, **19,** 491–497.

Silberberg, A., & Fantino, E. Choice, rate of reinforcement, and the changeover delay. *Journal of the Experimental Analysis of Behavior,* 1970, **13,** 187–197.

Silberberg, A., & Williams, D. Choice behavior on discrete trials: a demonstration of the occurrence of a response strategy. *Journal of the Experimental Analysis of Behavior,* 1974, in press.

Squires, N., & Fantino, E. A model for choice in simple concurrent and concurrent-chains schedules. *Journal of the Experimental Analysis of Behavior,* 1971, **15,** 27–38.

Ten Eyck, R. L., Jr. Effects of rate of reinforcement-time upon concurrent operant performance. *Journal of the Experimental Analysis of Behavior,* 1970, **14,** 269–274.

Tversky, A. Intransitivity of preferences. *Psychological Review,* 1969, **76,** 31–48.

Tversky, A., & Russo, J. E. Substitutibility and similarity in binary choices. *Journal of Mathematical Psychology,* 1969, **6,** 1–12.

Wardlaw, G. R., & Davison, N. C. Preference for fixed-interval schedules: effects of initial-links. *Journal of the Experimental Analysis of Behavior,* 1974, in press.

Wike, E. L. *Secondary reinforcement.* New York: Harper, 1966.

Young, P. T. *Motivation and emotion.* New York: Wiley, 1961.

Young, P. T. *Emotion in man and animal.* Huntington, N.Y.: Robert E. Krieger, 1973.

REINFORCING PROPERTIES OF ESCAPE FROM FRUSTRATION AROUSED IN VARIOUS LEARNING SITUATIONS

Helen B. Daly[1]

STATE UNIVERSITY OF NEW YORK COLLEGE AT OSWEGO,
OSWEGO, NEW YORK

I. Introduction

A great number and variety of experiments have been reported which indicate that nonreward in the presence of cues previously paired with reward arouses an aversive emotional-motivational response. This response has been called primary frustration (R_F), and Amsel has formulated a theory (Frustration Theory) within the

[1] The research reported in this chapter was supported by a NIH Postdoctoral Fellowship (1 F2 AM-34, 132-01) and NIMH Grants 16719 and 17398. I am indebted to James Ison, and Dorothy and Wallace McAllister for their guidance and help. Appreciation is also due to Abram Amsel and James McCroskery for their helpful comments following a critical reading of the manuscript, and to Len Johnson, Lynn Tondat, Jill Wallace, and Annette Hilland who helped run the experiments. I also wish to thank my colleagues for their helpful advice.

framework of neo-Hullian behavior theory which accounts for the effects of R_F as well as a conditioned form of frustration (r_f). Frustration Theory integrates a number of experimental findings and makes certain predictions concerning the effects of frustration in various learning situations such as extinction, incentive shifts, partial and varied reinforcement, discrimination, and acquisition of the "observing response."

The details of Frustration Theory have been provided elsewhere (Amsel, 1958, 1962, 1967; Amsel & Ward, 1965). One of the major assumptions of the theory is that when an expectancy for reward (r_r) has been classically conditioned, the absence of reward arouses a primary frustration response. The theory further assumes that frustration is motivating (energizing) and that its reduction is reinforcing. Therefore, the theory predicts that a response instrumental in reducing frustration should be learned. To test this implication about the reinforcing properties of frustration reduction, one must present the presumed frustration-arousing cues to a subject who has some opportunity to escape from them. If these stimuli are not aversive, then the organism should neither escape initially nor learn the escape response; if these stimuli are aversive and escape is reinforcing, then subjects should learn the response as indexed by an increase in the strength of the escape response with successive trials.

This chapter summarizes research from a number of different learning situations involving reward manipulations in which frustration has been typically introduced to account for the results. The goal of these studies has been to provide empirical support for the frustration interpretation by using an escape-from-frustration response to measure independently the relative amounts of frustration present. The general methodology of the studies is described first, followed by a statement of the purpose, specific methods, results, and conclusions of the individual experiments.

II. General Methodology

A. SUBJECTS

Hooded, Sprague-Dawley, or Holtzman albino male rats were kept at 85% body weight usually accomplished by feeding them laboratory chow for one hour/day. In sucrose reward studies rats were weighed each day and fed the appropriate amount to maintain them at 85%.

B. APPARATUS

One-way hurdle-jump apparatus were used during the escape-from-frustration training phase. They consisted of a startbox and a goalbox (both 27.9 cm long, 11.4 cm wide, and 14.0 cm high) separated by a vertically sliding door (10.2 × 6.4 cm) which rested on a hurdle 5.1 cm high. The startboxes were covered with sanded Plexiglas and were painted either black or white. The food cup in the startbox was a bent measuring spoon hanging from the wall next to the hurdle-jump door. The goalboxes were painted medium gray and had a wire mesh lid with Plexiglas attached to the top of the wire mesh. The sides and floors were made from pine board. In some studies the hurdle-jump latencies were measured from the time the hurdle-jump door was raised until the floor of the goalbox was depressed. In other studies speeds were measured from the time the hurdle-jump door was raised until a photobeam 10.2 cm within the goalbox was broken.

Training prior to the escape-from-frustration phase was done in straight alleys, where *the goalbox of an alley was the startbox of the hurdle-jump apparatus.* The width and height of the alleys were the same as the hurdle-jump apparatus and were also constructed from pine. The startboxes were 30.5 cm long and the runway sections were 139.7 cm long. The alleys were covered with sanded Plexiglas. Startbox doors which opened horizontally activated silent switches connected to a Hunter Klockounter. Interruption of photobeams 15.2, 137.2, and 157.5 cm from the door measured start, runway, and goal times, respectively. Horizontally sliding goalbox doors prevented retracing. Three alley and hurdle-jump apparatus have been used. The measurements of the apparatus used in the earlier studies differed only slightly from those reported here, and the alley and startbox of the hurdle-jump apparatus were painted white. The later studies used two identical alleys placed side by side, but one alley was painted white, the other black.

C. PROCEDURE

The alley training procedures were patterned after those used by Ison (e.g., Ison, Glass, & Daly, 1969). The hurdle-jump training procedures were patterned after those used by the McAllisters in their studies on escape-from-fear (e.g., McAllister & McAllister, 1962a). All rats were placed on the deprivation schedule eight days prior to the beginning of the experiment. On the seventh day animals were taken to the experimental room where they were allowed to eat the reward pellets or drink the sucrose solution and to explore the goalbox of the hurdle-jump apparatus for seven minutes. During alley training all subjects were given six trials/day. On each trial, subjects were placed in the startbox. The startbox door was opened when the subject had faced it for three seconds. The goalbox door was closed when the last photobeam was broken. Subjects were removed from the goalbox when they finished eating the reward pellets (37 mg, Noyes Co.), or were left in the goalbox for 10 sec if given a small reward or no reward. The intertrial interval varied from 6 to 10 min, during which the subjects were placed in individual retaining cages with water available. On the day following the last alley trial, subjects were given 12 or 15 hurdle-jump training trials, and either 9, 12, or 15 trials on the next day. During hurdle-jump training subjects were placed directly into the startbox of the hurdle-jump apparatus. The hurdle-jump door was raised 10 sec later. After jumping, the subject remained in the goalbox of the hurdle-jump apparatus for 10 sec and was then returned to the retaining cage. If the subject did not jump within 60 sec, he was removed from the startbox and a latency of 60 sec was recorded. The intertrial interval varied from 4 to 12 min.

D. STATISTICAL ANALYSES

Start, runway, goal, and hurdle-jump latencies were converted to reciprocals (speeds) in every study. The alley acquisition data were analyzed in blocks of six trials (mean speeds for each day of training). If the experiment included an alley phase in which reward magnitudes were changed, analyses were carried out on individual trials. Hurdle-jump speeds were analyzed in blocks of three trials. Repeated measures analyses of variance were done by computer, and appropriate analyses of simple main effects and/or Newman-Keuls tests were subsequently done when appropriate. Results reaching the .05 probability level were considered statistically significant, however, many of the results were significant beyond the .001 level.

III. Reward Manipulations Following Continuous Reinforcement

A. NONREWARD

Subjects given alley training on a continuous reinforcement schedule receive a reward in the goalbox of the alley on every trial. Although speeds are typically slow early in training, with additional trials subjects run quickly down the alley. When subjects are no longer rewarded in the goalbox of the alley, speeds are initially high, but they decrease with additional nonrewarded trials. Although a number of different theoretical analyses have been formulated to account for the acquisition and extinction of responses, the theoretical framework which gave rise to the following experiments was that aspect of Hull-Spence Theory (e.g., Hull, 1952; Spence, 1956), called Frustration Theory (e.g., Amsel, 1958). This theory accounts for appetitive (approach to food) learning in an alley by assuming that the unconditioned stimulus (UCS) is the food reward, the conditioned stimuli (CSs) are the cues of the goalbox (apparatus cues), and the unconditioned response (UCR) is the complex of consummatory responses made in the presence of the food. The conditioned response (CR) includes components of the UCR, and has been called anticipatory reward or expectancy for food (r_r). It is assumed that r_r is aroused not only by the goalbox stimuli, but also by the startbox and runway stimuli because of their similarity and temporal proximity to the goalbox stimuli. Feedback stimuli (s_r) from r_r are presumed to be present and thus to become part of the stimulus complex evoking the instrumental running response (see Spence, 1956).

When reinforcement is no longer given following acquisition of the expectancy for reward, there is a decrease in the strength of the instrumental running response. Although this decrease could reflect the simple extinction of r_r, several investigators have pointed to the agitated behavior of organisms during extinction as evidence for an active motivational interpretation of the effects of nonreward (see Terrace, 1972, for a review of this position). As mentioned earlier, the Frustration Theory analysis of extinction assumes that nonreward in the presence of r_r conditioned during the acquisition phase arouses an aversive emotional response. This response is presumed to be a UCR, and components of it are assumed to become classically conditioned to the stimuli present (r_f). Not only is r_f assumed to be aroused by the goalbox stimuli, but also by the runway and startbox stimuli because of their similarity and temporal proximity to the goalbox stimuli. Also, r_f is assumed to produce stimuli (s_f), and avoidance behaviors are presumed to be aroused by these stimuli. Thus, the avoidance responses associated with r_f-s_f compete with the approach responses conditioned during the acquisition phase, resulting in conflict. With repeated extinction trials, the strength of r_f increases, the resultant avoidance responses become stronger, and response speeds decrease.

If the Frustration Theory analysis of extinction is correct, the stimuli paired with nonreward should be aversive: subjects should learn a new response to escape from the stimuli which arouse frustration. Presumably, the reduction in frustration reinforces escape from frustration aroused by the absence of reward. The following studies provide support for this analysis.

Experiment 1 (Daly, 1969b) tested the reinforcing properties of escape from frustration aroused by nonreward following training on a continuous reinforcement schedule. Data from the hurdle-jump phase appear in Fig. 1. The group labeled EXP'T-0-NCS had been given 60 food-reinforced acquisition trials (15 pellets on each trial) and 18 extinction trials. Presumably r_r was conditioned during the 60 acquisition trials, and frustration, which became conditioned to the cues of the goalbox, was aroused during the 18 extinction trials. During hurdle-jump training the goalbox stimuli of the alley (now the startbox stimuli of the hurdle-jump apparatus) should have aroused both unconditioned and conditioned frustration. Escape from these stimuli following the hurdle-jump response to the neutral goalbox of the hurdle-jump apparatus should have reduced frustration and thus reinforced the hurdle-jump response. The data in Fig. 1 clearly indicate that Group EXP'T-0-NCS learned to jump the hurdle. The acquisition curve is similar to that obtained for most instrumental responses. This result replicates those obtained in an earlier study by Adelman and Maatsch (1956), but it extends the results since a nonreinforced control group was included. Group CONTROL-0-NCS had been given 78 trials in the alley, but had never received any food reward. If confinement in the startbox of the hurdle-jump ap-

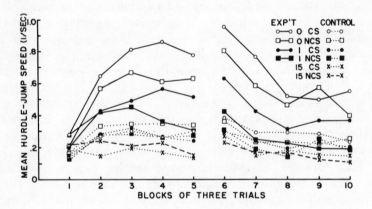

Fig. 1. Hurdle-jump speeds to escape nonreward (0) or a reduced (1) food reward following alley acquisition with (EXP'T) or without (CONTROL) a large food reward presented on a continuous reinforcement schedule, with (CS) or without (NCS) a discrete CS. (From Daly, 1969b; by permission of the American Psychological Association, Inc.)

paratus is aversive and the basis for the behavior of Group EXP'T-0-NCS, then the control group should also learn to jump the hurdle. The data in Fig. 1 show the Group CONTROL-0-NCS did not show much of an increase in hurdle-jump speeds across trial blocks, and that Group EXP'T-0-NCS jumped faster than Group CONTROL-0-NCS. Experience with nonreward per se in the alley was not sufficient to result in hurdle jumping, i.e., nonreward had to have been experienced in the presence of cues previously paired with reward. A second control group was also included which was given 78 food-reinforced alley trials, but was also given food in the startbox of the hurdle-jump apparatus during hurdle-jump training (CONTROL-15-NCS). This group was run because research had indicated that stimuli paired with food arouse conditioned excitement (e.g., Zamble, 1967). The data in Fig. 1 indicate that experience with rewards per se was not sufficient to result in hurdle jumping.

The previous analysis stated that Group EXP'T-0-NCS learned to jump the hurdle to escape both conditioned and unconditioned frustration. However, there is no way of differentiating how much of each source of frustration contributed to hurdle-jump performance. Additional groups were included to demonstrate that conditioned frustration did influence hurdle jumping. Group EXP'T-0-CS was given 60 food-reinforced acquisition trials followed by 18 extinction trials in the alley. However, a light over the goalbox of the alley was turned on as the subject broke the second photobeam in the alley on the 18 extinction trials. Thus, the conditioned stimuli (CSs) during the 18 r_f conditioning trials were both the apparatus cues and the light. During hurdle-jump training the light was on in the startbox of the hurdle-jump apparatus and was turned off after the hurdle-jump response. If the light provided another source of frustration (which would have to be conditioned frustration), this group should have jumped faster than the group not given this additional source of frustration (Group EXP'T-0-NCS). This prediction was based on the finding that subjects learned to jump a hurdle faster when fear was conditioned to both a discrete CS and apparatus cues than when conditioned only to the apparatus cues (McAllister & McAllister, 1962b). The data in Fig. 1 show that Group EXP'T-0-CS jumped faster than Group EXP'T-0-NCS. This difference was not due to any inherent aversiveness of the light: Groups CONTROL-0-CS and CONTROL-15-CS did not differ significantly from Groups CONTROL-0-NCS and CONTROL-15-NCS, respectively. The only procedural difference between the CS and NCS control groups was that for the former groups a light was turned on during the last 18 alley trials and 30 hurdle-jump training trials. It can, therefore, be concluded that conditioned frustration aroused by the light influenced hurdle-jump performance.

The Hull-Spence Theory states that the classical conditioning of an expectancy for reward (r_r) occurs during acquisition of an instrumental response. However, it should be possible to condition r_r in the absence of a required instrumental response. To determine whether nonreward is aversive when r_r is conditioned without the occurrence of a required instrumental response, subjects in Exp. 2 (Daly, 1969c) were simply placed 60 times into the goalbox of the alley used in the previous study and given the 15 reward pellets. This was followed by 12 placements into an empty goalbox (frustration-conditioning trials) during which a light was turned on (CS condition of Exp. 1). During the subsequent two days of hurdle-jump training, subjects could jump from the box in which food had previously been given to the goalbox of the hurdle-jump apparatus. The light was turned off following the response. The data in Fig. 2 show that this group (15-0 CS) learned to jump the hurdle, and jumped faster than a control group (0-0 CS) which had experienced the same number of goal placements and CS presentations as Group 15-0 CS, but had never received food. This result indicates that the conditioning of r_r and arousal of R_F occur even if no instrumental response is required. These data also provide evidence against an alternative explanation of the results obtained in Exp. 1; it could be argued that hurdle-jump performance was due to a transfer of the running response to

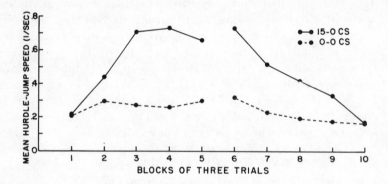

Fig. 2. Hurdle-jump speeds to escape nonreward following direct placements with (15-0 CS) or without (0-0 CS) a large food reward presented on a continuous reinforcement schedule. (From Daly, 1969c; by permission of the American Psychological Association, Inc.)

the jumping response. Since Group 15-0 CS in Exp. 2 learned to jump the hurdle without being required to learn an instrumental approach response during the r_r conditioning trials, the response transfer explanation for the data obtained in Exp. 1 can be ruled out.

The results which appear in Figs. 1 and 2 support the prediction that escape from frustration aroused by nonreward following reward given on a continuous reinforcement schedule can reinforce the learning of a hurdle-jump response. The results of Exp. 1 have been replicated twice (Exps. 15 and 18, reported later). However, in order to conclude that any response which leads to a reduction in frustration will be learned, one must demonstrate that responses other than the hurdle-jump response can be learned. Exp. 3 (Daly & McCroskery, 1973, second experiment) showed that a bar-press response can be learned to escape frustration-arousing cues. Following 75 r_r conditioning trials (15/day) using the placement procedure employed in Exp. 2, subjects were placed into the box with a bar present but no food reward. Subjects could escape (lifted out) from the nonrewarded box if they pressed the bar. The response measure was the reciprocal of the time from placement into the box until the bar was pressed. The data in Fig. 3 show that this group (15-0) learned to press the bar and pressed it faster than a control group (0-0) which had been given the same number of placement trials but had never received food. This result provides support for the prediction from Frustration Theory that any response instrumental in escaping frustration will be learned.

The rewards used in Exps. 1–3 were multiple food pellets. However, the reinforcing properties of escape from frustration should not depend on the type of rewarding agent. Experiment 4 (Daly,

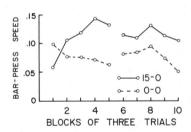

Fig. 3. Bar-press speeds to escape nonreward following direct placements with (15-0) or without (0-0) a large food reward presented on a continuous reinforcement schedule. (From Daly & McCroskery, 1973; by permission of the American Psychological Association, Inc.)

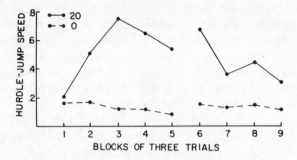

Fig. 4. Hurdle-jump speeds to escape nonreward following alley acquisition with (20) or without (0) a 20% sucrose reward presented on a continuous reinforcement schedule.

unpublished) demonstrated that subjects would learn to jump a hurdle to escape frustration when the reward used was 1 cc of a 20% sucrose solution. The alley acquisition procedures were identical to those used in Exp. 1 except for the type of reward. Following 12 alley extinction trials, subjects were given two days of hurdle-jump training using the procedures described earlier. A control group given the same number of alley and hurdle-jump trials but no sucrose reward was included. The data from the hurdle-jump phase appear in Fig. 4. The group previously given the sucrose reward (20) learned to jump the hurdle and jumped significantly faster than the control group (0). Thus, the finding that nonreward following continuous reinforcement is aversive and can be the basis for the learning of a new response is not restricted to solid food rewards. Presumably, any type of reward would provide the same result.

Subjects in Exps. 1–4 were run under high hunger drive; they were at about 85% of their ad lib. body weight and were run approximately 22 hr after their last feeding. Research has indicated that the effects of nonreward are greater under high-drive than under low-drive conditions (e.g., McHose & Ludvigson, 1964). To determine whether the conditioning of frustration and the subsequent learning to escape from frustration-arousing cues is influenced by drive level, Cohen (1973) used the direct placement procedures described for Exp. 2. Following 45 r_r conditioning trials (Phase 1), 12 r_f conditioning trials (Phase 2) were administered in which a light CS was presented. Then subjects were given hurdle-jump training (Phase 3) to escape from the CS to a neutral box. The experimental group given all three phases under the high-drive condition (22 hr since last feeding) jumped the hurdle faster than a control group treated identically except for the omission of food reward during the first phase. This result replicates the findings of Exp. 2. However, the experimental group given all three phases under a low-drive condition (3 hr since last feeding) did not jump the hurdle faster than a low-drive control group. The results obtained with the high-drive groups could have been due to the high-drive level during the frustration-conditioning phase and/or due to the high-drive level during the hurdle-jump phase. To test whether drive level during Phase 2 and/or Phase 3 was the determiner of hurdle-jump performance, Cohen included groups which were shifted to the opposite drive level during the frustration-conditioning phase. One group run under the high-drive condition during Phases 1 and 3 was given r_f conditioning trials under the low-drive condition. Another group run under the low-drive condition in Phases 1 and 3 was given r_f conditioning trials under the high-drive condition. Statistical comparisons (2×2 analyses of variance) included the data of the two experimental groups described earlier. Groups under the high-drive condition during hurdle-jump training jumped faster than the low-drive groups, indicating that drive level during hurdle-jump training influences performance. Groups given the r_f conditioning trials under the high-drive condition jumped faster than the groups given r_f conditioning trials under the low-drive condition, irrespective of drive level during the hurdle-jump phase (no interaction effect). This result indicates that drive level affected the conditioning of frustration which in turn influenced the learning of a response to escape the frustration-arousing stimuli.

To test whether the reinforcing effects of escape from frustration would combine with other sources of reinforcement, subjects in Exp. 5 (Daly, 1970) were given both frustration-conditioning and fear-conditioning trials prior to hurdle-jump training to escape from the fear- and frustration-arousing cues. The direct placement procedure was used for the 60 r_r conditioning and 12 r_f conditioning trials. Frustration was conditioned to the apparatus cues only. Subjects were then placed in a second box identical to the first one except that it contained a grid floor through which electric shocks were delivered. Subjects were given 35 tone-shock pairings. The following day they were given hurdle-jump training to escape from the box in which they had been given r_r and r_f conditioning trials. The tone was turned on as subjects were placed into the startbox and was turned off following the hurdle-jump response. The stimuli of the startbox of the hurdle-jump apparatus had been paired with nonreward in the presence of

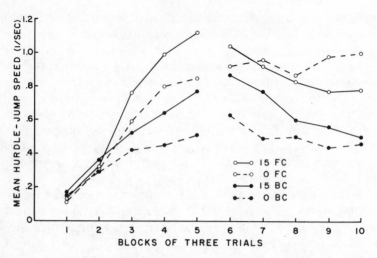

Fig. 5. Hurdle-jump speeds to escape nonreward following direct placements with (15) or without (0) a large food reward presented on a continuous reinforcement schedule, and forward (FC) or backward (BC) fear-conditioning (shock presentation) trials. (From Daly, 1970; by permission of the American Psychological Association, Inc.)

cues previously paired with reward (frustration arousal), the tone had been paired with shock (fear arousal). Jumping the hurdle was, therefore, instrumental in escaping both frustration- and fear-arousing stimuli. The data appear in Fig. 5. The group given both frustration- and fear-conditioning trials (15 FC) jumped the hurdle faster on the first day of hurdle-jump training than a nonfrustrated control group (0 FC) which had been given the identical number of fear-conditioning trials but had not received a food reward during the initial 60 trials. Acquisition of a new response was faster when two sources of learned motivation were present than if only one was present. This result was also obtained when a lower level of fear was combined with frustration. McAllister and McAllister (1962b) demonstrated that hurdle jumping to escape fear-arousing stimuli is faster following forward-conditioning (FC) than following backward-conditioning (BC) trials. Following backward-conditioning trials fear is not conditioned to the discrete CS but is conditioned to the apparatus cues. Following forward-conditioning trials fear is conditioned to both the discrete CS and the apparatus cues. It was concluded that when fear is conditioned to a compound stimulus a greater magnitude of fear is aroused than if fear is conditioned only to a single stimulus.

Experiment 5 included two groups which were given shock-tone pairings (backward-conditioning trials). One of these was also given r_r and r_f conditioning trials (15 BC), a second was not (0 BC). Groups given backward-conditioning trials jumped slower than the groups given forward-conditioning trials, which replicates the results obtained by McAllister and McAllister (1962b). Group 15 BC jumped faster than Group 0 BC, which supports the conclusion that fear and frustration combine to produce faster learning of the hurdle-jump response as compared with a group in which only fear is aroused.

B. Reduced Reward

Subjects typically show a rapid decrease in response strength when they are given a small reward following a series of trials on which they were given a large reward on a continuous reinforcement schedule. In fact, within three to six experiences with the small reward they usually run slower than a control group which had received the small reward throughout training. Crespi (1942) called this result the depression effect, and it has been replicated many times. If one assumes that a small reward in the presence of cues previously paired with a large reward arouses frustration, the depression effect can be accounted for by Frustration Theory in the same way it accounts for the effects of nonreward. The difference in speed between the shifted and nonshifted groups is presumably due to the avoidance behaviors aroused by the frustration stimuli in the shifted group which are not aroused in the control group (see Ison et al., 1969).

If a decrease in the magnitude of reward arouses frustration, then organisms should learn new responses to escape from the reduced reward. Experiment 1 (Daly, 1969b), which was described earlier, included groups shifted from 15 pellets to 1 pellet during alley training. The reduced reward was also given to the subjects in the startbox of the hurdle-jump apparatus during hurdle-jump training. All other aspects of the procedure were identical to those described previously for the extinction groups. The data appear in Fig. 1. The groups shifted from the large to the small reward (EXP'T-1-NCS) did learn to jump the hurdle to escape cues paired with the reduced reward and jumped faster than the control group (CONTROL-1-NCS) which had received the small reward during all phases of the experiment. A group given r_f conditioning trials in the presence of a light CS in addition to the apparatus cues was also included. This group (EXP'T-1-CS) jumped faster than the no-light CS group (EXP'T-1-NCS). Group CONTROL-1-CS, which was included to control for the effects of the light, was given 1 pellet throughout training and the light was turned on during the last 18 alley trials and all hurdle-jump trials. Group EXP'T-1-CS jumped faster than this control group, which did not differ from the control group run under the no-light CS condition (Group CONTROL-1-NCS). This result replicated the finding obtained with the extinction groups.

If any instrumental response can be learned to escape stimuli paired with frustration aroused by shifts from a large to a small reward, subjects should learn to press a bar to escape from the stimuli paired with the small reward. In Exp. 6 (Daly & McCroskery, 1973, first experiment) subjects were given 60 r_r conditioning placement trials (6 per day) and 42 trials of bar-press training in which escape (lifted out) from the stimuli paired with the reduced reward was possible only if they pressed the bar. A light, presented on all of the trials on which a small reward was given, was turned off when the subject pressed the bar. The data appear in Fig. 6. The group shifted to the small reward (15-1 CS) pressed the bar faster than a control group (1-1 CS) which was given the small reward throughout training. This indicates that bar-press speeds are increased by the aversiveness aroused by a shift from a large to a small reward. There was, however, some indication that escape from the light and/or confinement in the box influenced bar-press speeds, since the control group showed acquisition of the bar-press response. This complicates the analysis of the results, since it is unclear whether the reinforcement in Group 15-1 CS for the bar-press response was the reduction in frustration, the light, and/or confinement. If these subjects learned

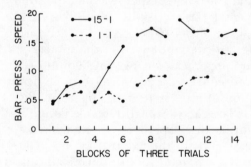

Fig. 6. Bar-press speeds to escape a reduced food reward following direct placements with (15-1) or without (1-1) a large food reward presented on a continuous reinforcement schedule. (From Daly & McCroskery, 1973; by permission of the American Psychological Association, Inc.)

the bar-press response to escape from the light or confinement, frustration could merely have acted as an irrelevant drive which energized a response reinforced by them rather than providing the source of reinforcement itself. Nevertheless, it can be concluded that frustration aroused by the reduction in reward magnitude did influence bar-press speeds, since Group 15-1 CS pressed the bar significantly faster than Group 1-1 CS.

In all of the previously reported experiments reward magnitude was reduced abruptly: subjects were given the large reward for a number of days and then shifted abruptly to the small reward on subsequent days. Since Gonzalez, Gleitman, and Bitterman (1962) did not obtain a depression effect when rewards were reduced gradually (two pellets each trial), it has been generally accepted that frustration is aroused following an abrupt reduction in reward magnitude, but not following a gradual reduction. This result implies that r_r is reduced during the gradual-shift phase, so that when a small reward is presented there is no substantial discrepancy between the expected and obtained reward magnitudes, and hence no basis for the arousal of frustration. However, Rosen, Glass, and Ison (1967) obtained a gradual decrease in alley speeds following an abrupt shift from 15 pellets to 1 pellet when the subjects had been given injections of sodium amobarbital. This drug is assumed to attenuate the effects of inhibitory emotional responses such as frustration (e.g., Barry, Wagner, & Miller, 1962). Therefore, the drugged subject's gradual change in performance presumably reflects the reduction in r_r uninfluenced by frustration. On the basis of this result, one might conclude that r_r is not extinguished rapidly and that a small reward following a gradual reduction in reward magnitude would arouse frustration. One difficulty in interpreting the result of the Gonzalez et al. (1962) experiment is that training was terminated after the subjects had been given the small reward only once. Therefore, the magnitude of frustration aroused by the small reward could not be ascertained. Experiment 7 (Daly, 1974) measured the magnitude of frustration aroused by a small reward following a gradual reduction in reward magnitude. After 60 alley acquisition trials, subjects were given the small reward for six trials following a gradual shift (one pellet less each trial) from 14 pellets to 1 pellet, and the size of the depression effect was compared with that following an abrupt reduction in reward magnitude. During the gradual-shift phase, speeds in the alley decreased only slightly, and there was no depression effect. These results replicate those of Gonzalez et al. (1962). However, during the last six alley trials when all groups were given the small reward, there

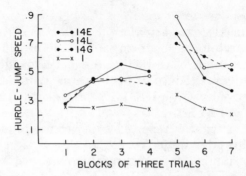

Fig. 7. Hurdle-jump speeds to escape a reduced food reward following gradual (14G), abrupt (14L and 14E), or no (1) reduction in food reward in an alley presented on a continuous reinforcement schedule. (From Daly, 1974; by permission of the American Psychological Association, Inc.)

was a further decrease in speed of approach to the reduced reward and a depression effect occurred. The magnitude of the depression effect for the groups given the abrupt reduction in reward magnitude and the group given the gradual reduction in reward magnitude did not differ. In the next phase, subjects were given hurdle-jump training to escape from the reduced reward. Only if frustration is aroused by the small reward following the gradual shift in reward magnitude should subjects learn to jump the hurdle. The data from the hurdle-jump phase appear in Fig. 7. The group given the gradual reduction in reward magnitude (14G) learned to jump the hurdle and jumped faster than the control group (1) which had been given the one-pellet reward throughout the experiment. There were no significant differences in hurdle-jump speeds between Group 14G and either of the groups given an abrupt reduction in reward magnitude. In one of these groups the abrupt shift to the small reward occurred after 60 alley acquisition trials and the small reward was presented for the next 18 alley shift trials (14E). In the second group, the large reward was presented for an additional 12 trials (14L), those trials on which Group 14G was receiving the gradual reduction in reward magnitude. Both Groups 14G and 14L received the small reward for the last six alley trials. The groups given the abrupt reduction in reward magnitude learned to jump the hurdle which replicates the results of Exp. 1. The fact that Group 14G learned to jump the hurdle indicates that frustration is aroused by a small reward even following a gradual reduction in reward magnitude. This conclusion is also supported by the data from the shift phase in the alley, since Group 14G did run slower than Group 1 (depression effect).

Results of some recent experiments have indicated that reward magnitude may be a less important determiner of response strength than the number of pieces of food received (e.g., McCain, 1969; McCain, Dyleski, & McElvain, 1971). In the studies discussed previously, subjects were given 14 or 15 small pellets as a large reward and one small pellet as the small reward. It is, therefore, possible that it was the decrease in the number of pellets rather than the decrease in the reward magnitude which was aversive. Experiment 8 (Daly, 1971) measured speed of hurdle jumping to escape one 20-mg pellet following 60 alley acquisition trials during which one group was rewarded with a single large (500 mg) pellet and a second group was rewarded with 25 small (20 mg) pellets. Following six r_f conditioning trials in the alley during which they were given one small (20 mg) pellet, the subjects were given hurdle-jump training to escape from the small reward. The hurdle-jump data appear in Fig. 8. The group which had received the one large pellet (1L) and the group which had received the 25 small pellets (25S) both learned to jump the hurdle and jumped faster than a control group (1S) which had been given one small pellet throughout training. However, Group 25S did jump faster than Group 1L, which indicates that decreases in both reward magnitude and number of pellets is more aversive than a decrease in reward magnitude only. However, a reduction in reward magnitude, with the number of pellets held constant, is also aversive.

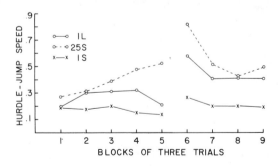

Fig. 8. Hurdle-jump speeds to escape a reduced food reward following alley acquisition with a large food reward of one large pellet (1L) or 25 small (25S) pellets presented on a continuous reinforcement schedule. (From Daly, 1972b; by permission of the Psychonomic Society, Inc.)

Experiment 4 indicated that nonreward in the presence of stimuli previously paired with a sucrose reward is aversive. Experiments 9–11 (Daly, unpublished) were conducted to determine if reductions in concentration of a sucrose reward are aversive. In Exp. 9 subjects were given 1 cc of a 20% sucrose solution for 60 alley acquisition trials, followed by 12 alley shift trials and 15 hurdle-jump trials. During the shift and hurdle-jump trials the reward was 1 cc of a 3% sucrose solution. The data from the hurdle-jump phase appear in Fig. 9. Subjects in this group (20) did not learn to jump the hurdle and did not jump faster than a control group given a 3% sucrose reward (3) throughout training. There had also been no change in performance in the alley following the shift in reward magnitude, which replicates a number of other studies (e.g., Homzie & Ross, 1962; Rosen, 1966). However, some recent experiments (e.g., Weinstein, 1970) obtained a depression effect following a decrease in sucrose concentration. Weinstein used smaller quantities of reward. Therefore, .125 cc of a 30% sucrose solution was used as the large reward, and .125 cc of a 3% sucrose solution was used as the small reward in Exp. 10. Subjects were given 60 alley acquisition, 12 shift, and 18 hurdle-jump trials. The data from the hurdle-jump phase appear in Fig. 10. This procedure resulted in acquisition of the hurdle-jump response for the group shifted from the 30% to the 3% solution (30), and this group jumped faster than the control group given the 3% sucrose solution in all phases of the experiment (3). However, the speeds of Group 30 did not decrease substantially during the alley shift phase. Group 30 was still running faster than Group 3 by the end of alley training. To ensure that the results of the hurdle-jump phase could not be attributed to the generalization of the running to the jumping response, the direct placement pro-

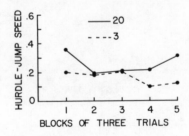

Fig. 9. Hurdle-jump speeds to escape a 3% sucrose reward following alley acquisition with a 20% (20) or 3% (3) sucrose reward (1 cc) presented on a continuous reinforcement schedule.

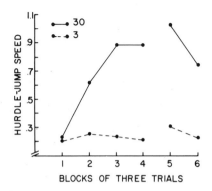

Fig. 10. Hurdle-jump speeds to escape a 3% sucrose reward following alley acquisition with a 30% (30) or 3% (3) sucrose reward (.125 cc) presented on a continuous reinforcement schedule.

cedure described in Exp. 2 was used in Exp. 11. Subjects were given 60 r_r and 6 r_f conditioning trials followed by 18 hurdle-jump trials. The data in Fig. 11 show that the group given .125 cc of a 30% sucrose solution (30) during the first phase of the experiment learned to jump the hurdle and jumped faster than the control group given .125 cc of a 3% sucrose solution throughout training (3). The results of Exps. 10 and 11 indicate that when a .125 cc quantity of a sucrose solution is used, a shift from a 30% to a 3% solution is aversive; subjects did learn the hurdle-jump response to escape from the reduced sucrose reward. There are, however, still a number of unanswered questions. It is unclear why the subjects in Exp. 9 did not learn to jump the hurdle and why there was no evidence of a depression effect in the alley in Exp. 10 despite the fact that the hurdle-jump data indicate that frustration was aroused.

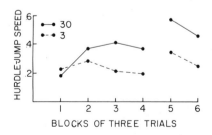

Fig. 11. Hurdle-jump speeds to escape from a 3% sucrose reward following direct placements with a 30% (30) or 3% (3) sucrose reward (.125 cc) presented on a continuous reinforcement schedule.

C. INCREASES IN DELAY OF REWARD

Subjects in the experiments discussed thus far were reinforced immediately upon entering the goalbox of the alley. Food was in the goal cup prior to placing the subject in the startbox, but subjects could not see the food until they were over the cup because it was bent up. There has been much interest in the effects of a delay of reward on the acquisition of a response and in the effects of an increase in delay of reward. If extinction training is viewed as placing the subject in a situation of infinite delay, then it is logical to predict that an increase to some finite delay would also be aversive. Attempts to demonstrate the aversiveness of an increase in the delay of reward have led to mixed results. The depression effect does not occur within a few trials as it does with a decrease in reward magnitude (e.g., Shanab, 1971), but it has been shown to occur within 12 to 36 experiences with the longer delay of reward (e.g., Shanab, 1971; Shanab & McCuistion, 1970). Increases in delay of reward have not resulted in faster running in the second alley of a double runway unless it has been combined with a reduction in reward magnitude (e.g., McHose, 1966; Sgro, Glotfelty, & Moore, 1970). Sgro *et al.* have suggested that the eventual receipt of the reward may attenuate the frustration response. If an increase in the delay of reward is not aversive, subjects should not learn to jump a hurdle to escape from the stimuli paired with the increase in the delay of reward. Experiment 12 (Daly, unpublished) tested this prediction. Subjects were given 60 alley acquisition trials in which a four-pellet food reward was delivered when the subject entered the goalbox. This was accomplished by having a measuring spoon pushed into the goalbox via a solenoid arrangement as the subject broke the last photobeam. Following 12 shift trials on which food was delivered 15 sec after the subject broke the last photobeam, subjects were given 30 hurdle-jump trials. Fifteen seconds after placement into the goalbox of the alley (the startbox of the hurdle-jump apparatus), the subject was given the four-pellet reward. Five seconds later the door over the hurdle was raised. The data appear in Fig. 12. This group (I-NE) jumped the hurdle faster than a control group which had been given the reward following a 15-sec delay throughout training (D-NE). However, the increase in speed of jumping across trials was small. This result had been anticipated because of the suggestion by Sgro *et al.* that the eventual receipt of reward may decrease the magnitude of the frustration response. Therefore, a group was shifted to an extinction condition during hurdle-jump training (no food in the

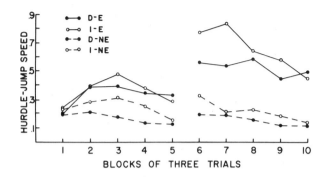

Fig. 12. Hurdle-jump speeds to escape a delayed food reward (NE) or nonreward (E) following alley acquisition with an immediate (I) or delayed (D) food reward presented on a continuous reinforcement schedule.

startbox of the hurdle-jump apparatus). This group (I-E) was given immediate reinforcement during alley acquisition and a 15-sec delay in reward for 12 shift trials. However, an empty food cup was presented in the goalbox 15 sec after the subject was placed into it, and the hurdle-jump door was raised 5 sec later. A second group was also given hurdle-jump training under the extinction condition but had been run under the delay of reward condition throughout alley training (D-E). These extinction groups jumped faster than the non-extinction groups, and both extinction groups showed an increase in speed over trials. The group which had been shifted to the delay of reward condition jumped faster than the group which had never been given the reward immediately, which indicates that an increase in delay of reward is aversive. Thus, the two sources of frustration (the increase in delay of reward and extinction) resulted in faster hurdle jumping than if only one source of frustration (the extinction condition) was present. These results indicate that an increase in the delay of reward is aversive.

IV. Reward Manipulations Following Intermittent Reinforcement

A. Partial and Varied Reinforcement

The results of experiments reported in Section III demonstrate the aversiveness of nonreward or a small reward in the presence of cues previously paired with a large reward on a continuous reinforcement schedule. Subjects given training on a partial reinforcement schedule are also given nonrewarded trials in the presence of stimuli paired with reward: nonrewarded trials are interspersed with the rewarded trials on an irregular schedule. Therefore, Frustration Theory (Amsel, 1962) would predict that an aversive emotional response would be aroused by nonreward during acquisition on a partial reinforcement schedule. On rewarded trials a portion of the response made to the reward is conditioned to the stimuli present. These stimuli then arouse anticipatory reward responses. Once r_r is conditioned, nonreward should arouse frustration, which should become conditioned to the stimuli present. Eventually, the stimuli of the alley should arouse both r_r and r_f. If this analysis is correct, nonreward during and following acquisition of a response reinforced on a partial reinforcement schedule should be aversive. Subjects should learn to escape from a nonrewarded box which had previously been paired with both reward and nonreward (partial reinforcement).

Other data indicate that the above analysis of the effects of a partial reinforcement schedule may be too simple. In Section III it was pointed out that two indices of the magnitude of frustration aroused are the rate of change of performance in approach to the nonreinforced goalbox during extinction training and the size of the depression effect. It has been well established that acquisition on a partial reinforcement schedule results in an increased resistance to extinction as compared with acquisition on a continuous reinforcement schedule. It has also been shown that alley acquisition on a partial reinforcement schedule as compared with a continuous reinforcement schedule retards the onset of the depression effect when subjects are shifted to a small reward (Ison et al., 1969). One interpretation is that nonreward or a reduced reward following acquisition on a partial reinforcement schedule is not an aversive event. Therefore, this analysis would predict that subjects would not learn to jump the hurdle to escape nonreward following acquisition on a partial reinforcement schedule. However, Frustration Theory (Amsel, 1958) accounts for the increase in resistance to extinction following acquisition on a partial reinforcement schedule by assuming that counterconditioning occurs. Approach rather than avoidance responses become associated with the frustration stimuli (s_f) because subjects do make approach responses toward the goalbox in the presence of frustration responses (r_f) and their stimuli (s_f) and are occasionally given a food reward on such trials. Therefore, approach responses become conditioned to s_f. Nonreward following acquisition on a partial reinforcement schedule arouses frustration, but the approach responses

conditioned to s_f retard the rate of extinction as compared with subjects given acquisition on a continuous reinforcement schedule. This
analysis is the basis of the notion of persistence as recently developed
by Amsel (1972). Subjects trained on a partial reinforcement schedule show an increased resistance to extinction because s_f arouses approach rather than avoidance responses, not because nonreward is not
aversive. This analysis predicts that subjects given acquisition on a
partial reinforcement schedule will learn to jump the hurdle to
escape from nonreward.

Experiment 13 (Daly, 1969a) included two groups given 60 alley
acquisition trials on a partial reinforcement schedule. One group was
given a large reward (15 pellets); the second, a small reward (one
pellet) on rewarded trials. Following alley training both groups were
given 30 hurdle-jump trials to escape from the nonrewarded goalbox
to a neutral box. The data appear in Fig. 13. Both the large (15 PR)
and the small (1 PR) reward groups learned to jump the hurdle, although Group 15 PR jumped faster than Group 1 PR. This result
substantiates the prediction of Frustration Theory that the magnitude of frustration aroused is a direct function of the size of the discrepancy between the expected and obtained reward: the larger the
reward magnitude the larger is the discrepancy between the expected
reward and nonreward. Both Groups 15 PR and 1 PR jumped faster
than the control groups given 15 (15 CR), one (1 CR), or zero (0)
pellets on a continuous reinforcement schedule in *both* the alley and

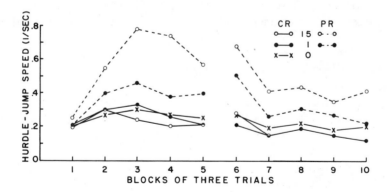

Fig. 13. Hurdle-jump speeds to escape nonreward following alley acquisition with
a large (15) or small (1) food reward presented on a partial reinforcement schedule
(PR). Control groups were given a large (15), small (1), or no (0) reward on a continuous reinforcement schedule (CR) during alley and hurdle-jump training. (From
Daly, 1969a, by permission of the American Psychological Association, Inc.)

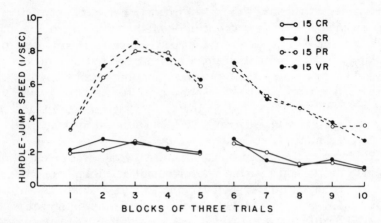

Fig. 14. Hurdle-jump speeds to escape nonreward or a small food reward following alley acquisition with a large food reward presented on a partial (15 PR) or varied (15 VR) reinforcement schedule. Control groups were given a large (15 CR) or small (1 CR) reward on a continuous reinforcement schedule during alley and hurdle-jump training. (From Daly, 1969a; by permission of the American Psychological Association, Inc.)

hurdle-jump phases. These results indicate that nonreward following alley acquisition on a partial reinforcement schedule is aversive.

Experiment 14 (Daly, 1969a) replicated the results of Exp. 13. In addition, a group given alley acquisition on a varied reinforcement schedule was included. On some trials this group was given a 15-pellet reward; on other trials, a one-pellet reward. Experiment 1 had indicated that a small reward in the presence of stimuli previously paired with a large reward is aversive. It was, therefore, predicted that a small reward presented in the presence of stimuli concurrently paired with a large reward would also be aversive. Hurdle-jump training was given following 60 alley acquisition trials. The data from the hurdle-jump phase appear in Fig. 14. The group which had been given alley acquisition on a partial reinforcement schedule (15 PR) was given no pellets in the startbox of the hurdle-jump apparatus. The group which had been given alley acquisition on a varied reinforcement schedule (15 VR) was given one pellet. Both groups learned to jump the hurdle and jumped faster than control groups given 15 pellets (15 CR) or one pellet (1 CR) during both phases of the experiment. From these studies it can be concluded that either a small reward following alley acquisition on a varied reinforcement

schedule, or nonreward following alley acquisition on a partial reinforcement schedule, is aversive.

B.   LIMITED PARTIAL REINFORCEMENT TRAINING

Frustration Theory assumes that approach responses become conditioned to s_f during alley acquisition on a partial reinforcement
schedule. Thus, approach responses are aroused during subsequent
extinction training, resulting in an increase in resistance to extinction as compared with a group given acquisition on a continuous reinforcement schedule. However, it is difficult for this analysis to
account for the small-trials partial reinforcement effect: subjects
given as few as two trials on a partial reinforcement schedule are
more resistant to extinction than subjects given two trials on a continuous reinforcement schedule (McCain, 1966). It is improbable
that the conditioning of r_r and r_f and counterconditioning could all
occur within such a small number of trials. Brooks (1969, 1971) has
stated that the Frustration Theory analysis of the small-trials partial
reinforcement effect should focus on the magnitude of frustration
aroused in the group given acquisition on a continuous reinforcement schedule and not on the magnitude of frustration aroused in
the group given acquisition on a partial reinforcement schedule. It
is possible that r_r is significantly greater following, for example, six
than following three reinforcements. Nonreward would thus arouse
a greater magnitude of frustration following six trials on a continuous reinforcement schedule than six trials on a partial reinforcement
schedule. The greater magnitude of frustration would arouse more
avoidance responses incompatible with approach responses and result
in more rapid extinction.

To test the aversiveness of nonreward following limited partial reinforcement acquisition training, Brooks (1969) used the direct placement technique described in Exp. 2. Subjects were given six placements either on a continuous or partial reinforcement schedule. One
group under each schedule received a large reward (30-sec access to
wet mash), and the other group received a small reward (one 45-mg
pellet). Brooks had predicted that nonreward following acquisition
with a small reward would not be aversive either for the continuously
or the partially reinforced groups, since differential r_r with such a
small reward would not develop in so few trials. A control group not
given any reinforcement was also included. During the subsequent 25
hurdle-jump trials the group which had been given the large reward

on the continuous reinforcement schedule jumped the hurdle faster
than all the other groups, which did not differ from each other. This
result thus supported Brooks' analysis of the small-trials partial reinforcement effect. In a second experiment, Brooks (1971) showed that
this result was obtained when the number of reinforcements was
equated. Subjects given 6 trials on a continuous reinforcement schedule jumped the hurdle faster to escape nonreward than a group given
12 trials (6 rewarded) on a partial reinforcement schedule. The same
result was obtained when a group given 3 trials on a continuous reinforcement schedule was compared with a group given 6 trials (3 rewarded) on a partial reinforcement schedule. It thus appears that the
conditioning of r_r is slower on a partial reinforcement schedule than
on a continuous reinforcement schedule, which results in nonreward
being more aversive following limited acquisition on a continuous
reinforcement schedule than on a partial reinforcement schedule.

V. Reward Manipulations Following Discrimination Training

A. Escape from S—

During discrimination learning subjects are reinforced for responding in the presence of one stimulus (S+) and are not reinforced
for responding in the presence of a second stimulus (S—). When both
stimuli are presented from the beginning of training there is typically
an increase in response strength in the presence of both stimuli followed by a subsequent decrease in response strength in the presence
of S—. The Frustration Theory analysis of discrimination learning
(Amsel, 1958) assumes that r_r is conditioned to S+. The increase in
response strength in the presence of S— early in training is presumed
to be due to the generalization of r_r from S+ to S—. Therefore, the
subject experiences nonreward in the presence of the generalized r_r.
Nonreward is assumed to arouse frustration which should become
conditioned to S—, the stimuli of the nonreinforced goalbox in the
case of alley training. The frustration response should be aroused by
the startbox and runway stimuli because of their similarity and temporal contiguity with the goalbox stimuli. The avoidance responses
associated with s_f underlie the decrease in response strength in the
presence of S—. This analysis thus states that an aversive emotional
state is aroused by S—. Terrace (1972) has summarized in a previous
volume in this series the data indicating some of the aversive proper-

ties of S— (emotional responses to S—, inhibitory stimulus control, peak shift) and has also summarized some studies showing the reinforcing properties of escape from S— (Rilling, Askew, Ahlskog, & Kramer, 1969; Terrace, 1971; Wagner, 1963). Therefore these studies will not be reviewed here in detail. The Rilling *et al.* and Terrace studies showed that pigeons will learn to peck a key to turn off S—. Terrace (1971) further showed that a group which learned to respond in the presence of S+ without responding in the presence of S— (errorless learning) did not show acquisition of the response instrumental in turning off S—, thus indicating that S— was not aversive under these conditions. Rilling, Kramer, and Richards (1973) have partially replicated this finding. These results readily follow from the Frustration Theory analysis of discrimination learning. Any technique which prevents generalization of r_r from S+ to S—, or prevents responding in the presence of S— and thus prevents the experience of nonreward in the presence of the generalized r_r, should preclude the arousal and conditioning of frustration. Therefore, S— should not be aversive, and subjects should not learn a response to escape from S—.

Wagner (1963) was the first to use the hurdle-jump technique to measure the aversiveness of S—. He did not, however, obtain an increase in the magnitude of hurdle jumping across trials. The procedures used in Exp. 15 (Daly, 1971) were a modification of Wagner's. A one-way rather than a two-way hurdle-jump procedure was used. The goalbox of the alley was the startbox of the hurdle-jump apparatus, and as a control, a group which was never reinforced was run rather than one which had been given alley acquisition on a partial reinforcement schedule. The data from Exp. 15 appear in Fig. 15. The groups labeled DR had been given either 30 or 60 (as labeled) alley acquisition trials, half in the white alley and half in the black alley. Half of the subjects were always reinforced in the white goalbox and not reinforced in the black goalbox, and vice-versa for the other half. All subjects were given hurdle-jump training from the nonreinforced goalbox to a neutral box. Both DR groups learned to jump the hurdle. They did not differ significantly from groups labeled CR and PR. These latter groups were given hurdle-jump training to escape nonreward following alley acquisition on a continuous (CR) or partial (PR) reinforcement schedule. Groups DR, PR, and CR jumped faster than the control groups (ZR) which had not been given any food reward during the alley acquisition phase. Thus, the hurdle-jump technique used by Wagner with the modifications described can be used to demonstrate that stimuli previously

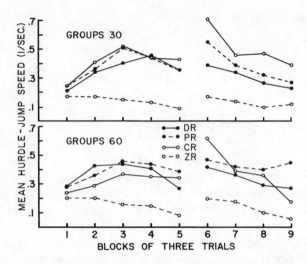

Fig. 15. Hurdle-jump speeds to escape nonreward in the presence of S— following discrimination learning (DR) or following partial reinforcement (PR), continuous reinforcement (CR), or no reinforcement (ZR). (From Daly, 1971; by permission of the American Psychological Association, Inc.)

paired with nonreward during discrimination learning are aversive: subjects in Groups DR did learn the hurdle-jump response.

Experiment 16 (Daly, 1971) replicated Exp. 15 in part. Groups given either 24 or 96 discrimination learning trials (15-0) learned to jump the hurdle to escape from the nonreinforced goalbox and jumped faster than the control groups (0-0) which had never received food in either alley (see Fig. 16). This experiment also included groups which were given 15 pellets in one goalbox and one pellet in the other goalbox during alley acquisition. Therefore, discrimination was between a large reward and a small reward, rather than between a large reward and no reward. Since Exps. 1 (incentive shift) and 14 (varied reinforcement schedule) had shown that a small reward in the presence of an expectancy for a large reward is aversive, it was predicted that subjects would learn to jump the hurdle to escape from the small reward following discrimination learning. These groups given either 24 or 96 discrimination learning trials (15-1) learned to jump the hurdle and jumped faster than the control groups (1-1) given one pellet throughout alley and hurdle-jump training. The results of Exps. 15 and 16, and those of Terrace and Rilling *ét al.*, clearly indicate that subjects will learn a response to escape from S—.

B. Extended Training

Experiments 15 and 16 varied the number of discrimination learning trials prior to hurdle-jump training. Groups in Exp. 15 were given either 30 or 60 trials, and groups in Exp. 16 were given either 24 or 96 trials. In both experiments there was little, if any, effect of the number of discrimination learning trials on hurdle-jump speeds. This result was contrary to the prediction derived from Frustration Theory, which assumes that frustration is aroused on the basis of the generalization of r_r from the reinforced to the nonreinforced alley. Since there should be a decrease in the generalization of r_r from S+ to S— as discrimination learning progresses, the magnitude of frustration aroused by nonreward (or a small reward) should also decrease. Each additional nonreinforced trial on which unconditioned frustration is not aroused, conditioned frustration should extinguish.

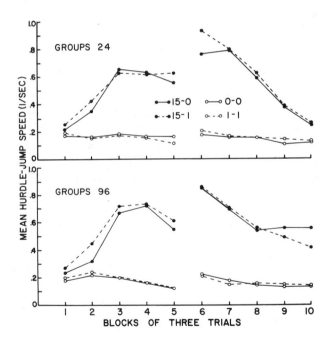

Fig. 16. Hurdle-jump speeds to escape nonreward or a small food reward in the presence of S— following acquisition of a discrimination between a large food reward and nonreward (15-0) or a large food reward and a small food reward (15-1). Control groups were given a small reward (1-1) or no reward (0-0) during alley and hurdle-jump training. (From Daly, 1971; by permission of American Psychological Association, Inc.)

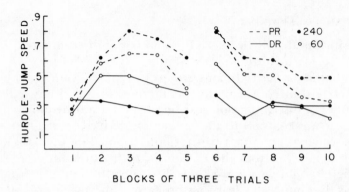

Fig. 17. Hurdle-jump speeds to escape nonreward in the presence of S— following discrimination learning (DR) or alley acquisition with a large food reward on a partial reinforcement schedule (PR) following two levels of training (240 or 60 trials).

Therefore, following extended discrimination training, S— should no longer be aversive. In support of this prediction, Amsel and Ward (1965) have shown that speeds in the second runway of a double runway are not increased by nonreward in the first goalbox following extended discrimination training. Terrace (1972) has also shown that the peak shift and behavioral contrast effects diminish, which has been taken to indicate that the aversiveness of S— decreases following extended discrimination training. Therefore, subjects given extended discrimination training should not learn a response to escape from S—. It is possible that not enough discrimination training was given in Exps. 15 and 16 for the decrease in generalization of r_r and resultant extinction of r_f to occur. In Exp. 17 (Daly, unpublished) one group received 60 and a second group received 240 discrimination learning trials. The data from the subsequent hurdle-jump phase appear in Fig. 17. The group given 60 discrimination learning trials (60 DR) learned to jump the hurdle, replicating the results of Exp. 15. Group 60 DR jumped faster than Group 240 DR, which did not learn to jump the hurdle. Therefore, following limited discrimination training (at least up to 96 trials, Exp. 16) nonreward is aversive, but following extended discrimination training (240 trials) nonreward is no longer aversive.

It is possible that the results obtained in Exp. 17 were due to "habituation" of the frustration response. Repeated experience with frustrative nonreward in any situation may result in a decrease in the magnitude of the unconditioned frustration response. To rule out this alternative explanation, groups given 60 or 240 alley acquisition trials on a partial reinforcement schedule prior to hurdle-jump training were included. Group 240 PR was, thus, given just as many nonrewarded and rewarded trials as Group 240 DR, but half were in the white alley and half in the black alley. Frustration Theory predicts that there should be no decrease in r_r with extended acquisition on a partial reinforcement schedule, and, therefore, frustration should be aroused by nonreward even following extended training. Only if the magnitude of the unconditioned frustration response habituates with repeated arousals should Group 240 PR not jump the hurdle. The data of these groups also appear in Fig. 17 (60 PR and 240 PR). Both groups learned to jump the hurdle, and Group 240 PR did not jump more slowly than Group 60 PR. Thus, repeated experiences with nonreward on a partial reinforcement schedule do not result in a decrease in the aversiveness of nonreward.

C.   OVERLEARNING REVERSAL EFFECT

Subjects will learn to reverse a discrimination if they are reinforced for responding in the presence of a former S— and not reinforced for responding in the presence of a former S+. Many studies have indicated that subjects given extended discrimination learning prior to reversal training will learn the discrimination reversal faster than subjects not given extended training on the original discrimination task (e.g., Paul, 1965; Sperling, 1965). This result, called the overlearning reversal effect, has not always been obtained. It has been difficult to isolate the critical variable(s) which determines the rate of reversal learning. One possible explanation can be derived from Frustration Theory. During acquisition of the original discrimination, r_r is conditioned to the stimuli paired with the reward (S+). This reward expectancy is classically conditioned, and thus the expectancy response presumably grows with each additional rewarded trial until it reaches an asymptotic level. During the subsequent discrimination reversal phase, nonreward is presented in the presence of the stimuli eliciting r_r. Thus, frustration should be aroused. The magnitude of frustration aroused is presumed to be a direct function of the magnitude of r_r. Therefore, if r_r is not at asymptote for a criterion-trained group (lenient criterion), the overtrained group should have a larger r_r than the criterion-trained group. Nonreward should thus arouse a greater magnitude of frustration in the group given overtraining, which in turn should elicit more avoidance responses and slower alley speeds in the previously reinforced alley. If r_r is at asymptote in the criterion-trained group (strict criterion), additional training should not increase r_r, and equal amounts of frustration should be aroused: overtraining beyond a strict criterion should not result in faster reversal learning. Sperling (1970) and Richman and Coussens (1970) have both shown that the speeds to S+ and S— reversed faster when the overtrained group was compared with a group run to a lenient criterion on the original discrimination task. No difference in the speed of reversal learning was found when the overtrained group was compared with a group trained to a strict criterion. These results support the prediction of Frustration Theory.

If the aversiveness of nonreward in the presence of S+ is the basis for the overlearning reversal effect, then subjects given overtraining on the original discrimination should jump a hurdle faster to escape from nonreward in the presence of S+ than a group trained to a lenient criterion. However, there should be no difference in hurdle-jump speeds between an overtrained group and one trained to a strict criterion. Experiment 18 (Daly, 1972a) gave hurdle-jump training following different amounts of original discrimination learning. Groups were given either 30, 60, or 120 discrimination learning trials, half in each alley, and 12 discrimination reversal trials to condition frustration to the previously reinforced stimulus. They were then given 30 hurdle-jump training trials to escape from the originally reinforced goalbox (S+). All three groups learned the discrimination, even the group given only 30 discrimination learning trials. It had been hoped that 30 trials could be considered a lenient criterion, 60 trials a strict criterion, and 120 trials overtraining, and that performance would be the same following 60 and 120 trials. The discrimination acquisition data indicate that these results were obtained. The groups given 60 and 120 trials ran faster in the reinforced alley and slower in the nonreinforced alley than the group given 30 trials. Differences between the groups given 60 and 120 trials were minimal (see Daly, 1972a). All three groups learned to reverse their discrimination within the 12 reversal trials, but no differences were found in speeds in the formerly reinforced alley. Presumably with additional trials differences would have appeared. During the subsequent hurdle-jump phase, the predictions of Frustration Theory were substantiated. The data appear in Fig. 18. The groups given 60 and 120 discrimination trials (10 DR and 20 DR) both learned the hurdle-jump response and did not differ from each other. Both of these groups jumped faster than the group given only 30 discrimination learning trials (5 DR). Control groups given 30, 60, or 120 alley trials but with no food reinforcement on any trial (5 ZR, 10 ZR, and 20 ZR,

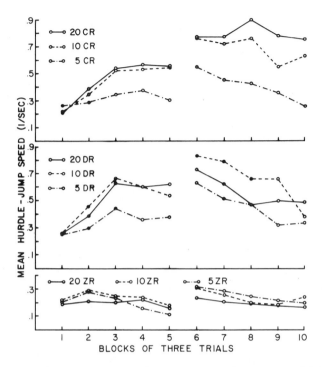

Fig. 18. Hurdle-jump speeds to escape nonreward in the presence of S+ following different levels (20, 10, or 5 days) of discrimination training (DR), continuous (CR), or no reinforcement (ZR). (From Daly, 1972a; by permission of American Psychological Association, Inc.)

respectively) showed no acquisition of the hurdle-jump response. These results thus indicate that nonreward is more aversive for an overtrained group as compared with a group trained to a lenient criterion but is not more aversive when compared with one trained to a strict criterion. Thus, support is provided for the prediction that the difference in the magnitude of frustration aroused by nonreward in the presence of S+ can be the basis for the overlearning reversal effect.

This analysis of the overlearning reversal effect is based on the assumption that greater magnitudes of frustration are aroused by greater magnitudes of r_r. Therefore, the same results should be obtained following alley acquisition on a continuous reinforcement schedule. To test this prediction additional groups were given 15, 30, or 60 alley acquisition trials on a continuous reinforcement schedule (3 trials per day, Groups 5 CR, 10 CR, and 20 CR) and 6 extinction trials prior to hurdle-jump training. The data from the hurdle-jump phase also appear in Fig. 18. As with the groups given discrimination training, Groups 10 CR and 20 CR did not differ from each other but jumped faster than Group 5 CR. All CR groups jumped faster than the ZR control groups. These data are consistent with the notion that once r_r has reached an asymptotic level, either on a continuous reinforcement schedule or during discrimination learning, additional training does not increase the magnitude of frustration aroused by nonreward.

VI. A Frustration Theory Analysis of the "Observing Response"

Pigeons will learn to press a pedal during training of a key peck reinforced on an intermittent reinforcement schedule if the pedal press is instrumental in presenting stimuli which are correlated with the presence or absence of reinforcement following a subsequent key peck (Wykoff, 1952). Rats given a choice between two arms of an E maze will choose the arm where stimuli are presented which are correlated with the presence or absence of reward in the goalbox rather than the arm where these stimuli are not correlated with reward (e.g., Perkins, 1955; Prokasy, 1956). The pedal press and the choice in the E maze are called "observing responses." If subjects make an "observing response" they are exposed to stimuli which differentially signal reward and nonreward. If they do not make the "observing response," stimuli correlated with reward and nonreward are not presented, but subjects are reinforced on an intermittent reinforcement schedule. Wykoff (1952, 1969), Perkins (1955), Wilton (1972), and others have presented theoretical accounts of the "observing response" elsewhere and they will not be repeated here. None of these analyses, however, focuses on the fact that during acquisition of the "observing response" nonreward is presented in the presence of stimuli paired with reward, which should, according to Frustration Theory, arouse frustration. In this type of experiment, nonreward occurs under two sets of circumstances. If the "observing response" is not made, the subject is reinforced on a partial reinforcement schedule. If the "observing response" is made, stimuli are presented which are correlated with reward and nonreward, a situation which is exactly comparable to discrimination learning. Reward is presented in the presence of one stimulus and not in the presence of another stimulus. Thus, it is possible to analyze "observing response" experiments as requiring subjects to make a choice between partial reinforcement and discrimination. Subjects placed in conflict situations typically choose the least aversive or the most positive alternative. Although it is possible to speculate that r_r is greater during discrimination learning than during partial reinforcement training, it is also possible to argue that it is the aversiveness of nonreward that differs between discrimination and partial reinforcement. This position is based on the findings of experiments reported previously. Experiments 13, 14, 15, and 17 showed that nonreward following alley acquisition on a partial reinforcement schedule is aversive. Experiment 17 showed that nonreward is aversive even following 120 experiences with nonreward on a partial reinforcement schedule. Experiments 15, 16, 17, and the Rilling et al. (1969) and Terrace (1972) studies showed that S— is aversive following acquisition of discrimination. The results of Exp. 15 showed that for at least 60 trials, there is very little, if any, difference in the magnitude of frustration aroused by nonreward following discrimination and partial reinforcement training. However, Exp. 17 showed that following 240 discrimination trials (120 with nonreward), nonreward no longer arouses frustration. The results of Exp. 17 thus indicate that nonreward is aversive following extended training on a partial reinforcement schedule but not following extended discrimination training. The theoretical analysis of this result was presented earlier. The Frustration Theory analysis of the "observing response" situation predicts that following extended training of the "observing response" subjects will choose the situation in which discrimination is possible because nonreward is aversive following extended training on a partial reinforcement schedule but is no longer as aversive following extended discrimination learning.

The Frustration Theory analysis of the "observing response" is appealing because it makes no additional assumption about enhancement of reward value under some conditions and not others, about preparatory responses, or about the value of information. It only assumes that the magnitude of frustration aroused by nonreward is greater following extended partial reinforcement than following extended discrimination training, an assumption supported by experimental evidence. However, empirical support for the analysis must be obtained. The following experiment provides such evidence. An E maze (Fig. 19) similar to that used by Perkins, Prokasy, and others was employed. The dimensions did not differ greatly from those reported in Wehling and Prokasy (1962). In this situation the "observing response" is a turn in a particular direction at the choice point

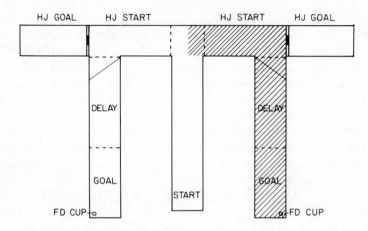

Fig. 19. Floor plan of E maze. The delay and goalboxes of the E maze had removable black or white inserts. The rest of the apparatus was gray. The shaded area had a wire mesh floor and sides. The dotted lines indicate placement of horizontally sliding doors. HJ stands for hurdle-jump startboxes and goalboxes.

of the E maze. Following the choice the subject is detained in the delay chambers which have removable inserts which are painted either black or white. If for a given subject a right turn at the choice point is designated the "observing response," then the colors of the delay chamber following a right turn are correlated with the presence or absence of food in the goalbox of the E maze. If the "observing response" is not made, that is, if the subject turns to the left, the delay chamber is also black on half of the trials and white on the other half, but the colors are not correlated with the presence or absence of food: on half of the trials on which it is white he will receive food and on half of the trials on which it is black he will receive food. The floor of the maze on the right side is covered with wire mesh; on the left side, with smooth metal. Therefore, if the "observing response" is a turn to the right, the wire mesh floor is paired with the "observing response" and the smooth floor is paired with the absence of the "observing response." In Frustration Theory terminology, the wire mesh floor and a right turn are paired with discrimination, and the smooth floor and a left turn are paired with partial reinforcement. If the Frustration Theory analysis of the "observing response" is correct, the stimuli associated with nonreward presented in the partial reinforcement situation are more aversive than the stimuli associated with nonreward in the discrimination situation. Therefore, subjects should learn a new response to escape the stimuli associated with the "nonobserving response" and should perform the response faster than subjects allowed to escape from the stimuli associated with the "observing response." To test this prediction, subjects in Exp. 19 (Daly, unpublished) were given hurdle-jump training trials to escape from the smooth floor or the wire mesh floor to a neutral box (HJ goal) with a ridged plastic floor. The gray startboxes of these hurdle-jump apparatus were the sections of the E maze just after the choice point but before the delay chambers (labeled HJ start). Guillotine doors separated the start and goal boxes of the hurdle-jump apparatus.

All subjects were first given 240 trials (8 per day) in the E maze. They were given four free trials followed by four forced trials. Subjects were forced to the side not chosen on the free trials, so that each day four turns were made to the right and four turns to the left. The schedule was also arranged so that two of the four trials to each side were reinforced and two were not reinforced, and two of the four trials to each side were to the black delay chamber and two were to the white delay chamber. For half of the subjects the "observing response" was a turn to the right, for the other half it was a turn to the left. For half of the subjects reinforcement was associated with the black delay box, for the other half it was associated with the white delay box on the "observing response" side. Subjects could not see the colors of the delay chamber from the choice point because the corner of the delay chamber visible from the choice point was painted gray (section above diagonal line drawn in the delay boxes in Fig. 19). Once the subject made a choice a horizontally sliding door was closed behind him to prevent retracing. Subjects were detained in the delay chamber for 15 sec. Half of the subjects in each group were given hurdle-jump training from the hurdle-jump box with the smooth floor, half from the hurdle-jump box with the wire mesh floor.

Thirty-two of the 38 subjects run reached the strict criterion of 11 out of 12 choices to the "observing response" side on the last three days of E-maze acquisition. None showed any preference for the "observing response" side until the twentieth day of training (160 trials). Of the six subjects who did not meet the criterion, none chose the "nonobserving response" side more than 7 out of 12 times on the last three days (they showed no preference for either side). Only those subjects reaching criterion were used in the hurdle-jump phase, since the purpose of the experiment was to test the aversiveness of the smooth versus wire mesh floor once the preference was established. On the last day of E-maze training the number of seconds taken to enter the delay chamber after the subject made the right or left turn

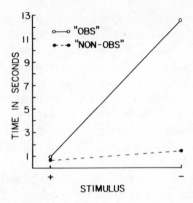

Fig. 20. Time (in seconds) taken to enter the delay chambers following an "observing response" ("OBS") or a "nonobserving response" ("NON-OBS") in the E maze, in the presence of the stimulus paired with reward (+) or nonreward (−).

was recorded. These data appear in Fig. 20. On the "observing response" side ("OBS") there was a clear-cut discrimination formed. Subjects took as long as 32 sec to enter the delay chamber when the color was the one associated with nonreward (−). However, on the "nonobserving response" side ("NON-OBS"), these same colors did not result in differential performance. These data support the Frustration Theory analysis of the "observing response." The color associated with nonreward in the presence of stimuli paired with the discrimination situation ("observing response" side) did not elicit approach responses. The same color in the presence of stimuli paired with the partial reinforcement situation ("nonobserving response" side) elicited approach responses. The slow speeds in approach to S— are presumably not caused by avoidance responses, since Groups 240 DR in Exp. 17, who also ran slowly in the presence of S—, did not learn the hurdle-jump response to escape from S—.

Following E-maze acquisition, subjects were given five days of hurdle-jump training. The training procedures described in Section II were used. The data appear in Fig. 21. The group given hurdle-jump training from the "observing response" side ("OBS") did not learn to jump the hurdle, whereas the group given hurdle-jump training from the "nonobserving response" side ("NON-OBS") did. A control group (CONTROL), given 240 E-maze trials (four free and four forced trials per day) but not given any food reinforcement on any trial, did not learn to jump the hurdle. This result indicates that the situation per se was not aversive. On the fourth day subjects

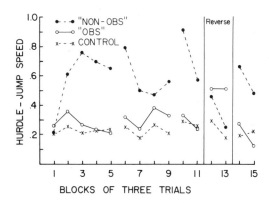

Fig. 21. Hurdle-jump speeds to escape from the stimuli associated with the presence ("OBS") or absence ("NON-OBS") of the "observing response." The control group received no food during E-maze or hurdle-jump training.

were given hurdle-jump training from the opposite side; that is, subjects given hurdle-jump training from the stimuli associated with the "observing response" side on the first three days were given hurdle-jump training from the stimuli associated with the "nonobserving response" side, and vice versa. Again, subjects jumped faster from the "nonobserving response" side than those jumping from the "observing response" side. They were switched back to the original side on the fifth day and performance reversed back. These results support the Frustration Theory analysis of acquisition of the "observing response." Stimuli associated with partial reinforcement or the "nonobserving response" side were sufficiently aversive to be the basis for the learning of a new response. Stimuli associated with discrimination or the "observing response" side were not aversive, since subjects did not learn the response.

VII. Summary and Conclusions

The experiments summarized in this chapter indicate that subjects will learn a new response to escape from frustration-arousing stimuli. It was demonstrated that rats will learn a hurdle-jump response to escape stimuli paired with nonreward or a reduced reward previously paired with a large reward. This result was obtained under

many different conditions and in various learning situations: following alley acquisition or direct placements on a continuous reinforcement schedule with solid food or sucrose rewards, in combination
with stimuli paired with shock or with an increase in delay of reward,
and following alley acquisition on a partial or varied reinforcement
schedule. It was also shown that amount of discrimination training
influences escape behavior from both S+ and S—, and that the
stimuli associated with the absence of an "observing response" are
more aversive than the stimuli associated with the presence of an
"observing response."

Rats given hurdle-jump training to escape frustration-arousing
stimuli are hard to distinguish from rats given hurdle-jump training
to avoid shock or escape stimuli previously paired with shock. After
nosing the food cup, they typically sit facing the door or scratch the
door, and leap over the hurdle as the door is raised. Occasionally,
subjects will turn around in the startbox and scratch at the door
which leads back into the alley. Some subjects jump across the hurdle
in less than one-half second. Subjects also demonstrate definite acquisition of the hurdle-jump response. On the early trials many subjects sniff around the entire startbox, and after many seconds slowly
climb over the hurdle. Some subjects do not jump over the hurdle
on the first few trials within the 60-sec limit, but there has been no
subject in an experimental group (except for Exp. 9 in which there
were no differences between the experimental and control groups)
which did not jump the hurdle with additional training. As was
pointed out by Daly (1969b), the poorest learner in any experimental
group in Exp. 1 jumped faster than the control group. It is therefore unclear why Terrace (1972) expressed concern about the performance of individual subjects when discussing this study. It has
also been suggested that hurdle-jump behavior may be due to increased activity of frustrated subjects. Patten (1971) has demonstrated
that frustrated subjects are more active than nonfrustrated control
subjects in the presence of frustration-arousing stimuli when they are
not given the opportunity to escape. The activity explanation is especially plausible if subjects do not show an increase in response
strength over trials as occurred in Wagner's (1963) study. If hurdle-
jump behavior is simply due to increased activity, then the frustrated
subjects should jump over the hurdle faster than nonfrustrated subjects on the very first trial. Differences between experimental and
control subjects on Trial 1 have not been obtained. However, with
additional training the hurdle-jump speeds of the experimental subjects increase. This pattern of results is what is obtained in most

learning situations. Unless one wants to interpret all learning data as due to increases in activity, then the present author sees no reason to adopt the activity explanation of the present data which are indistinguishable from those typically accepted as being performance changes due to learning.

Subjects not only show acquisition of the escape response, but also typically show extinction of the response with continued training. The decline usually begins partway through the second day of hurdle-jump training. According to Frustration Theory extinction of the hurdle-jump response reflects the extinction of both r_r and r_f. During hurdle-jump training, subjects are presented with stimuli presumed to arouse r_r. However, this classically conditioned expectancy response should extinguish when the CS is presented in the absence of the USC (food). Once the expectancy response extinguishes, unconditioned frustration is no longer aroused by nonreward or a reduced reward. Since r_f is also classically conditioned, it too must extinguish when the CS arousing r_f is presented but UCS (nonreward) no longer arouses unconditioned frustration. As the magnitude of both the unconditioned and conditioned frustration response decreases, the motivational basis for the hurdle-jump response declines. Therefore, the magnitude of the escape response should also decrease. This analysis also predicts that one should be able to vary the speed of hurdle jumping and the point at which extinction of the escape response begins by varying the number of nonrewarded trials prior to the beginning of hurdle-jump training. If extended trials were given during the alley extinction phase, subjects should not learn to jump the hurdle. Following 22 placements to a wet mash reward, Brooks and Goldman (1971) gave subjects 0, 10, or 20 nonrewarded trials prior to hurdle-jump training. Results indicated that the greater the number of nonrewarded trials prior to hurdle-jump training, the slower were the hurdle-jump speeds. These results accorded with the theoretical prediction.

Most of the experiments reported used a three-stage design: conditioning of r_r, r_f conditioning trials, and hurdle-jump training. In the experiments studying the effects of partial and varied reinforcement schedules and discrimination learning, the first two stages occurred simultaneously. However, the third stage was run concurrently with the first two stages only in the Rilling et al. (1969) and Terrace (1972) experiments. In these experiments the escape response (response on the left key) could be made during acquisition of the discrimination (responding on the right key). When using this latter procedure one must be careful that the opportunity to make the escape response does not influence the learning of the other response. It is, therefore, reassuring that their results were similar to those obtained with the successive stage procedure.

There are still a number of studies which must be carried out to obtain a complete picture of all the variables which influence the arousal of frustration and the reinforcing properties of escape from frustration-arousing stimuli. Studies should be conducted using reward other than solid food or sucrose, drives other than hunger, responses other than hurdle-jumping, bar-pressing, or key-pecking, and species other than rats or pigeons. More work needs to be done on the influence of reward magnitude during the r_r conditioning phase, and on increases in delay of reward (longer delays and other techniques for introducing delay of reward). There are also a number of experimental manipulations which influence behavior which the present formulation of Frustration Theory cannot account for: the effect of intertrial reinforcements (e.g., Brooks, 1971; Capaldi, Hart, & Stanley, 1963), N-R versus R-N transitions (Capaldi, 1967), and the method of presenting S— (e.g., Rilling et al., 1973).

Almost all of the studies reported were designed to test some prediction derived from Amsel's Frustration Theory. Although some researchers may want to formulate alternative theoretical explanations for the data presented in this chapter or may not want to integrate the results within any theoretical framework, the present author found Frustration Theory and Hull-Spence Theory a valuable guide in the formulation of the experiments and in the analysis of the results. Frustration Theory was able to predict the reinforcing effects of escape from nonreward or a small reward following continuous, partial, and varied reinforcement, following limited, moderate, and extended training in these situations and following discrimination learning, and the aversiveness of stimuli paired with the absence of the "observing response." Thus, the results of research in such varied areas as extinction, incentive shifts, the small-trials partial reinforcement extinction effect, the overlearning reversal and overlearning extinction effects, and the "observing response" were accounted for within one theoretical framework.

REFERENCES

Adelman, H. M., & Maatsch, J. L. Learning and extinction based upon frustration, food reward, and exploratory tendency. *Journal of Experimental Psychology,* 1956, **52,** 311–315.

Amsel, A. The role of frustrative nonreward in noncontinuous reward situations. *Psychological Bulletin*, 1958, **55**, 102–119.

Amsel, A. Frustrative nonreward in partial reinforcement and discrimination learning: Some recent history and a theoretical extension. *Psychological Review*, 1962, **69**, 306–328.

Amsel, A. Partial reinforcement effects on vigor and persistence. In K. W. Spence, & J. T. Spence (Eds.), *The psychology of learning and motivation*. Vol. 1. New York: Academic Press, 1967.

Amsel, A. Behavioral habituation, counterconditioning, and a general theory of persistence. In A. H. Black & W. F. Prokasy (Eds.), *Classical conditioning II: Current theory and research*. New York: Appleton, 1972.

Amsel, A., & Ward, J. S. Frustration and persistence: Resistance to discrimination following prior experience with the discriminanda. *Psychological Monographs*, 1965, **79** (4, Whole No. 597).

Barry, H., Wagner, A. R., & Miller, N. E. Effects of alcohol and amobarbital on performance inhibited by experimental extinction. *Journal of Comparative and Physiological Psychology*, 1962, **55**, 464–468.

Brooks, C. I. Frustration to nonreward following limited reward experience. *Journal of Experimental Psychology*, 1969, **81**, 403–405.

Brooks, C. I. Frustration considerations of the small-trials partial reinforcement effect: Experience with nonreward and intertrial reinforcement. *Journal of Experimental Psychology*, 1971, **89**, 362–371.

Brooks, C. I., & Goldman, J. A. Changes in the intensity of primary frustration during continuous nonreward. *Journal of Experimental Psychology*, 1971, **90**, 153–155.

Capaldi, E. J. A sequential hypothesis of instrumental learning. In K. W. Spence & J. T. Spence (Eds.), *The psychology of learning and motivation*. Vol. 1. New York: Academic Press, 1967.

Capaldi, E. J., Hart, D., & Stanley, L. R. Effect of intertrial reinforcement on the aftereffect of nonreinforcement and resistance to extinction. *Journal of Experimental Psychology*, 1963, **65**, 70–74.

Cohen, J. M. Drive level effects on the conditioning of frustration. *Journal of Experimental Psychology*, 1973, **98**, 297–301.

Crespi, L. P. Quantitative variation in incentive and performance of the white rat. *American Journal of Psychology*, 1942, **55**, 467–517.

Daly, H. B. Aversive properties of partial and varied reinforcement during runway acquisition. *Journal of Experimental Psychology*, 1969, **81**, 54–60. (a)

Daly, H. B. Learning of a hurdle-jump response to escape cues paired with reduced reward or frustrative nonreward. *Journal of Experimental Psychology*, 1969, **79**, 146–157. (b)

Daly, H. B. Is responding necessary for nonreward following reward to be frustrating? *Journal of Experimental Psychology*, 1969, **80**, 186–197. (c)

Daly, H. B. Combined effects of fear and frustration on acquisition of a hurdle-jump response. *Journal of Experimental Psychology*, 1970, **83**, 89–93.

Daly, H. B. Evidence for frustration during discrimination learning. *Journal of Experimental Psychology*, 1971, **88**, 205–215.

Daly, H. B. Hurdle jumping from S+ following discrimination and reversal training: A frustration analysis of the ORE. *Journal of Experimental Psychology*, 1972, **92**, 332–338. (a)

Daly, H. B. Learning to escape cues paired with reward reductions following single- or multiple-pellet rewards. *Psychonomic Science*, 1972, **26**, 49–52. (b)

Daly, H. B. Arousal of frustration following gradual reductions in reward magnitude. *Journal of Comparative and Physiological Psychology*, 1974, **86**, 1149–1155.

Daly, H. B., & McCroskery, J. H. Acquisition of a bar-press response to escape frustrative nonreward and reduced reward. *Journal of Experimental Psychology*, 1973, **98**, 109–112.

Gonzalez, R. C., Gleitman, H., & Bitterman, M. E. Some observations on the depression effect. *Journal of Comparative and Physiological Psychology*, 1962, **55**, 578–581.

Homzie, M. J., & Ross, L. E. Runway performance following a reduction in the concentration of a liquid reward. *Journal of Comparative and Physiological Psychology*, 1962, **55**, 1029–1033.

Hull, C. L. *A behavior system.* New Haven, Conn.: Yale University Press, 1952.

Ison, J. R., Glass, D. H., & Daly, H. B. Reward magnitude changes following differential conditioning and partial reinforcement. *Journal of Experimental Psychology*, 1969, **81**, 81–88.

McAllister, W. R., & McAllister, D. E. Postconditioning delay and intensity of shock as factors in the measurement of acquired fear. *Journal of Experimental Psychology*, 1962, **64**, 110–116. (a)

McAllister, W. R., & McAllister, D. E. Role of the CS and of apparatus cues in the measurement of acquired fear. *Psychological Reports*, 1962, **11**, 749–756. (b)

McCain, G. Partial reinforcement effects following a small number of acquisition trials. *Psychonomic Monograph Supplements*, 1966, **1** (12), 251–270.

McCain, G. Different levels of performance with equivalent weights of reward. *Psychonomic Science*, 1969, **14**, 2–3.

McCain, G., Dyleski, K., & McElvain, G. Reward magnitude and instrumental responses: Consistent reward. *Psychonomic Monograph Supplements*, 1971, **3** (16, Whole No. 48).

McHose, J. H. Incentive reduction: Simultaneous delay increase and magnitude reduction and subsequent responding. *Psychonomic Science*, 1966, **5**, 215–216.

McHose, J. H., & Ludvigson, H. W. Frustration effect as a function of drive. *Psychological Reports*, 1964, **14**, 371–373.

Patten, R. L. Frustrative facilitation effects of nonzero reward magnitude reduction on goal-box activity and runway locomotion. *Journal of Experimental Psychology*, 1971, **90**, 160–162.

Paul, G. Effects of overlearning upon single habit reversal in rats. *Psychological Bulletin*, 1965, **63**, 65–72.

Perkins, C. C., Jr. The stimulus conditions which follow learned responses. *Psychological Review*, 1955, **62**, 341–348.

Prokasy, W. F., Jr. The acquisition of observing responses in the absence of differential external reinforcement. *Journal of Comparative and Physiological Psychology*, 1956, **49**, 131–134.

Richman, C. L., & Coussens, W. Undertraining reversal effect in rats. *Journal of Experimental Psychology*, 1970, **86**, 340–342.

Rilling, M., Askew, H. R., Ahlskog, J. E., & Kramer, J. J. Aversive properties of the negative stimulus in a successive discrimination. *Journal of the Experimental Analysis of Behavior*, 1969, **12**, 917–932.

Rilling, M., Kramer, T. J., & Richards, R. W. Aversive properties of the negative stimulus during learning with and without errors. *Learning and Motivation*, 1973, **4**, 1–10.

Rosen, A. J. Incentive-shift performance as a function of magnitude and number of sucrose rewards. *Journal of Comparative and Physiological Psychology,* 1966, **62,** 487–490.

Rosen, A. J., Glass, D. H., & Ison, J. R. Amobarbital sodium and instrumental performance changes following reward reduction. *Psychonomic Science,* 1967, **9,** 129–130.

Sgro, J. A., Glotfelty, R. A., & Moore, B. D. Delay of reward in the double alleyway: A within-subjects versus between-groups comparison. *Journal of Experimental Psychology,* 1970, **84,** 82–87.

Shanab, M. E. Positive transfer between nonreward and delay. *Journal of Experimental Psychology,* 1971, **91,** 98–102.

Shanab, M. E., & McCuistion, S. Effects of shifts in magnitude and delay of reward upon runway performance in the rat. *Psychonomic Science,* 1970, **21,** 264–266.

Spence, K. W. *Behavior theory and conditioning.* New Haven, Conn.: Yale University Press, 1956.

Sperling, S. E. Reversal learning and resistance to extinction: A review of the rat literature. *Psychological Bulletin,* 1965, **63,** 281–297.

Sperling, S. E. The ORE in simultaneous and differential reversal: Acquisition tasks, acquisition criterion, and reversal task. *Journal of Experimental Psychology,* 1970, **84,** 349–360.

Terrace, H. S. Escape from S–. *Learning and Motivation,* 1971, **2,** 148–163.

Terrace, H. S. By-products of discrimination learning. In G. H. Bower (Ed.), *The psychology of learning and motivation.* Vol. 5. New York: Academic Press, 1972.

Wagner, A. R. Conditioned frustration as a learned drive. *Journal of Experimental Psychology,* 1963, **66,** 142–148.

Wehling, H. E., & Prokasy, W. F. Role of food deprivation in the acquisition of the observing response. *Psychological Reports,* 1962, **10,** 399–407.

Weinstein, L. Negative incentive contrast with sucrose. *Psychonomic Science,* 1970, **19,** 13–14.

Wilton, R. N. The role of information in the emission of observing responses and partial reinforcement acquisition phenomena. *Learning and Motivation,* 1972, **3,** 479–499.

Wykoff, L. B. The role of observing responses in discrimination learning. Part 1. *Psychological Review,* 1952, **59,** 431–442.

Wykoff, L. B. The role of observing responses in discrimination learning. In D. P. Hendry (Ed.), *Conditioned reinforcement.* Homewood, Ill.: Dorsey Press, 1969.

Zamble, E. Classical conditioning of excitement anticipatory to food reward. *Journal of Comparative and Physiological Psychology,* 1967, **63,** 526–529.

CONCEPTUAL AND NEUROBIOLOGICAL ISSUES IN STUDIES OF TREATMENTS AFFECTING MEMORY STORAGE[1]

James L. McGaugh and Paul E. Gold

DEPARTMENT OF PSYCHOBIOLOGY
UNIVERSITY OF CALIFORNIA, IRVINE, CALIFORNIA

I. Introduction

There is extensive evidence that in man, as well as the other animals, the retention of learned responses can be influenced by post-training treatments such as centrally acting drugs and electrical stimulation of the brain. In general, the treatments are most effective if they are administered shortly after the learning experience. That is, the effect of a given treatment on subsequent retention performance varies with the time, after training, at which the treatment is administered (Gibbs & Mark, 1973; Glickman, 1961; McGaugh & Herz, 1972). In the most general sense, these findings support the view that the processes underlying the formation of memory traces are time-dependent (McGaugh, 1966; McGaugh and Dawson, 1971).

However, studies of such time-dependent effects address several different kinds of issues. First, many studies in this area attempt to examine the perseveration-consolidation hypothesis proposed by Mueller and Pilzecker in 1900. These studies attempt to determine whether memory-storage processes become more resistant to modulating influences as the time interval between the training and treat-

[1] Supported by Research Grant MH 12526 from the National Institute of Mental Health, United States Public Health Service. We thank John Haycock, Mark Handwerker, and Roderick Van Buskirk for their contributions to the experimental findings reported in this paper.

ment is increased. Further, many studies concerned with the memory consolidation hypothesis attempt to determine whether there are alternative interpretations of the time-dependent effects which are either more adequate or more parsimonious. Second, other studies in this area attempt to determine whether, as suggested by Hebb (1949) and Gerard (1949), the processes underlying recent memory are different from those of older memories. Third, many experimental studies of time-dependent effects in memory, particularly those conducted in the past few years, have attempted to use these findings to make inferences about the neurobiological bases of memory-storage processes.

While the findings of any experiment concerned with time-dependent effects may have implications for each of these issues, the issues are quite independent. For example, the finding that a particular treatment, such as electrical stimulation of the brain produces retrograde amnesia or retrograde enhancement of retention may or may not shed any light on the question of whether the treatment has different effects on short-term memory and long-term memory processes. Further, such a finding may or may not shed light on the neurobiological basis of the effects. Thus, in assessing the contribution of studies in this area of research it is essential to consider separately the type of question addressed by each study in question.

At one level of analysis it is quite appropriate to inquire whether a particular treatment such as electroconvulsive shock (ECS) produces retrograde amnesia. Further, it is useful to determine what other treatments which affect neural activity produce behavioral effects comparable to those produced by ECS. Such experiments can provide data which are important for theory at one level of analysis: They can provide an assessment of the consolidation hypothesis. However, such experiments, by themselves, do not necessarily provide any understanding of the basis of the behavioral effects observed. Even if the mechanism of action of the specific treatment which is used to affect memory is fairly well understood, the major contribution of a study may be to clarify a conceptual question rather than to provide a neurobiological explanation of the effect. Again, the contribution of a particular study depends upon the appropriateness of the technique used for answering the questions under consideration. Techniques appropriate for investigating the neurobiological basis of retrograde amnesia and retrograde enhancement of memory are not necessarily the most effective or efficient techniques for answering questions at another theoretical level.

In this paper we have attempted to characterize the contributions of recent studies in the general area of time-dependent studies of memory storage to each of the three major theoretical issues outlined above. The first section assesses the contributions of studies of the gradient of retrograde amnesia and retrograde enhancement of memory. The second section considers the usefulness of such studies for attempting to understand the nature of short-term and long-term memory. The third section considers the contributions of studies attempting to investigate the neurobiological bases of treatments which influence memory-storage processes. In the final section, we summarize our assessment of the contribution of studies in this area to an understanding of memory processes.

II. Memory Modulation and Consolidation

The central assumption of the consolidation hypothesis as proposed by Mueller and Pilzecker (1900) is that the memory trace of an experience increases in strength after the experience. There is, in fact, evidence that, following training, retention increases with time (Deutsch, 1973). More often, however, the hypothesis has been examined by experimental studies of retrograde amnesia and retrograde enhancement of memory. Of course, as the term "retrograde" implies, it is of central importance for the hypothesis that the effectiveness of the modulating influence decreases as the interval between the training and treatment is increased. This evidence, that retention is modulated by posttrial treatments, has provided the primary support for the consolidation hypothesis. However, we wish to stress that consolidation is only inferred from, not directly measured by, such evidence. The findings of such studies merely indicate the effectiveness of a given treatment, administered at a particular time, on retention performance. It seems reasonable to assume that the longest time after training at which a treatment can significantly modulate subsequent retention should vary with the experimental treatment, depending upon the degree to which the treatment affects the neural systems involved in the hypothesized consolidation processes. In addition, there is no *a priori* reason to expect that comparable "consolidation times" are initiated under different training conditions. More simply, this logic suggests that experimental studies of retrograde disruption and enhancement of retention should not be expected to yield any time-constant for consolidation.

The results of studies of retrograde amnesia are consistent with the general view. Under some conditions, for example, treatments such as ECS and convulsant drugs affect retention only if they are administered within a few seconds or minutes after training. Under other conditions, effects are obtained with treatments administered as long as 2 or 3 days after training (McGaugh & Herz, 1972; Mah & Albert, 1973). Such findings are, of course, perplexing only if it is assumed that retrograde amnesia directly reflects the time needed for completion of consolidation processes. There is now clear evidence that the gradients depend upon the specific experimental conditions used. Cherkin has shown, for example, that the retrograde amnesia gradients produced by treating neonatal chicks with the convulsant drug flurothyl (which is inhaled) varies directly with the concentration of the fluorothyl and the duration of the treatment (Cherkin, 1969). Gradients obtained with ECS vary directly with the intensity and duration of the current (Alpern & McGaugh, 1968; Buckholtz & Bowman, 1972; Haycock & McGaugh, 1973). Jamieson (1972) found that the gradient is greatly extended by administering a series of 5 ECS treatments administered at 1-min intervals. In general, the degree of modulation of memory produced by posttrial treatments depends upon the severity of the treatment (i.e., the dose, intensity, duration, etc.).

Recent findings by Gold, Macri, and McGaugh (1973c) illustrate the degree of variation in RA gradients that is produced by electrical stimulation applied directly to the brain in rats. Current (.5 sec, 60 Hz) of intensities varying from 1 to 8 mA (.5 sec, 60 Hz) were administered directly to either the frontal or posterior cortex of rats either immediately or at a delay of up to 4 hr following a single training trial on an inhibitory (passive) avoidance task. As Fig. 1 shows, the retention performance measured 24 hr later varied systematically with the cortical region stimulated, the current intensity, and the treatment delay. For example, with frontal cortex stimulation 2 mA produced only a brief (5 sec) gradient and 4 mA stimulation produced a somewhat longer gradient (between 30 sec and 5 min), while virtually complete amnesia was produced by 8 mA administered 15 min after training. With posterior cortex stimulation 4 mA produced significant amnesia even when administered 1 hr after training.

The findings suggest that retrograde amnesia gradients reflect time-dependent changes in the thresholds for modulating memory processes with particular experimental treatments. This interpretation raises the interesting question as to whether there might be treatments which can produce effects on memory if administered at even longer posttrial intervals (i.e., days or weeks). It is clear, however, that there are limits to the effectiveness of a given treatment under specific experimental conditions. For example, Paolino and

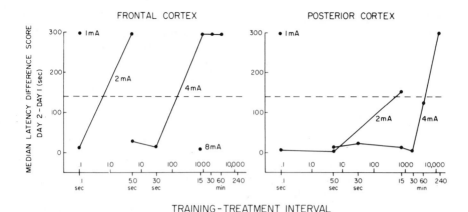

Fig. 1. The effect of direct electrical stimulation of the cortex in rats on retention of an inhibitory avoidance response as a function of the current intensity, training-treatment delay, and cortical region stimulated. Retention is indexed by the differences between response latencies on Day 2 and Day 1. All median latency difference scores less than 140 sec (dotted line) are significantly lower (indicating retention impairment) than the latencies of animals given only footshock on the training trial (300 sec). (From Gold *et al.*, 1973c.)

Hine (1973) were unable to produce amnesia gradients of greater than 1 min by direct cortical stimulation, even if very intense (i.e., 10, 50, and 100 mA) current was used. We have also obtained evidence that retrograde amnesia gradients cannot be extended in unlimited fashion merely by increasing the intensity of cortical stimulation (Gold, McDonald, & McGaugh, 1974b). Such results need not imply a maximal retrograde amnesia gradient; these findings merely reveal a limitation in the amount of disruption produced by a given treatment.

As we have noted, there is also extensive evidence that retention can be enhanced by posttrial treatments including CNS stimulants and low-intensity electrical stimulation of the brain (Bloch, 1970; McGaugh, 1968a, 1973a, 1973b). The gradient of retrograde enhancement varies with the particular experimental condition and the type of treatment used.

Thus, the findings of studies of the effects, on retention, of posttrial treatments, are generally quite consistent with the interpretation that the treatments modulate time-dependent processes underlying memory. The most essential finding is that degree of modulation decreases as the interval between training and treatment is increased. However, while such findings are consistent with the consolidation hypothesis, numerous alternative interpretations of the basic findings of these studies have been proposed. Since many of the alternative interpretations are considered in detail in recent papers (Lewis, 1969; Dawson & McGaugh, 1971; McGaugh & Herz, 1972; Mah & Albert, 1973; Miller & Springer, 1973), we will not review them in detail here.

A common assumption of many of the alternate interpretations is that the treatments affect retention not by influencing the storage of memory but, rather, by affecting retrieval processes. In view of the facts of time-dependency in the treatment effects on memory, it cannot be assumed that the treatments have a general effect on memory retrieval. Since the treatments selectively affect recently acquired information it must be assumed that they somehow affect the retrievability of recently stored information without affecting the storage itself. Without additional evidence, such an interpretation would be very difficult to assess. It is not clear how one could distinguish time-dependent storage effects from time-dependent retrieval effects. However, the retrieval hypothesis need not assume that the information is permanently irretrievable. It might be that the information can be retrieved if special experimental procedures are used.

For example, the findings of several studies (Lewis, Misanin, & Miller, 1968; Miller & Springer, 1973; Quartermain, McEwen, & Azmitia, 1970) have suggested that rats which are rendered amnesic by a posttrial treatment can subsequently display retention of the response if they are given some kind of a treatment which will "remind" them of the original training. However, in assessing the effect it is important to examine in detail the specific experimental procedures used. Typically the animals are trained on a 1-trial inhibitory avoidance task. They are punished with a footshock for stepping from one compartment to another. Retention is indexed by high-response latencies on the retention test trial. The "reminder" treatment usually consists of a footshock administered in a different apparatus. Evidence from several recent studies (Cherkin, 1972; Gold, Haycock, Macri, & McGaugh, 1973b; Haycock, Gold, Macri, & McGaugh, 1973b) indicates that the "reminder" treatment can have punishing effects which influence response latencies on the retention test. Further, "reminder" treatments are effective only if the animals have some residual memory of the original training. The "reminder" effect can be readily explained as resulting from the summation, through generalization, of the punishing effects of the reminder stimulus with a weak memory of the original inhibitory avoidance training. It is not necessary to assume that the "reminder" treatment acts on retrieval processes.

Of course, such evidence is not proof that reminders do not act as proposed by a retrieval hypothesis. The evidence does indicate that it is equally reasonable to assume that "reminders" affect behavior simply because they are mildly punishing. If this is the case, then "reminder" effects do not shed any light on the question as to whether posttrial treatment effects are due to influences on storage or retrieval of memory. The evidence remains consistent with the view that posttrial treatments affect memory storage.

Another alternative interpretation of the posttrial treatment effects on retention is that the memory may be stored under the brain state produced by the treatment and, consequently, be irretrievable under normal conditions. Evidence supporting this "state-dependency" hypothesis has been obtained by several investigators (Kurtz & Palfai, 1973; Nielson, 1968; Thompson & Neely, 1970). In our laboratory, however, we have not obtained support for the "state-dependent" interpretation of posttrial effects (McGaugh & Landfield, 1970; Zornetzer & McGaugh, 1969). In one study, for example, we gave mice an ECS treatment (transcorneal, 15 mA, 800 ms) or a sham ECS (no current) 20 sec after a single training trial on an inhibitory avoidance task. Some groups received a footshock on the training trial and some did not. A retention test was given 6 days later. One hour before the test half the animals in each group received an ECS and half did not. Thus, the ECS-treated animals were tested under a "brain-state" comparable to that elicited by the posttrial ECS treatment. The results are shown in Fig. 2. Contrary to the prediction of the state-dependency hypothesis the ECS given before the retention test decreased the response latencies in all groups. The ECS treatment given before the retention test did not eliminate or even attenuate the amnesia produced by the posttrial treatment (two groups on the left in Fig. 2) and did not cause amnesia in animals which received sham ECS following the original training. Thus, these results do not support the "state-dependency" interpretations of retrograde amnesia. Of course, our findings do not rule out the possibility that there might be conditions under which posttrial treatments can produce "state-dependent" learning. They do, however, indicate that such an interpretation does not provide a general explanation of retrograde amnesia produced by posttrial treatments.

Further, the findings of retrograde facilitation of learning produced by drugs and electrical stimulation of the brain (Bloch, 1970;

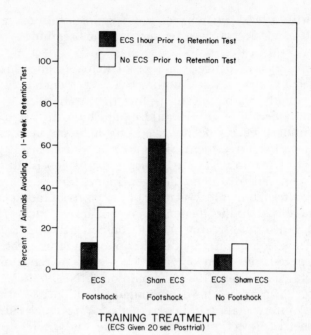

Fig. 2. The effect on retention performance of administering an ECS treatment 1 hr before the retention test. Mice (15 per group) received ECS (15 mA, 800 msec) or "sham" ECS 20 sec after training on an inhibitory avoidance task and were tested 1 week later. The percent of animals showing retention of the response was not significantly affected by ECS treatments administered before the retention test. (From McGaugh & Landfield, 1970.)

McGaugh, 1973a), are not easily interpreted in terms of a "state-dependent" hypothesis. If memories are stored in the brain state produced by the posttrial stimulation then retrieval should be impaired when the animals are subsequently tested. The evidence that retention is enhanced, rather than impaired, is inconsistent with the "state-dependent" hypothesis.

In summary, the basic finding of studies of the effects of posttrial treatments on memory is that the effects are time-dependent. Thus, the findings are, in general, consistent with the view that memory storage processes are time-dependent. While there have been many alternative interpretations of the time-dependent effects, the findings of experimental tests of alternative hypotheses have not produced critical evidence against the view that memory-storage processes are time-dependent. Studies of retrograde modulation of memory such as those discussed in this section bear only on the question of the adequacy of the consolidation hypothesis. They are not designed to provide any direct evidence concerning the way or ways in which the treatments act to produce the effects on memory-storage processes.

III. Memory Modulation and Memory Processes

The findings of studies of retrograde amnesia raise some interesting and important conceptual questions concerning memory processes. If, as the evidence suggests, memories are consolidated over time following training, how is it that we are able to recall experiences almost immediately after they occur? The successful integration and organization of behavior clearly requires that we use recently acquired memories. Several solutions to this problem have been proposed. The dual-trace hypothesis (Gerard, 1949; Hebb, 1949) proposes that recent memory and older memory may be based on different neural processes. This hypothesis provides a convenient neural basis for the behavioral distinction between short-term memory (STM) and long-term memory (LTM). The hypothesis also provides an interpretation of the modulating influences of posttrial treatments. If it is assumed that STM is required for LTM, then disruption of STM processes would be expected to produce amnesia. Or, amnesia might be produced by impairing LTM processes directly. If STM and LTM are based on different processes, it is also possible that the processes are independent and in parallel—rather than sequentially organized (Barondes, 1970; Kesner, 1973; Mc-Gaugh, 1968b). A third possibility is that STM and LTM are not based on different processes but merely refer to two stages of a single process (Gold and McGaugh, 1974). Although this issue has been the focus of much recent research the problem is, as yet, far from being resolved.

One of the most interesting findings of research in this area is that, under many conditions, amnesia develops over a period of time after animals are treated with an amnesic treatment (Agranoff, 1972; Barondes & Cohen, 1966; Geller & Jarvik, 1968; McGaugh & Landfield, 1970; Miller & Springer, 1971; Swanson, McGaugh, & Cotman, 1969). One possible interpretation of this effect (which is referred to as "short-term decay") is that the amnesic treatment does not affect STM, but rather acts directly to impair LTM storage processes. The results do indicate that treatments which produce retrograde amnesia do not necessarily immediately disrupt all retention. Thus, amnesia

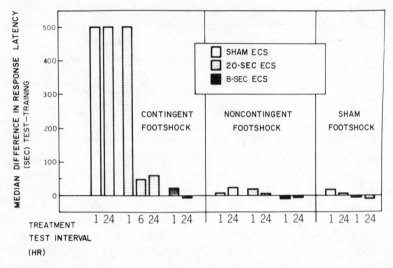

Fig. 3. Decline of retention of a one-trial inhibitory avoidance response following an ECS treatment. The groups given ECS 20 sec following training show good retention 1 hr later but less retention at 6 and 24 hr. No comparable effect is seen in groups given ECS 8 sec after training or in groups given only ECS or noncontingent footshock or both treatments. (From McGaugh & Landfield, 1970.)

is not due to a total disruption of STM at the time of treatment. However, the rate of development of amnesia following a treatment does vary depending upon the experimental treatment. For example, in one study from our laboratory (Fig. 3), we found that mice showed good retention of an inhibitory avoidance response for 1 hr, and less retention on a 6-hr test, if an ECS was administered 20 sec after training. No retention was found, however, if the ECS was administered within 8 sec after training (McGaugh & Landfield, 1970). These findings suggest that amnesia may be produced by impairing processes underlying recent memory. If so, this would argue for a sequential organization of STM and LTM (McGaugh & Dawson, 1971). However, the findings are also consistent with the view that STM and LTM are both based on the same process and that newly acquired memories are simply more labile (Gold & McGaugh, 1974).

At the present time, the most that can be concluded from studies of this kind is that amnesic treatments do not necessarily produce a memory loss which is either immediate or complete. Amnesia may develop over a period of seconds, hours, or days, depending upon the experimental conditions. At present, the findings have not provided any clear-cut understanding of the basis of the effect. Whether STM and LTM are based on the same process or different processes remains to be determined. Experiments employing posttrial treatments can only indicate the conditions under which retention can be modulated. It seems likely that clarification of this issue will require several different kinds of experimental approaches.

IV. Neurobiological Aspects of Memory Modulation

Much of the interest in studies of retrograde amnesia and retrograde enhancement of memory is based on the assumption that understanding the mechanisms by which treatments modulate memory will contribute to an understanding of the neurobiology of memory-storage processes. Why do treatments modulate memory? What neural processes underlie the time-dependent processes which are inferred from the studies of memory modulation? This question has been approached by two different types of research strategies. The first approach utilizes treatments which are known to affect memory and attempts to determine the neural effects of the treatments which are responsible for the effects on memory. Electrical stimulation of the brain and convulsant drugs are examples of treatments which are emphasized in studies using this strategy. A second strategy uses treatments which are thought to have some specific mechanism of action in order to test specific hypotheses concerning mechanisms involved in memory storage. Treatments used in studies which emphasize this strategy include antibiotic drugs which interfere with the synthesis of RNA and protein, drugs affecting transmitter systems, and hormones.

In this section we review some of the findings of research employing these two strategies in attempts to understand the neurobiological bases of treatments which modulate memory storage.

A. Effects of Electrical Stimulation of the Brain

Although the perseveration-consolidation hypothesis was proposed in 1900, the first experimental studies of the hypothesis using animal subjects were first conducted almost 50 years later (Duncan, 1949). The studies grew out of an interest in investigating the behavioral effects of the then newly developed technique of electroconvulsive shock (ECS) (McGaugh, 1974). The early studies demonstrated that ECS produced retrograde amnesia. From the outset, it was assumed that the amnesia was due to the convulsions or the brain seizures produced by the current. Studies of the neural bases of ECS-induced amnesia were begun only in the last decade. The recent research has attempted to determine (1) what effects of the stimulation are critical for producing the memory effects, and (2) whether the effects can be produced by localized stimulation of specific brain regions. The findings of this research are summarized in detail in recent reviews (Gold, Zornetzer, & McGaugh, 1974d; Kesner & Wilburn, 1974; McGaugh & Herz, 1972; McGaugh, Zornetzer, Gold, & Landfield, 1972).

Obviously, electrical brain stimulation produces many effects on neural functioning. The problem is that of determining which of the many possible effects are responsible for or at least correlated with the effects of brain stimulation on memory. In a series of studies, we examined the relationship between brain-seizure activity and retrograde amnesia produced by electrical stimulation delivered through transcorneal and cortical electrodes. We found that, in mice, the threshold for producing amnesia is generally very close to the brain-seizure threshold. Further, if the brain-seizure threshold is elevated by administering diethyl ether, the amnesic threshold is also raised (McGaugh & Zornetzer, 1970; Zornetzer & McGaugh, 1971a). More recently, Gehres, Randall, Riccio, and Vardaris (1973) reported that, in rats, the amnesic effect of hypothermia is blocked by drugs which prevent the brain seizures elicited by hypothermia. However, brain seizures are neither necessary nor sufficient conditions for producing amnesia. Amnesia is sometimes produced by electrical stimulation which is below the brain-seizure threshold (Zornetzer & McGaugh, 1971b) and, in some strains of mice, amnesia is not produced by current which is well above the brain-seizure threshold (Van Buskirk & McGaugh, 1974). Nonetheless, the fact that the thresholds for producing amnesia and brain seizures with ECS treatments are often quite similar suggests that the behavioral and neural effects may result from some basic disturbance in neural functioning. ECS current which produces seizures and amnesia also produces significant, but small (approximately 30%), inhibition of brain protein synthesis (Cotman, Banker, Zornetzer, & McGaugh, 1971; Dunn, 1971). Whether all of these effects are due to a common disturbance remains to be determined.

In rats, direct electrical stimulation of the cortex produces amnesia if the current is above the brain-seizure threshold. However, under many conditions elicitation of a brain seizure is not a suffi-

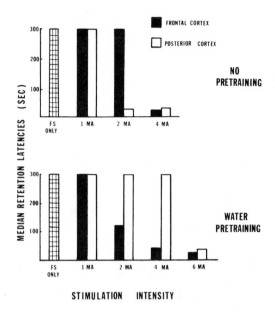

Fig. 4. Inhibitory avoidance response retention latencies of animals which received either frontal or posterior cortex stimulation 5 sec after training. In the top graph, animals were trained in a simple two-compartment inhibitory avoidance task. In the lower graph, water-deprived animals were pretrained to drink from a water spout and later received a footshock while drinking. As can be seen, the lowest intensity which produces amnesia differs for both frontal and posterior cortical stimulation in these tasks. Other findings indicate that water deprivation and pretraining exposure to the behavioral apparatus account for the altered thresholds. (From Gold *et al.*, 1973a.)

cient condition for producing retrograde amnesia (Gold & McGaugh, 1973; Gold *et al.*, 1973a, 1974b; Zornetzer, 1972).

The threshold for elicitation of a brain seizure by electrical stimulation of a region of the cortex is quite stable. Seizures are elicited by stimulation of either frontal or posterior cortex with current intensities at and above 2 mA (.5 sec, 60 Hz). However, as is shown in Fig. 4, the threshold for producing amnesia by immediate post-trial stimulation of the cortex varies considerably in different tasks. In one task (Fig. 4), stimulation of the posterior cortex produced amnesia only at current intensities above 6 mA. Under different experimental conditions, 2.0-mA stimulation of the posterior cortex is sufficient to produce amnesia. Since all stimulation above 2.0 mA produced seizures in both experiments, the effects cannot be explained by differences in brain seizures. The differences in amnesia threshold in the two studies are produced by differences in the motivational and training procedures used (Gold et al., 1973a).

In summary, the findings of our studies of direct cortical stimulation, like those of our ECS studies summarized above, indicate that while amnesia thresholds are often similar to seizure thresholds, brain seizures are not a sufficient condition for producing retrograde amnesia. Electrical stimulation of the cortex has many effects on brain activity. For example, cortical stimulation decreases the amount of EEG slow-wave activity in the theta range (4–7 Hz) for a period of several minutes following stimulation. It may be, as some experimental findings suggest (Landfield, McGaugh, & Tusa, 1972), that the amnesia produced by brain stimulation is due to an alteration brain functioning which is indexed by the shift in EEG frequencies away from the theta range. Whether such effects are causal or only correlational remains to be determined. Thus, while there are several kinds of neural changes that are correlated with retrograde amnesia, as yet, none has been shown to be a critical determinant of amnesia. Although further studies of neural correlates of amnesia induced by ECS and cortical stimulation are clearly needed the fact that such stimulation has many effects suggests that it will not be an easy task to determine the neural alterations which underlie the amnesia effect of such stimulation.

However, it is clear from these studies that memory is modulated by brain stimulation. Numerous recent studies have begun to explore the effects on memory of low-intensity electrical stimulation of specific brain regions. These studies have attempted to determine whether amnesia is produced by subseizure stimulation and whether stimulation of different brain regions has different effects on memory. There is extensive evidence that memory is influenced by posttrial stimulation of subcortical brain regions (Gold et al., 1974d). Facilitation has been produced by stimulation of the mesencephalic reticular formation (Bloch, 1970; Denti, McGaugh, Landfield, & Shinkman, 1970) and hippocampus (Destrade, Soumireu-Mourat, & Cardo, 1973; Landfield, Tusa, & McGaugh, 1973). Retrograde amnesia has been produced by stimulation of several brain regions including the hippocampus (Haycock, Deadwyler, Sideroff, & McGaugh, 1973a; Kesner & Conner, 1972; McDonough & Kesner, 1971; Shinkman & Kaufman, 1972), amygdala (Bresnahan & Routtenberg, 1972; Kesner, 1973; Kesner & Doty, 1968), caudate putamen complex (Herz & Peeke, 1971; Peeke & Herz, 1971; Wyers & Deadwyler, 1971;

Wyers, Peeke, Welliston, & Herz, 1968), and substantia nigra (Routtenberg & Holzman, 1973).

At one level of analysis, these experiments are conceptually similar to those using ECS or cortical stimulation. They provide additional evidence that memory-storage modulation can be produced by brain stimulation and they show in many cases that the effects can be produced with current that does not produce brain seizures. However, at another level, these studies can determine the brain structures in which stimulation is most effective in modulating memory and may lead to an understanding of brain systems which can modulate storage.

These possibilities are illustrated by our recent studies of the effects of stimulation of the amygdala in rats. An initial study (Gold, Macri, & McGaugh, 1973d) investigated the effect of bilateral stimulation of the amygdala through bipolar electrodes (25-μA, .1 msec-pulses, 100-Hz, 10-sec train) on retention of an inhibitory avoidance response. As is shown in Fig. 5, retention was impaired if the stimulation was delivered within an hour after the training. A subsequent study demonstrated that amnesia could also be produced by posttrial unilateral stimulation of the amygdala (Gold, Edwards, & McGaugh, 1974a). Because the stimulation was delivered unilaterally it was possible to examine the relationship between the degree of amnesia and the location of the tip of the electrode within the amygdala. The results of this analysis are shown in Fig. 6. Clearly, the greatest

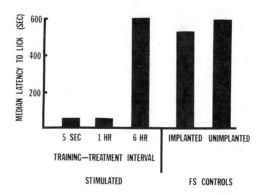

Fig. 5. Retention performance of animals trained in a one-trial inhibitory avoidance task. Rats received bilateral subseizure electrical stimulation of the amygdala at various times after training. Retention was impaired if the stimulation was administered within 1 hr of training. (From Gold et al., 1973d.)

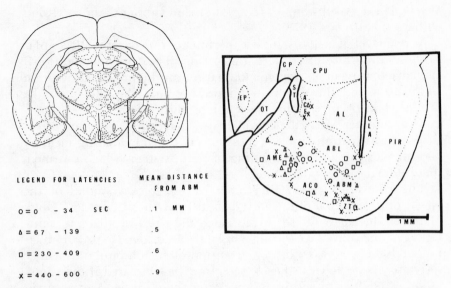

Fig. 6.   Retention performance of animals which received low-level unilateral electrical stimulation of the amygdala 5 sec after training on an inhibitory avoidance task.
Sites of electrode tips within the amygdala are shown on right, superimposed on the
appropriate figure from Pelligrino and Cushman (1967). The circles, triangles, squares,
and X's indicate the response latencies, shown on left, of individual animals. Each
group in the legend represents approximate quartiles. Lowest response latencies (i.e.,
greatest amnesia) were obtained with stimulation in or near the basomedial nucleus.
(From Gold *et al.*, 1974a.)

degree of amnesia (as indexed by retention latencies) was produced
by electrodes located within or adjacent to the basomedial nucleus.
Further, the degree of amnesia decreased as the distance of the electrode from the nucleus increased. These findings clearly suggest
that the basomedial nucleus is a highly effective stimulation site
for producing retrograde amnesia by electrical stimulation.

   Inhibitory (passive) avoidance tasks are used in most studies of
memory-storage modulation. If the findings are interpreted in terms
of the influence of treatments on memory processes, it is essential
that the generality of the effect be studied. Consequently, we have
also investigated the effects of posttrial electrical stimulation of the
amygdala on retention of an active avoidance task (Handwerker,
Gold, & McGaugh, 1974). In this study, rats were first implanted
with bilateral bipolar electrodes in the amygdala. They were given
8 trials (30-sec intertrial interval) in a one-way shuttle box. On each
trial a footshock (1.0 mA) could be avoided by moving to the safe

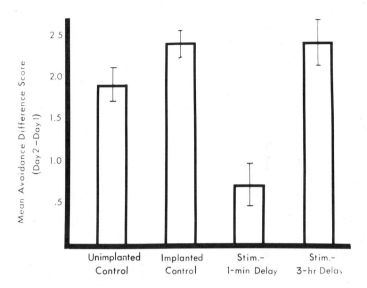

Fig. 7. Retention performance of animals which received bilateral electrical stimulation of the amygdala after training on a one-way active avoidance task. Animals which received the stimulation immediately after training had poor retention when tested 24 hr later. Animals which received the stimulation 3 hr after training had no retention deficit. (From Handwerker *et al.*, 1974.)

end of the box within 10 sec. Amygdala stimulation (0.1-msec pulses, 100 pps, 45–55 μA for 10 sec) was delivered either immediately after training or 3 hr later. The animals were then given 8 additional trials the following day. Figure 7 shows the mean improvement in avoidance scores (Day 2–Day 1) for the two stimulated groups and two nonstimulated controls. The immediate posttrial stimulation produced significant impairment while the performance of the 3-hr group was comparable to controls. An analysis of the location of the electrode tips indicated that the electrodes were located in several nuclei in the amygdala. In order to determine whether the basomedial nucleus was a particularly effective stimulation site, we examined the relationship between the difference scores of individual animals and the average distance of the two electrodes from the basomedial nucleus. The results are shown in Fig. 8. The basomedial nucleus appears to be a highly effective site for producing retrograde amnesia by electrical stimulation in both inhibitory and active avoidance tasks. It remains to be determined whether comparable effects can be obtained with different tasks including tasks using appetitive motivation.

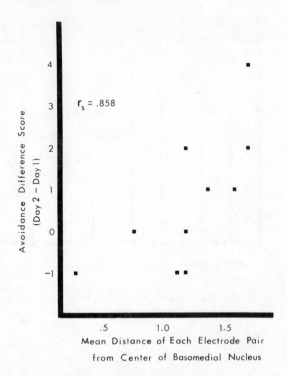

Fig. 8. Relationship between electrode placement within the amygdala and the degree of retention deficit produced by posttrial bilateral electrical stimulation. For each animal, the mean distance was determined between each animal's electrodes and the basomedial nucleus. (From Handwerker *et al.*, 1974.)

As we have indicated, the basomedial nucleus of the amygdala is not the only effective brain site for producing memory modulation. Fairly localized effects of stimulation of other brain regions have been reported by other investigators. For example, Routtenberg and Holzman (1973) found that amnesia can be produced by stimulation of the substantia nigra, pars compacta while stimulation of adjacent neural regions was ineffective. Bresnahan and Routtenberg (1972) found that the medial nucleus was the most effective stimulation site for producing amnesia in an inhibitory avoidance task. Zornetzer, Chronister, and Rose (1973) found that in mice amnesia was produced by bilateral electrical stimulation of the area dentata of the hippocampus. However, the effect was obtained only if both electrodes were in the area dentata.

These findings leave little doubt that memory-storage processes can be modulated by subseizure electrical stimulation of several subcortical regions. The effects are time-dependent and they show some degree of localization. However, not all brain regions are effective. Why are some regions particularly effective stimulation sites? There are two types of interpretations of the findings of localized effects. First, it might be that the region stimulated is part of the neural system involved in memory storage and that the stimulation directly modulates the activity of the neural system. This type of interpretation has been proposed by Kesner (1973). The findings of one study, for example (Kesner & Conner, 1972), indicate that posttrial stimulation of the midbrain reticular formation and the hippocampus produces quite different effects on retention. With hippocampal stimulation, animals display retention a minute after the treatment and amnesia a day later. With reticular formation stimulation, the animals show poor retention 1 min after training but memory a day later. On the basis of these findings, Kesner and Conner proposed that the midbrain reticular formation is part of the neural system mediating short-term memory and that the hippocampus is part of the neural system mediating long-term memory.

While the interpretation offered by Kesner and Conner (1972) is consistent with the findings, the results of their study as well as other studies of localized effects of brain stimulation are open to other interpretations (Gold *et al.*, 1974d). The localized stimulation may produce effects because of excitation or inhibition of neural activity in other neural systems connected with the stimulated regions, and/or the stimulation may cause the release of hormones which produce widespread effects on brain activity. The function of a given brain region is not easily determined by studying the behavioral effects of treatments applied to the region. However, since modulating influences on memory can be obtained by highly localized stimulation it should be possible to determine whether the effects are due to influences on other neural systems. It seems likely that different brain regions have different roles in the processing and utilization of memory. It may well be that stimulation of some regions directly affects "memory" neurons while stimulation of other regions produces influences which modulate activity in "memory" neurons. Further systematic study of the critical changes necessary for producing memory modulation by stimulation of specific brain regions should provide some useful leads to understanding the neurobiological bases of memory.

B. CHEMICAL INFLUENCES ON MEMORY MODULATION

Another approach to the problem of understanding the neuro-biological bases of memory-storage modulation involves the use of drugs. Drugs with fairly well-understood specific mechanisms of action can be used to investigate specific hypotheses concerning the neurobiology of memory-storage processes. The rationale for such studies is clear: if a specific alteration in neural functioning can be shown to influence consolidation, then it can be concluded that the function which is altered is somehow involved in or plays a modulating role in memory storage. Thus, in order to contribute to our understanding of memory-storage processes, pharmacological studies must (1) demonstrate that the drugs produce retrograde amnesia or enhancement of retention, (2) relate the behavioral effects to measured changes in the specific system in question, and (3) provide evidence that the behavioral effect is not due to other actions of the drug. There have been numerous studies of drug effects on memory-storage processes (Dawson & McGaugh, 1973; McGaugh, 1973a; McGaugh & Petrinovich, 1965). It has, however, proved to be extremely difficult to provide convincing evidence that the effects on memory are due to the "primary" mechanism of action of the drugs used.

Investigators in many laboratories have conducted extensive studies of the effects on memory of drugs which affect RNA and protein synthesis in the brain (Agranoff, 1972; Barondes, 1970; Barondes & Squire, 1972; Flexner, & Roberts, 1967; Flood, Bennett, Rosenzweig & Orme, 1973). The findings of these studies clearly demonstrate that drugs which impair RNA and protein synthesis produce amnesia. In general, the behavioral effects are similar to those produced by electrical stimulation of the brain. The effects are time-dependent. Further the magnitude of disruption depends upon the percent of inhibition of synthesis, as well as the duration of inhibition. Generally, memory is impaired only if the inhibition of protein synthesis is greater than 90%. Thus, the findings of these experiments have met the first two conditions listed above. They demonstrate the critical behavioral phenomena and they relate the behavioral effect to the hypothesized mechanism of action.

These results are consistent with the hypothesis that the drugs disrupt consolidation by inhibiting RNA and protein synthesis. Control studies indicate that the effects are not due to general malaise or other nonspecific effects. However, many alternative interpretations remain. For example, Flexner, Serota, and Goodman (1973) reported that two of the antibiotics used to inhibit protein synthesis inhibit the activity of tyrosine hydroxylase, the rate-limiting enzyme in the synthesis of dopamine and norepinephrine. This finding together with evidence that the amnesic effects of these antibiotics can be blocked by adrenergic stimulants suggests that the amnesic effects of antibiotics might be due to an inhibition of norepinephrine biosynthesis. It is possible that memory storage is impaired by both of these proposed mechanisms. At least this possibility cannot be ruled out. But, since the studies have not as yet shown which of the possible mechanisms contribute to the drugs' effects on memory, the hypothesis that the amnesia is due to the "primary" effect of inhibition of protein synthesis requires additional study. If the effect is due to inhibition of protein synthesis, it will be essential to know which proteins are required for storage and whether protein synthesis is required in all or only restricted brain regions. Most of the important questions concerning the possible involvement of protein synthesis in memory storage remain to be investigated.

A series of recent studies have attempted to determine whether catecholamines, particularly norepinephrine, play a role in memory storage. Kety (1972) has suggested that biogenic amines released in affective states may modulate storage by regulating synaptic activity at synapses activated by a training experience. As we pointed out above, there is some evidence that protein synthesis inhibitors might act by inhibiting the synthesis of dopamine and norepinephrine. Evidence from a number of recent studies indicates that amnesia is produced by the drug diethyldithiocarbamate (DDC) which is an inhibitor of dopamine beta hydroxylase (the enzyme responsible for synthesizing norepinephrine from dopamine) (Dismukes & Rake, 1972; Hamburg & Cohen, 1973; Osborne & Kerkut, 1972; Randt, Quartermain, Goldstein, & Anagnosti, 1971). We have obtained evidence confirming these findings in a series of studies in mice and rats (Gold, Van Buskirk, Haycock, & McGaugh, 1974c; Van Buskirk, Haycock, & McGaugh, 1974). The findings of our studies with mice are shown in Fig. 9. The mice were trained on an inhibitory avoidance task, injected with DDC, and tested a week later. The figure on the left indicates the dose-response effects obtained when DDC is administered immediately after training. The most effective dose was 900 mg/kg. The effect of varying the time of administration is shown in the right figure. Retention is significantly impaired by

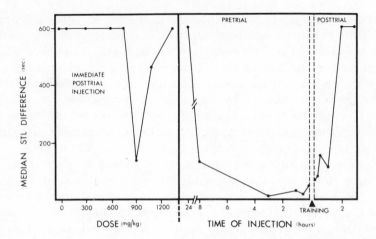

Fig. 9. The effect of diethyldithiocarbamate (DDC) on retention of an inhibitory avoidance response in mice. Retention was tested 1 week after the training trial. The results on the left indicate the dose-response effect of DDC injections administered (I.P.) immediately after training. The results on the right indicate the effects of time of administration, before or after training, with a dose of 900 mg/kg. Note that a retention deficit results from injections administered up to 8 hr before training, or 1 hr after training. (From Van Buskirk *et al.*, 1974.)

injections administered within 3 hr before training and 1 hr after training. Figure 10 shows the results of similar experiments in rats. Immediate posttrial injections produce amnesia at doses greater than 680 mg/kg. When DDC in a dose of 680 mg/kg is administered before training, retention is impaired even if the injection is given 10 days before training. Posttrial injections impair retention if administered within 1 day after training. Thus, while the effects of DDC in rats are similar to those obtained with mice, the effects with rats are much more severe.

The results of these studies of DDC on retention clearly indicate that the drug impairs retention. The effects are time-dependent and dose-dependent. Further, the doses which affect retention significantly reduce levels of norepinephrine. With a dose of 900 mg/kg, for example, norepinephrine levels are reduced to about 25% of control levels for a period of at least 8 hr (Van Buskirk *et al.*, 1974). These findings indicate that the behavioral effects of DDC are correlated with reduction of norepinephrine.

Consequently, these findings are consistent with the interpretation that norepinephrine is involved in memory-storage processes. However, DDC has a variety of influences on neural activity. For example, DDC is a chelating agent and, thus, will affect any process which involves heavy metals. Until the contribution of these other influences to the behavioral effects are investigated, many alternative interpretations of the basis of the behavioral effects are possible. Evaluation of the hypothesis that catecholamines are involved in memory-storage processes will require additional control studies as well as studies using many other drugs which influence catecholamine levels and biosynthesis.

We have considered several of many possible specific central neurobiological effects which may underlie retrograde amnesia. However, there is, in addition, the possibility that some treatments which modify memory processes do so indirectly, via peripheral mechanisms. This view is detailed in a recent review (Gold & McGaugh, 1973). Briefly, we suggested the hypothesis that the relatively nonspecific consequences of an experience, e.g., arousal or hormonal levels, may modulate the efficiency of memory-storage processes. Accordingly, it should be possible to modify—either enhance or dis-

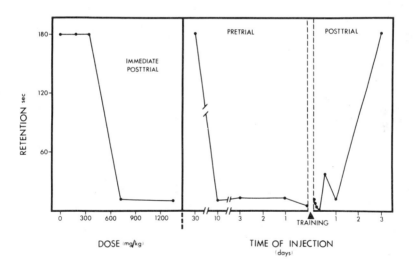

Fig. 10. The effect of diethyldithiocarbamate (DDC) on retention of an inhibitory avoidance response in rats. (The doses were 170, 340, 680, and 1360 mg/kg I.P.) Retention was measured 6 days after training. The results on the left indicate the dose-response effect obtained with immediate posttrial injections. The results on the right indicate the effects of time of administration (680 mg/kg) on retention. Note that a retention deficit is produced by injections which precede training by up to 10 days. Retrograde amnesia is produced with injections delayed by as much as 1 day but not 3 days. (From Gold et al., 1974c.)

rupt—memory storage by experimentally modifying an animal's nonspecific physiological responses following a training experience.

There is some evidence which indicates that some amnesic treatments may act by affecting nonspecific consequences of training. For example, Barondes and Cohen (1968) found that amnesia developed over time following training and either ECS or cycloheximide. Corticosteroid injections, as well as amphetamine injections, administered during the period of retention decay compensated for the amnesic treatment. Those animals which received the compensatory treatments within a few hours of training did not develop amnesia. One interpretation of these results is that the amnesic treatment produced rapid forgetting because of interference with the nonspecific consequences of training, perhaps pituitary-adrenal activity in this case.

Another possible mechanism underlying memory disruption has been found empirically. Recently, we found that ACTH or epinephrine administered after training will produce amnesia at doses which do not produce brain seizures or other obvious electrocorticographic alterations (Fig. 11). If these preliminary results are confirmed, they suggest a possible mechanism by which any severe stressor—including such diverse treatments as ECS, anoxia, and protein synthesis inhibitors—may produce RA. This provides a second possible interpretation of the results obtained by Barondes and

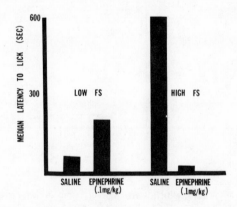

Fig. 11. Interaction of footshock level and effect of epinephrine on retention. Animals were trained on an inhibitory avoidance task using either a weak (.7 mA, .35 sec) or strong (2 mA, 1 sec) footshock. Immediately after training, saline or epinephrine injections (.1 mg/kg) were administered. Under the low footshock condition, epinephrine facilitated retention (p < .01); under the high footshock condition, the same dose of epinephrine disrupted retention. (From Gold and Van Buskirk, 1974a).

Cohen (1968). It is possible that the amnesic treatments disrupted memory processes by increasing the levels of ACTH. Corticosteroids would, of course, decrease ACTH secretion via negative feedback mechanisms. Interestingly, amphetamine also reduces ACTH levels (Ganong, 1973). In summary then, although the evidence is as yet sparse, it suggests that we must not exclude indirect effects of amnesic treatments on memory processes, possibly via hormonal alterations.

The results shown in Figure 10 also indicate that, under appropriate conditions, hormones can facilitate memory-storage processes. If the behavioral situation is such that the nonspecific consequences of training are minimal, then posttrial hormone administration may improve retention by experimentally increasing the consequences of training.

We have obtained some initial findings which are consistent with this view. In this study, water-deprived rats were pretrained to lick from a water spout at the end of a two-compartment alley. When the latency to drink reached a low asymptote, each rat received a weak footshock while drinking, followed by injections of saline or epinephrine (.1 mg/kg). Animals then received a retention test the next day. The measure of retention was the latency to drink from

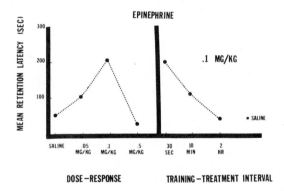

Fig. 12. Effect of posttrial epinephrine injections on retention of an inhibitory avoidance response. Rats were pretrained to drink from a water spout at the end of an alley. On the training trial, each rat received a weak footshock followed immediately by saline or epinephrine (.1 mg/kg) injections or by epinephrine injected 10 min or 2 hr after training. The retention measure was the latency to lick from the water spout on a test trial 24 hr after training. Animals which received immediate posttrial epinephrine injections showed retention performances which were significantly better than that of saline controls. Delayed epinephrine injections did not significantly improve retention performance. (From Gold and Van Buskirk, 1974b).

the water spout. As shown in Fig. 12, animals which received saline immediately after the footshock avoided the water for approximately 50 sec. However, those animals which received epinephrine after the footshock avoided the water spout for approximately 200 sec. Animals which received the epinephrine at delayed intervals after training did not show significantly improved retention; that is, the memory facilitation was time-dependent. However, at high foot-shock levels which produce very good retention in control animals, the same dose of epinephrine disrupts retention (refer to Fig. 11). Of course, the dose injected after training adds to the natural hormonal response of the animal to training, indicating that there is an inverted-U dose-response curve for memory facilitation. We have obtained similar behavioral results with ACTH and pentylene-tetrazol (Krivanik, 1971; cf. McGaugh, 1973a).

Many hormones are released after footshock, including epinephrine, ACTH, vasopressin, thyroid hormone, and gonadotrophic hormones (cf. Mangili, Motta, & Martini, 1966). At this time all must be considered to be agents which may possibly modulate memory-storage processes, and it now appears that at least some hormones can indeed facilitate or disrupt memory-storage processes. Peripheral alterations have, in general, not been examined as possible underlying mechanisms for retrograde amnesia or facilitation. However, preliminary results suggest that these mechanisms may be important in both amnesia and facilitation and are worthy of further investigation.

V. Concluding Comments

In this paper we have attempted to (1) review some of the conceptual issues involved in studies of retrograde amnesia and retrograde facilitation of memory and (2) summarize recent findings which have implications for the neurobiological bases of memory-storage processes.

The findings of research in this area clearly indicate that retention is modified by treatments administered after training. The modulating influences are clearly time-dependent. Thus, the evidence provides strong support for the hypothesis that memory-storage processes are time-dependent. While there have been several alternative interpretations of the time-dependent posttrial treatment effects, none has as yet replaced the venerable consolidation hypothesis.

However, studies in this area have not as yet provided any understanding of the nature of the processes underlying consolidation. It is not clear whether treatments affect consolidation by modulating short-term memory processes or whether the treatments directly affect long-term storage processes. The results of studies of electrical stimulation of the brain have shown that some correlates, such as brain seizures, play no critical role in modulating storage. But such studies have not revealed the influences which *are* critical in affecting memory. The studies which use stimulation of specific brain regions suggest that brain stimulation can be an effective technique for investigating the role of specific neural systems in modulating memory-storage processes. Recent pharmacological studies have provided additional evidence that drugs can influence memory-storage processes. The major problem facing such studies is that of determining the neurobiological effect which underlies the observed behavioral effect. Obtaining critical evidence to support the current hypotheses *re* the role of protein synthesis, catecholamine synthesis, and hormones in memory storage will be a difficult task. It seems likely, however, that further studies of the neurobiological bases of treatments which modulate memory storage should contribute to an eventual understanding of the neurobiology of memory.

References

Agranoff, B. W. Further studies on memory formation in the goldfish. In J. L. McGaugh (Ed.), *The chemistry of mood, motivation and memory.* New York: Plenum, 1972. Pp. 175–185.

Alpern, H. P., & McGaugh, J. L. Retrograde amnesia as a function of duration of electroshock stimulation. *Journal of Comparative and Physiological Psychology,* 1968, **65,** 265–269.

Barondes, S. H. Multiple steps in the biology of memory. In F. O. Schmitt (Ed.), *The neurosciences.* New York: Rockefeller University Press, 1970. Pp. 272–278.

Barondes, S. H., & Cohen, H. D. Puromycin effect on successive stages of memory storage. *Science,* 1966, **151,** 594–595.

Barondes, S. H., & Cohen, H. D. Arousal and the conversion of "short-term" to "long-term" memory. *Proceedings of the National Academy of Sciences, U.S.,* 1968, **61,** 923–929.

Barondes, S. H., & Squire, L. R. Slow biological processes in memory storage and "recovery" of memory. In J. L. McGaugh (Ed.), *The chemistry of mood, motivation and memory.* New York: Plenum, 1972. Pp. 207–216.

Bloch, V. Facts and hypotheses concerning memory consolidation. *Brain Research,* 1970, **24,** 561–575.

Bresnahan, E., & Routtenberg, A. Memory disruption by unilateral low level, subseizure stimulation of the medial amygdaloid nucleus. *Physiology and Behavior,* 1972, **9,** 513–525.

Buckholtz, N. S., & Bowman, R. E. Incubation and retrograde amnesia studies with various ECS intensities and durations. *Physiology and Behavior,* 1972, **8,** 113–117.

Cherkin, A. Kinetics of memory consolidation: Role of amnesic treatment parameters. *Proceedings of the National Academy of Sciences, U.S.*, 1969, **63**, 1094–1101.

Cherkin, A. Retrograde amnesia in the chick: Resistance to the reminder effect. *Physiology and Behavior*, 1972, **8**, 949–955.

Cotman, C., Banker, G., Zornetzer, S., & McGaugh, J. L. Electroshock effects on brain protein synthesis: Relation to brain seizures and retrograde amnesia. *Science*, 1971, **173**, 454–456.

Dawson, R. G., & McGaugh, J. L. Drug facilitation of learning and memory. In J. A. Deutsch (Ed.), *The physiological basis of memory*. New York: Academic Press, 1973. Pp. 77–111.

Denti, A., McGaugh, J. L., Landfield, P. W., & Shinkman, P. Effects of posttrial electrical stimulation of the mesencephalic reticular formation on avoidance learning in rats. *Physiology and Behavior*, 1970, **5**, 659–662.

Destrade, C., Soumireu-Mourat, B., & Cardo, B. Effects of posttrial hippocampal stimulation on acquisition. *Behavioral Biology*, 1973, **8**, 713–724.

Deutsch, A. J. The cholinergic synapse and the site of memory. In A. J. Deutsch (Ed.), *The physiological basis of memory*. New York: Academic Press, 1973.

Dismukes, R. R., & Rake, A. V. Involvement of biogenic amines in memory formation. *Psychopharmacologia*, 1972, **23**, 17–25.

Duncan, C. P. The retroactive effect of electroshock on learning. *Journal of Comparative and Physiological Psychology*, 1949, **42**, 32–44.

Dunn, A. Brain protein synthesis after electroshock. *Brain Research*, 1971, **35**, 254–259.

Flexner, L. B., Flexner, J. B., & Roberts, R. B. Memory in mice analyzed with antibiotics. *Science*, 1967, **155**, 1377–1383.

Flexner, L. B., Serota, R. G., & Goodman, R. H. Cycloheximide and acetoxycycloheximide: Inhibition of tyrosine hydroxylase activity and amnestic effects. *Proceedings of the National Academy of Sciences, U.S.*, 1973, **2**, 354–356.

Flood, J. F., Bennett, E. L., Rosenzweig, M. R., & Orme, A. E. The influence of duration of protein synthesis on inhibition of memory. *Physiology and Behavior*, 1973, **10**, 555–562.

Ganong, W. F. Catecholamine and the secretion of senin, ACTH, and growth hormone. In E. Usdin and S. H. Snyder (Eds.), *Frontiers in Catecholamine Research*. New York: Pergamon, 1974.

Gehres, L. D., Randall, C. L., Riccio, D. C., & Vardaris, R. M. Attenuation of hypothermic retrograde amnesia produced by pharmacologic blockage of brain seizures. *Physiology and Behavior*, 1973, **10**, 1011–1017.

Geller, A., & Jarvik, M. E. The time relations of ECS-induced amnesia. *Psychonomic Science*, 1968, **12**, 169–170.

Gerard, R. W. Physiology and psychiatry. *American Journal Psychiatry*, 1949, **106**, 161–173.

Gibbs, M. E., & Mark, R. F. *Inhibition of memory formation*. New York: Plenum, 1973.

Glickman, S. E. Preservative neural processes and consolidation of the memory trace. *Psychological Bulletin*, 1961, **58**, 218–233.

Gold. P. E., Bueno, O. F., & McGaugh, J. L. Training and task-related differences in retrograde amnesia thresholds determined by direct electrical stimulation of the cortex in rats. *Physiology and Behavior*, 1973, **11**, 57–63. (a)

Gold, P. E., Edwards, R., & McGaugh, J. L. Amnesia produced by unilateral, subseizure, electrical stimulation of the amygdala in rats, 1974, in preparation. (a)

Gold, P. E., Haycock, J. W., Macri, J., & McGaugh, J. L. Retrograde amnesia and the "reminder effect": An alternative interpretation. *Science,* 1973, **180,** 1199–1201. (b)

Gold, P. E., McDonald, R., & McGaugh, J. L. Direct cortical stimulation: A further study of treatment intensity effects on retrograde amnesia gradient. *Behavioral Biology,* 1974, **10,** 485–490. (b)

Gold, P. E., & McGaugh, J. L. Relationship between amnesia and brain seizure thresholds in rats. *Physiology and Behavior,* 1973, **10,** 41–46.

Gold, P. E., & McGaugh, J. L. A single-trace, two-process view of memory storage processes. In D. Deutsch & A. J. Deutsch (Eds.), *Short term memory.* New York: Academic Press, 1974, in press.

Gold, P. E., Macri, J., & McGaugh, J. L. Retrograde amnesia gradients: Effects of direct cortical stimulation. *Science,* 1973, **179,** 1343–1345. (c)

Gold, P. E., Macri, J., & McGaugh, J. L. Retrograde amnesia produced by sub-seizure amygdala stimulation. *Behavioral Biology,* 1973, **9,** 671–680. (d)

Gold, P. E., & Van Buskirk, R. Facilitation and disruption of memory storage processes with posttrial injections of ACTH and epinephrine. 1974, in preparation. (a)

Gold, P. E. & Van Buskirk, R. Facilitation of time-dependent memory processes with posttrial epinephrine injections. 1974, submitted for publication. (b)

Gold, P. E., Van Buskirk, R., Haycock, J., & McGaugh, J. L. Effects of diethyldithio-carbonate on retention of an inhibitory response in rats. 1974, in preparation. (c)

Gold, P. E., Zornetzer, S. F., & McGaugh, J. L. Electrical stimulation of the brain: Effects on memory storage. In G. Newton & A. Riesen (Eds.), *Advances in psychobiology.* Vol. 2. New York: Wiley (Interscience), 1974, in press. (d)

Hamburg, M. D., & Cohen, R. P. Memory access pathway: Role of adrenergic versus cholinergic neurons. *Pharmacology, Biochemistry & Behavior,* 1973, **1,** 295–300.

Handwerker, M., Gold, P. E., & McGaugh, J. L. Effects of posttrial electrical stimulation of the amygdala on retention of an active avoidance response. *Brain Research,* 1974, in press.

Haycock, J. W., Deadwyler, S. A., Sideroff, S. I., & McGaugh, J. L. Retrograde amnesia and cholinergic systems in the caudate-putamen complex and dorsal hippocampus of the rat. *Experimental Neurology,* 1973, **41,** 201–213. (a)

Haycock, J. W., Gold, P. E., Macri, J., & McGaugh, J. L. Noncontingent footshock "attenuation" of retrograde amnesia: A generalization effect. *Physiology and Behavior,* 1973, **11,** 99–102. (b)

Haycock, J. W., & McGaugh, J. L. Retrograde amnesia gradients as a function of ECS-intensity. *Behavioral Biology,* 1973, **9,** 123–127.

Hebb, D. O. *The organization of behavior.* New York: Wiley, 1949.

Herz, M. J., & Peeke, H. V. S. Impairment of extinction with caudate nucleus stimulation. *Brain Research,* 1971, **33,** 519–522.

Jamieson, J. L. Temporal patterning of electroshock and retrograde amnesia. Unpublished doctoral dissertation, University of British Columbia, 1972.

Kesner, R. P. A neural system analysis of memory storage and retrieval. *Psychological Bulletin,* 1973, **80,** 177–203.

Kesner, R. P., & Connor, H. S. Independence of short- and long-term memory: A neural systems approach. *Science,* 1972, **176,** 432–434.

Kesner, R. P., & Doty, R. W. Amnesia produced in cats by local seizure activity initiated from the amygdala. *Experimental Neurology,* 1968, **21,** 58–68.

Kesner, R. P., & Wilburn, M. W. A review of electrical stimulation of the brain in the context of learning and retention. *Behavioral Biology,* 1974, **10,** 259–293.

Kety, S. S. Brain catecholamines, affective states and memory. In J. L. McGaugh (Ed.), *The chemistry of mood, motivation, and memory.* New York: Plenum, 1972. Pp. 65–80.

Krivanek, J. Facilitation of avoidance learning by pentylenetetrazol as a function of task difficulty, deprivation and shock level. *Psychopharmacologia,* 1971, **20,** 213–229.

Kurtz, P., & Palfai, T. State-dependent learning produced by metrazol. *Physiology and Behavior,* 1973, **10,** 91–95.

Landfield, P. W., McGaugh, J. L., & Tusa, R. J. Theta rhythm: A temporal correlate of memory storage processes in the rat. *Science,* 1972, **175,** 87–89.

Landfield, P. W., Tusa, R., & McGaugh, J. L. Effects of posttrial hippocampal stimulation on memory storage and EEG activity. *Behavioral Biology,* 1973, **8,** 485–505.

Lewis, D. J. Sources of experimental amnesia. *Psychological Review,* 1969, **76,** 461–472.

Lewis, D. J., Misanin, J. R., & Miller, R. R. Recovery of memory following amnesia. *Nature (London),* 1968, **220,** 704–705.

McDonough, J. H., & Kesner, R. P. Amnesia produced by brief electrical stimulation of the amygdala or dorsal hippocampus in cats. *Journal of Comparative and Physiological Psychology,* 1971, **77,** 171–178.

McGaugh, J. L. Time-dependent processes in memory storage. *Science,* 1966, **153,** 1351–1358.

McGaugh, J. L. Drug facilitation of memory and learning. In D. H. Efron, J. O. Cole, J. Levine, and J. R. Wittenborn (Eds.), *Psychopharmacology: A review of progress. 1957–1967.* PHS Publ. No. 1836. Washington, D.C.: U.S. Government Printing Office, 1968. Pp. 891–904. (a)

McGaugh, J. L. A multi-trace view of memory storage. In D. Bovet, F. Bovet-Nitti, & A. Oliverio (Eds.), *Recent advances on learning and retention.* Quaderno N. 109, Anno CCCLXV. Rome: Roma Accademia Nazionale Dei Lincei, 1968. Pp. 13–24. (b)

McGaugh, J. L. Drug facilitation of learning and memory. *Annual Review of Pharmacology,* 1973, **13,** 229–241. (a)

McGaugh, J. L. Modification of learning and memory by CNS stimulants and electrical stimulation of the brain. In F. E. Bloom & G. H. Acheson (Eds.), *Brain, nerves, and synapses.* Fifth International Congress on Pharmacology, Vol. 4. Basel: Karger, 1973. (b)

McGaugh, J. L. Electroconvulsive shock: Effects on learning and memory in animals. In M. Fink, S. S. Kety, J. L. McGaugh, & T. A. Williams (Eds.), *Psychobiology of convulsive therapy.* Washington, D. C.: Winston, 1974, 85–97.

McGaugh, J. L., & Dawson, R. G. Modification of memory storage processes. *Behavioral Science,* 1971, **16,** 45–63.

McGaugh, J. L., & Herz, M. J. *Memory consolidation.* San Francisco: Albion, 1972.

McGaugh, J. L., & Landfield, P. W. Delayed development of amnesia following electroconvulsive shock. *Physiology and Behavior,* 1970, **5,** 1109–1113.

McGaugh, J. L., & Petrinovich, L. F. Effects of drugs on learning and memory. *International Review of Neurobiology,* 1965, **8,** 139–196.

McGaugh, J. L., & Zornetzer, S. Amnesia and brain seizure activity in mice: Effects of diethyl ether anesthesia prior to electroshock stimulation. *Communications in Behavioral Biology, Part A,* 1970, **5,** 243–248.

McGaugh, J. L., Zornetzer, S. F., Gold, P. E., & Landfield, P. W. Modification of memory systems: Some neurobiological aspects. *Quarterly Review of Biophysics,* 1972, **5,** 163–186.

Mah, C. J., & Albert, D. J. Electroconvulsive shock-induced retrograde amnesia: An analysis of the variation in the length of the amnesia gradient. *Behavioral Biology,* 1973, **9**, 517–540.

Mangili, G., Motta, M., & Martini, L. Control of adrenocorticotrophic hormone. In L. Martin & W. Ganong (Eds.), *Neuroendocrinology.* Vol. 1. New York: Academic Press, 1966.

Miller, R. R., & Springer, A. D. Temporal courses of amnesia in rats after electroconvulsive shock. *Physiology and Behavior,* 1971, **6**, 229–233.

Miller, R. R., & Springer, A. D. Amnesia, consolidation and retrieval. *Psychological Review,* 1973, **80**, 69–79.

Mueller, G. E., & Pilzecker, A. Experimentelle beitrage zur lehre von gedachtniss. *Zeitschrift für Psychologie,* 1900, **1**, 1–288.

Nielson, H. C. Evidence that electroconvulsive shock alters memory retrieval rather than memory consolidation. *Experimental Neurology,* 1968, **20**, 3–20.

Osborne, R. H., & Kerkut, G. A. Inhibition of noradrenalin biosynthesis and its effects on learning in rats. *Comparative and General Pharmacology,* 1972, **3**, 359–362.

Paolino, R. M., & Hine, B. EEG seizure anomalies following supramaximal intensities of cortical stimulation: relationships with passive-avoidance retention in rats. *Journal of Comparative and Physiological Psychology,* 1973, **83**, 285–293.

Peeke, H. V. S., & Herz, M. J. Caudate nucleus stimulation retroactivity impairs complex maze learning in the rat. *Science,* 1971, **173**, 80–82.

Pelligrino, L. J., & Cushman, A. J. *A stereotaxic atlas of the rat brain.* New York: Appleton, 1967.

Quartermain, D., McEwen, B. S., & Azmitia, E. C., Jr. Amnesia produced by electroconvulsive shock or cycloheximide: Conditions for recovery. *Science,* 1970. **169**, 683–686.

Randt, C. T., Quartermain, D., Goldstein, M., & Anagnosti, B. Norepinepherine biosyntheses inhibition: Effects on memory in mice. *Science,* 1971, **172**, 498–499.

Routtenberg, A., & Holzman, N. Memory disruption by electrical stimulation of substantia nigra, pars compacta. *Science,* 1973, **181**, 83–86.

Shinkman, P. G., and Kaufman, K. P. Posttrial hippocampal stimulation and CER acquisition in the rat. *Journal of Comparative and Physiological Psychology,* 1972, **80**, 283–292.

Swanson, R., McGaugh, J. L., & Cotman, C. Acetoxycycloheximide effects on one-trial inhibitory avoidance learning. *Communications in Behavioral Biology, Part A,* 1969, **4**, 239–245.

Thompson, C. I., & Neely, J. E. Dissociated learning in rats produced by electroconvulsive shock. *Physiology and Behavior,* 1970, **5**, 783–786.

Van Buskirk, R., Haycock, J., & McGaugh, J. L. Effects of diethyldithiocarbonate on retention of an inhibitory avoidance response in mice. 1974, in preparation.

Van Buskirk, R., & McGaugh, J. L. Pentylenetetrazol-induced retrograde amnesia and brain seizures in mice. *Psychopharmacologia,* in press.

Wyers, E. J., & Deadwyler, S. A. Duration and nature of retrograde amnesia produced by stimulation of caudate nucleus. *Physiology and Behavior,* 1971, **6**, 97–103.

Wyers, E. J., Peeke, H. V. S., Welliston, J. S., & Herz, M. J. Retroactive impairment of passive avoidance learning by stimulation of the caudate nucleus. *Experimental Neurology,* 1968, **22**, 350–366.

Zornetzer, S. F. Brain stem and RA in rats: A neuroanatomical approach. *Physiology and Behavior,* 1972, **8**, 239–244.

Zornetzer, S. F., Chronister, R. B., & Ross, B. The hippocampus and retrograde amnesia: Localization of some positive and negative memory disruptive sites. *Behavioral Biology,* 1973, **8,** 507–518.

Zornetzer, S. F., & McGaugh, J. L. Effects of electroconvulsive shock upon inhibitory avoidance: The persistence and stability of amnesia. *Communications in Behavioral Biology, Part A,* 1969, **3,** 173–180.

Zornetzer, S. F., & McGaugh, J. L. Retrograde amnesia and brain seizures in mice. *Physiology and Behavior,* 1971, **7,** 401–408. (a)

Zornetzer, S. F., & McGaugh, J. L. Retrograde amensia and brain seizures in mice: A further analysis. *Physiology and Behavior,* 1971, **7,** 841–845. (b)

THE LOGIC OF MEMORY REPRESENTATIONS

Endel Tulving and Gordon H. Bower

UNIVERSITY OF TORONTO, TORONTO, ONTARIO, CANADA
AND YALE UNIVERSITY, NEW HAVEN, CONNECTICUT

AND

STANFORD UNIVERSITY, STANFORD, CALIFORNIA

I. Introduction

One of the most pervasive primitive distinctions men have made in their quest for understanding nature has been that between being and becoming, between substance and change. Theoretical specu-

[1] This paper was initiated and partly written while both authors were resident Fellows at the Center for Advanced Study in the Behavioral Sciences in Stanford, California. Gordon Bower's research is supported by the National Institutes of Mental Health, Grant MH-13950, Endel Tulving's by the National Science Foundation, Grant GB-40208X, and by the National Research Council of Canada, Grant A8632. The authors are grateful to Fergus Craik and Ronald Okada for helpful comments on an earlier draft of the paper.

lation in cognitive psychology, too, centers on the dual nature of mind, mind as an entity and mind as a process. A long tradition has held that "contents" of the mind in some sense exist independently of the "processes" that create the contents, change them, and make use of them. Thus, in studying memory we are concerned with two broad questions: what the structure of a memory is, and what processes operate upon it. Although the currently popular information processing approach to remembering has been focused primarily on the functioning of the memory system, it has not entirely neglected the problem of the nature and properties of the information that is processed. One cannot for long continue asking questions about how memory traces are formed, what encoding and recoding consist of, or what the processes of retrieval are like, without wanting to know what it is that is retained in the memory "store" and retrieved from it.

It seems indisputable that something—some thing or some change —endures after an experience has ceased, making possible the subsequent remembering of the experience. That something, whatever its form or substance, is the memory trace. A central problem of long standing has to do with its description. How can it be characterized? On what basis are we to do it? And how are we to know that our descriptions are useful for ordering facts and hypotheses about memory?

The purpose of this essay is to review developments in research on the nature of stored mnemonic information. We will be concerned with questions about the properties of the memory traces, and, specifically, with the problem of how memory traces can be studied. Much evidence has become available recently that is clearly relevant to the nature of representation of information in memory; moreover, interest in the problem is increasing, so a review of the current state of knowledge on this topic might be useful and appropriate.

An introductory section outlining the boundaries of our inquiry will be followed by the major section of the essay, which reviews the methods that have been used in attempts to describe memory traces. In this review we are especially interested in the rules of inference on which investigators have relied in bridging the gap between experimental operations and empirical observations, on the one hand, and the assumed nature and characteristics of the hypothetical memory traces on the other. In the final section we discuss some of the general aims of trace theory in the light of the accomplishments and shortcomings of the research to date.

A. Introspection, Copy Theory, and Trace Strength

Since the problem of representation of memory traces is an old one in psychology, having been anticipated in the works of many philosophers and scholars, a few words are in order about some early ideas. We will mention one popular method for describing memory traces and two popular characterizations of them.

The method is introspection. For a long time it was supposed that the only possible window into the mind was provided by introspection. The proposition that one could look inward and observe the contents of one's perceptions, memories, and thoughts was accepted as self-evident truth. Even today some people still believe that the shape of the mind can be revealed to the inward gaze much as the external world is revealed to immediate sensory experience. The naïve form of this view likens the mind to an architectural structure and introspection to a flashlight beam that lights up portions of otherwise dark goings-on in its nether regions. Such naïve beliefs persist despite the concerted attack by analytic philosophers (e.g., Ryle, 1949) upon the special-status role traditionally assigned to introspection.

Current theories of self-perception and how self-descriptive repertoires are acquired (see Bem, 1972) cast "introspective reports" in an entirely different perspective. The fact that introspections today are no more revealing, precise, or significant than they were in ancient Greek times should have been the signal that the method had its limitations. The major limitation on introspection is that it can tell us something only about the *products* ("conscious contents") of the mind. These products are determined not only by the information stored "in the mind" but also by the operations performed on the stored information to bring it into consciousness. The point is that although introspection can serve as a source of data reflecting certain characteristics of the memory system—as is recall behavior, or reaction time—it does not tell us what the memory traces are like prior to their retrieval. This is why we must reject it as a method for studying memory traces.

One of the two popular characterizations of memory traces is the "copy theory" that stems from introspections about memory images. In a simple form it holds that memory traces are more-or-less perfect copies of input events. Thus, with respect to word-events, the traces have some or all of the same properties as the stimulus words themselves: meaning or meanings, graphemic structure, acoustic pattern, perhaps size, length, spatial position on the display device, and the like. The conceptualization is unsatisfactory for several reasons (see also Pylyshyn, 1973). For one thing, relations among memory units and their properties do not depend solely on the characteristics of the stimuli presented, but also on the kinds of mental activities or encoding operations that the system carries out in dealing with these stimuli. These encoding operations, as yet poorly specified, intervene between perception of a stimulus and the creation of its representation in memory. The encoding process does not just select existing features of the stimulus; it may actively change, elaborate, and restructure the input in a manner that renders the notion of trace as a copy of the initial event rather meaningless. Second, it is difficult to imagine that the memory coding system stores the physical, linguistic, and semantic attributes of a word as such. A great deal of evidence suggests that what is stored is something else and that the attributes of input and output events are only correlated with this something and not identical with it. A memory trace is no more a copy of the input stimulus (or of the retrieved response) than the pattern of magnetization of ferromagnetic particles on a tape is a copy of some spoken message recorded on the tape.

The second popular characterization of memory traces we will reject is that the trace is a unidimensional entity whose sole property relevant to memory phenomena is its strength. This idea served as a part of the foundation of study of memory for centuries, but it has been almost totally abandoned in recent years. The concept of trace "strength" never acquired sufficient surplus meaning to make it anything more than a descriptive term referring to some measurable aspect of memory performance or some transformation of it.

B. LIMITING OUR INQUIRY

Human beings can remember a very large number of things. These include objects, places, events, facts, movements, patterns, relations, feelings, beliefs, and many other aspects of perceptual phenomena and their conceptual correlates. It is quite possible that the internal representations of all of these things, whether immediately experienced or stored in memory, share common properties and are composed of common elements. Eventually a general trace theory may be developed that encompasses the substrata of all mental phenomena. So far, however, most of the evidence about the format and characteristics of memory traces has been derived from research using verbal materials, and hence we will limit our inquiry to representations of verbal symbols such as words.

A further limitation on our inquiry is imposed by the fact that verbal units such as words play a somewhat different role in memory experiments than they do in language. What the subject in a memory experiment has to remember is not the word as such but rather its occurrence in a particular place at a particular time. The properties of a word-event stored in memory thus are not identical with those of the word's representation in the subject's mental lexicon. At the very least, the internal representation of the word-event must contain some additional information not contained in the representation of the word itself, and it is not inconceivable that under certain circumstances the two representations differ drastically. Regardless of whether one finds the distinction between the two classes of memories sufficiently sharp to warrant formalizing the difference (e.g., Tulving, 1972), the distinction between a verbal unit as a meaningful part of language and as a part of a temporally dated and spatially located episode experienced by a person is unavoidable. Given the distinction, the nature of the relation between semantic information and episodic information in the memory store becomes one problem to be dealt with by experiment and theory.

II.   Methods for Studying Memory Traces

A rather general and atheoretical conception of the memory trace of an event regards it as a collection of features or a bundle of information. This view has been proposed and elaborated by many writers (e.g., Anisfeld & Knapp, 1968; Bower, 1967; Bregman & Chambers, 1966; Underwood, 1969; Wickens, 1970) and is now generally accepted as one of the basic pretheoretical assumptions. The consensus also holds that the trace is determined at least by three classes of variables (a) characteristics of the focal element or elements of the event, (b) the conditions and general context of its occurrence, and (c) specific operations performed on the elements-in-context by the system. Different memory performances are supported by different components of this informational collection. Performance may be conceived of as an answer the system supplies in a particular retrieval situation to an explicit or implied query addressed to it (Norman, 1968). It is at least partly a product of the information contained in the query and the information contained in the memory trace. Thus, although the informational content of the memory trace and its specific characteristics are not directly observable, inferences can be made about the trace in terms of the relation between properties of the retrieval situation, including the query, and the properties of observed memory performance.

A wide variety of experimental situations have been used by students of memory as a source of information about the properties of memory traces. In this section of the paper we will briefly review these situations, the nature of evidence derived from them, and the logic used in them. We will refer to these situations as methods, to emphasize the fact that with respect to the problem at hand—specification of properties of traces—the memory experiment serves a special function. It is not used as an instrument for evaluating hypotheses or for determining the effect of a variable X on some aspect of behavior Y. Rather, it is used as a probe to provide information about something that cannot be observed directly.

The methods we will briefly discuss present a reasonably fair cross section of contemporary research. But our listing of the methods is not exhaustive, nor can we pretend that the methods we do discuss are mutually exclusive. Rather than attempting to systematically classify or integrate the various approaches that have been used, an attempt that seems premature now, we will simply try to describe the field as it appears to us. It is somewhat disorganized and fragmented, there are obvious difficulties with language and terminology, and it is not always clear exactly what can be concluded from a given set of data. But the sheer volume of work and the great variety of methods that have been used testify to the importance of the problem. It seems, therefore, appropriate to review this work and these methods.

There are essentially two aspects of mnemonic performance that can be observed in experiments: first, the *contents* of what the subject retrieves (recalls or recognizes) about a particular input; and second, the *time* that he requires for the retrieval of these contents. Thus, all inferences about the nature and characteristics of internal representations are based either on probabilities of various types of retrieved contents (or response classes) or latencies of retrieving these contents. The first method we will consider involves measurement of retrieval times, while the remainder deals with response probabilities.

A. DECISION LATENCIES

When the subject has studied some material, the experimenter can ask him questions about it and record the time he requires to initiate or produce the answer. In initial experiments conducted within an experimental paradigm introduced and developed by Sternberg (1966, 1969) the studied material consisted of simple verbal units—digits, letters, words, and the like—and the questions posed to the subjects concerned nominal identity and order relations among study-set items. In subsequent work by many other investigators, the types of study and test items, as well as to-be-judged relations between them, have been greatly extended to cover a much wider range of possibilities. But most of this work has been directed at questions about processes rather than structure. The basic assumption in this work has been that reaction times reflect the number and complexity of successive steps involved in processing of the information.

A notable exception to this general process-orientation has been the work of Michael Posner. Together with his associates, Posner has been explicitly concerned with "representational systems for storing information in memory" (Posner, 1969b) and has used decision latencies in his own work on memory "codes" (e.g., Posner, 1969a; Posner, Boies, Eichelman, & Taylor, 1969; Posner & Keele, 1967; Posner & Taylor, 1969). In a typical experiment the subject is presented with a single item, such as the capital letter A, which he stores in memory. Then a probe item is presented and the subject decides whether it is the same as or different from the stored item with respect to a particular level of categorization. For example, the two letters may be the "same" if they are physically identical (A and A), if they share the same name (A and a), if they are both vowels (A and E), or if they are both letters (A and E). For a given level, such as "same name" judgments, it has been found that decisions are faster for physical identity matches (A and A) than for the name matches (A and a); however, this difference becomes smaller as the interval increases between the presentation of the stored and the probe item. Such data, together with outcomes of other converging operations, have been interpreted by Posner as suggesting that the initial representation of the study item is in a form closely tied to its physical form, while related information, such as the name or membership in a certain category, becomes available later.

While Posner's work has shown that reasonable inferences about properties of stored information can be made on the basis of decision latencies, certain apparent limitations of the method should be mentioned. First, it is almost always possible to translate any set of statements about the format of some stored information into a set of statements about processing operations carried out on a literal copy of the input, and it is not always easy to decide which set of statements makes more sense. Second, decision latencies in many tasks are known to be drastically changeable by instructions emphasizing either speed or accuracy, and the trade-off between these two aspects of performance may radically change the outcome of experiments (e.g., Lively, 1972). Third, because of these accuracy-speed trade-off relations, the method of decision latencies seems to be limited to situations in which the subjects never make any mistakes in answering the test questions, that is, either to small sets of immediately tested materials or to very well-learned sets of materials tested at any retention interval. Ideally, only a single item should be stored in memory in experiments using decision latencies to make inferences about its characteristics. So far it has been a rare experiment on decision latencies that reports error rates of 0%.

B. MATERIALS VARIATIONS

One method for inferring characteristics of memory traces is employed in experiments varying the type of materials. For example, the events to be remembered might consist in the presentation of a list of words as contrasted to a set of pictured objects whose names are the words of the other list. Paivio (1971) and his associates have consistently found that presentations of object pictures are better remembered than are presentations of their names; furthermore, names of concrete objects are usually remembered better than names of abstract concepts.

The standard inference drawn from these studies is that there are two "representational systems" or two "modes of representation," the imagery system and the verbal system. Pictorial inputs and picturable verbal stimuli are stored in both systems, while verbal inputs, particularly if their referents cannot be readily imagined, are stored only in the verbal system. Retrievability of a stored event is a direct function of the availability of relevant information in one or both systems. Paivio and Csapo (1973), for instance, have shown that free recall of a given name, if both the name and the picture are presented, is predictable by adding up of the contributions from independent verbal and pictorial inputs.

Paivio (1969) has attempted to further distinguish the verbal and imagery systems according to their specialization for handling temporally ordered (sequential) versus unordered information. It has been found, at fast input rates, that whereas pictures exceed words in free (unordered) recall, the reverse holds for serially ordered recall. So, picture codes are said to be effective for item information, whereas sequential word-to-word associations are specialized for reproducing serial-order information. Supporting the conclusions based on the method of materials variations, there is some neurological evidence (see, e.g., Gazzaniga, 1972) that suggests cerebral hemispheric lateralization of verbal versus nonverbal functions.

One logical problem that arises in connection with the method of materials variations concerns the rules for postulating different "memory systems." For instance, modality of presentation is surely one of the attributes about an event that is stored in memory and the evidence is quite clear that retrievability of an event frequently depends upon its modality of presentation. But it is not clear how one gets from this evidence to two "memory systems" or two memory "stores." It seems to us that the evidence for a "visual imagery" store is no better than that for a "tactual store," "olfactory store," "proprioceptive store," "color store," and the like. The question is whether we should postulate a distinct memory system for every discriminable stimulus variable and for every variation of events along values of that variable that produces differences in memory for those events. If we did, we would soon have more memory systems or memory stores than we could name. If we did not, it is necessary to spell out the rules for such postulation when it is deemed appropriate or necessary. In this connection it is also of interest to note that it has not yet been made clear by anyone how the task of explaining memory phenomena is materially aided by the hypothesized existence of different memory stores and systems (cf. Pylyshyn, 1973).

C. ORIENTING TASKS

It is easy to show that recall and recognition of a given word event may depend greatly on the "orienting task" performed by the subject when he studies a word (e.g., Craik, 1973; Hyde & Jenkins, 1969; Till & Jenkins, 1973). For instance, the subject will remember the word much better when he makes some sort of a semantic judgment about it at input than when the judgment entails only the acoustic pattern of the spoken word.

One might want to assume that the nature of the orienting task, or the nature of the encoding operation performed on the input stimulus, determines the characteristics of the memory trace. Thus, a semantic operation creates a trace rich in semantic information, while an "acoustic" task produces a trace with prominent acoustic attributes and relatively lower semantic content. If one further assumes that semantically encoded traces endure longer or that they can be more readily retrieved than acoustically encoded traces, the performance differences resulting from these orienting tasks can be understood. Similar reasoning applies to other tasks and encoding dimensions.

The logic here is plain and simple, and the available data neat and clear. And yet there remains an apparent gap in the reasoning: why do "deeply" encoded traces endure longer, and why do more superficially encoded traces yield lower probabilities of retrieval? Why, for instance, does "semantic" encoding result in higher recall and recognition than "acoustic" encoding? Somehow the matter is intuitively rather obvious, perhaps even too obvious. Whenever such a situation arises, one has to guard against the tendency to achieve understanding merely by labeling the facts differently. As matters stand now, the data on orienting tasks followed by free-recall or recognition tests could quite readily be "explained" in terms of the vacuous concept of trace "strength": certain orienting tasks or encoding operations produce stronger traces and hence greater probability of subsequent retrieval than do some others, as does increasing the study time or reducing the amount of interfering material. References to qualitative differences among traces seem to be superfluous, as long as appropriate converging operations are lacking. Some such converging operations have been performed in terms of measurement of semantic clustering (Hyde & Jenkins, 1969), but the fact that clustering measures, as we will argue later in the paper, are not particularly useful for making inferences about all the properties of stored information, means that there is room left for improvement.

The method of orienting tasks would have to be combined with a more direct manipulation of retrieval conditions before it can be successfully distinguished from other situations in which merely the "strength" of traces is manipulated. Experimental variation of encoding operations is a potentially powerful means for influencing the properties of stored information but assumptions about these properties need to be tested in more specific retrieval conditions than those provided by free-recall or recognition tests.

D. FEATURE REPETITION

If a presented item is repeated in a study list and the subject can subsequently not only recall its name but also knows that it was presented twice (e.g., Madigan, 1969), it seems reasonable to assume that the trace of the item has been somehow changed by repetition. Historically, facilitative effects of repetition on recall and recognition have been interpreted in terms of "strengthened" traces or associations. This approach, as we have mentioned, is not particularly enlightening for it does not encourage further questions about the nature and characteristics of the trace.

More revealing, however, are experimental treatments in which it is not the whole unit that is repeated, but rather a particular feature of the unit (although response measures are still probabilities of recall or recognition of the name of the whole unit). Included here would be two-list paired-associate transfer paradigms denoted as A–B, A–B' (response similarity) and as A–B, A'–B (stimulus similarity). The primed members (A' or B') are related to their unprimed mates (A or B) along any of a number of "similarity dimensions"— semantic, phonetic, orthographic, and the like. In most cases, one expects mutual facilitation of the two pairs, with A–B' being learned faster and A–B being remembered at a higher level than appropriate control pairs. A second set of examples are free-recall experiments showing that conceptually categorized words are more readily recalled than unrelated words.

The facilitative effects of similarity of items along one or more specified dimensions can be interpreted as reflecting either informational overlap among stored traces or mediational processes at the time of retrieval. The former involves references to trace structures or trace characteristics, while the latter implies a particular process of recovery of independently stored information. But the process of mediation, too, must be governed by trace properties, even if relations between traces are conceptualized as independent. Thus the logic of the method of feature repetition holds that facilitative effects of specifiable similarity among to-be-remembered events can be regarded as direct evidence for the events' internal representations containing information correlated with the similarity dimension. The argument is strengthened by the converging operation of presenting a retrieval cue embodying the information common to the stored events. For instance, if a category name serves as an effective retrieval cue, the information it contains can be assumed to overlap with that contained in the representations of the category instances as target items.

Similar reasoning may apply to transfer effects such as those described by Laurence (1970) and Nelson and Rothbart (1972). The

latter authors, for instance, had their subjects learn a paired-associate list consisting of number-word pairs, such as 17–PAIN, and
tested them seven days later. Following the recall test, subjects
learned a second list, in which the same stimulus terms were paired
with homonyms of first-list response terms, such as 17–PANE. Even
when subjects had failed to recall the response PAIN to the stimulus
17 in the first-list recall test, they learned the 17–PANE pair in the
transfer list more rapidly than did control subjects who had earlier
learned an unrelated first list. The interpretation here is that some
information about the acoustic form of the response term from the
17–PAIN pair was retained even though the total amount of available information was insufficient to support recall. The retained
acoustic information may have served as a retrieval cue or a mediator
in the recall of the transfer-list pair. Again, the observed transfer
effect can be used in drawing inferences about features of memory
traces of learned verbal items.

Sometimes feature repetition produces interference rather than
facilitation. Thus, perhaps paradoxically, in some situations evidence for the nature of information available in a memory trace is
derived from observations of performance decrements attributable
to interitem similarity. For instance, Baddeley (1966) showed that
subjects had great difficulty in immediate reconstruction of the serial
order of a short list of acoustically similar words, although they had
no such difficulty when the list items were related semantically or
were unrelated. In one experiment, for instance, subjects had only
10% correct serial reconstructions for acoustically similar words,
65% for semantically related words, and 71% for unrelated lists.
Baddeley concluded from these data that subjects use "an almost
exclusively acoustic coding system" in remembering words over very
short intervals of time.

The reasoning here has never been spelled out in detail. It seems
somehow self-evident that if a variable X has an effect on recall of
certain material while variables W, Y, and Z do not, then the features implicated by X are represented in the trace while those implicated by W, Y, and Z are not. Although many researchers seem
quite content to accept the reasoning without wondering what kind
of a process model would explain interference attributable to stimulus similarity along some but not other dimensions, in the absence
of such a model the logical steps that get us from the data to theory
are uncertain. The consequence is that the implications of findings
for the trace theory have remained questionable.

E. FEATURE PROBING

The subject need not always recall the name or recognize a literal copy of an experimental unit of the material for the experimenter to be able to make inferences about properties of stored traces. Recall of certain other aspects of stored word-events, certain "parts" or features thereof, can also provide useful evidence. Indeed, some of the most widely used techniques for the description of memory traces are of this type.

The most straightforward of the feature probing methods consists in simply asking the subjects questions about specific features, properties, or "tags." Experiments investigating various memory "judgments" rely on this method (e.g., Hintzman & Block, 1971; Kirsner, 1974; Light, Stansbury, Rubin, & Linde, 1973). During testing the subject is shown a whole item and asked to judge its earlier frequency of occurrence in the list, or its recency, mode of presentation (visual or auditory, verbal or pictorial, male or female voice, etc.), and other attributes of this kind. To the extent that subjects can accurately provide this information, the inference can be made that the relevant features were stored as part of the memory trace of the item.

One problem with the method of feature probing concerns the distinction between direct and derived information, a problem shared by many other methods. In the present context it refers to the possibility that feature X is not directly represented in the trace but rather judgments made about feature X are derived from evidence about feature Y. Thus, for instance, some researchers (e.g., Morton, 1968; Peterson, Johnson, & Coatrey, 1969) have argued that recency judgments can be based on information about the "strength" of the memory trace where strength reflects the consequences of some other factor, such as frequency of repetition. Thus, the argument would be that recency information need not be directly contained in the memory trace and that it can be derived from some other feature of the trace. Another possible limitation of the method lies in the fact that it can provide information only about those memory traces that can be successfully retrieved in response to a literal copy of the stored verbal item; that is, the method requires item recognition as a precondition for the judgment about its features. But we know of circumstances in which whole-item recognition fails when the context is changed (e.g., Tulving & Thomson, 1973) yet the subject probably could satisfactorily respond

to certain feature probes provided the test conditions insured contact with the trace. Finally, possible trade-off between information
about various physical features and the names of word-events may
create complications in interpreting data. Madigan and Doherty
(1972), for instance, have shown that subjects retain modality and
frequency information about words only at the expense of the ability
to freely recall the names of words.

F. RECALL INTRUSIONS

A popular technique for studying memory traces has been based
on the examination of the errors subjects make while recalling. In
a classic paper, Conrad (1964) reported an analysis of intrusion
errors in recall of visually presented strings of consonants. These
errors were highly systematic, with incorrect responses being similar
acoustically to the correct item. Conrad suggested that the memory
traces of the visually presented consonants in his experiment had
an "acoustic or verbal basis" (p. 82). Similar data and comparable
conclusions were reported by Wickelgren (1965). Although it is
possible to argue that "acoustic" confusions in recall are not caused
by acoustic overlap but rather by motor overlap of the articulatory
musculature in vocalizing the items (Hintzman, 1967), and although
there is evidence that acoustic confusion errors can be eliminated
by suppressing vocalization (e.g., Estes, 1973), the phenomenon of
recall intrusions is a real one. Moreover, it is by no means limited
to the acoustic dimension in very short-term retention of order information. When subjects are presented with categorized words for
free recall, for instance, most intrusion errors are new words from
the presented conceptual categories (e.g., Tulving & Pearlstone,
1966), implying that part of the stored information used at recall
is category-specific but not item-specific.

It is assumed that recall intrusions reflect the properties of stored
information. The logic here is that traces of any two events, A and
B, contain both features that distinguish them from one another
and features that are common to them. If the distinguishing features
are lost but the common ones retained, B may be given as an intrusion in place of A.

One problem with the method of recall intrusions lies in the
uncertainty whether all incorrect responses convey information
about what has been stored, or whether only some of them do.
Frequently an item cannot be recalled and the subject makes no
overt response whatsoever, although his ability to recognize the

same item implies existence of some appropriate information in the store at the time of the test. Why then does the subject not use that information for "guessing" the item in the recall situation? "To guess or not to guess" a response requires among other things some kind of internal criterion set by the subject, presumably on the basis of payoff incentives and penalties for intrusions. To the extent that "pure guesses" occur, the intrusion data will be contaminated by some random noise and to a degree varying with explicit or implicit payoffs. It is not obvious how to "correct" intrusion data for such guesses.

G. FALSE POSITIVE RECOGNITION ERRORS

One of the most popular methods has involved the analysis of errors in recognition tests. When a subject in a memory experiment makes an error of incorrectly identifying a new test item as old, it can be assumed that he does so because the test item shares certain critical features with one or more actually presented list items and that the incorrect identification of the test item as old is based on its informational overlap with the stored information in terms of these specific features. The method has been applied to recognition of individual words (e.g., Anisfeld & Knapp, 1968; Eagle & Ortof, 1967; Fillenbaum, 1969; Underwood, 1965; Walter, 1973) as well as sentences (e.g., Begg & Paivio, 1969; Bransford & Franks, 1971; Kosslyn & Bower, 1974; Sachs, 1967). Much of the work done with this technique is simply to demonstrate that systematic recognition errors are made and that the results are consistent with the notion that words and other verbal units are stored as bundles or collections of features. But some more analytical work has also been done, investigating how the features of stored units, as estimated from recognition errors, are affected by experimental treatments. Eagle and Ortof (1967) studied the effect of distracting the subject during input on the characteristics of resulting memory traces; Cermak, Schnorr, Buschke, and Atkinson (1970) and Elias and Perfetti (1973) examined the effect of different encoding operations on the types of later recognition errors; Anisfeld (1970) found that presentation of to-be-remembered nouns in meaningful adjective-noun phrases rendered antonyms as lures ineffective, although in earlier experiments (e.g., Anisfeld & Knapp, 1968; Fillenbaum, 1969) antonyms had been found to be as effective distractors as had been synonyms; and Bach and Underwood (1970) have reported relative rates of decay in features of stored information over time.

Since this is a popular method, likely to be even more widely used in the future, it is particularly important that the rules of inference connecting the data to the theory be worked out and made clear. It sounds plausible enough to say that subjects are more likely to identify new items as old if these new items share certain critical features with the traces of old items, but obviously it cannot be simply the amount of overlap between the sets of features of traces and test items that is responsible for false positive responses. The following thought experiment illustrates the problem. Suppose that a subject is shown a word, asked to remember it, and then immediately presented a probe word that is either a close synonym of the first word, a homonym, or is very similar in orthography to the first word. Our hypothetical subject is asked whether this was the word that he just saw before. With sane adults, there will surely be no false positive responses, even though there would be considerable overlap between the old word and the probe word. The hypothetical result means that the subject's recognition response depends not only upon the similarity or overlap of certain features, but also on the differences in memorable properties between the trace and the probe item. Thus, only if the subject lacks appropriate information about these uniquely identifying features—if he has "forgotten" them—might he make a recognition error on the basis of remembered overlapping features.

To consider an important implication of this explanation, let us entertain the simple assumption (although there is good evidence that the assumption is wrong) that the subject makes recognition judgments only on the basis of two kinds of information about a word, information corresponding to phonetic and semantic attributes. After studying a target word (e.g., CHAIR), the subject will be presented with two new test words, one phonetically related to the target (e.g., PAIR), the other semantically related (e.g., TABLE). If the features are remembered as all-or-none descriptors, then the subject should never identify both the phonetically related *and* the semantically related lure as old, since the "recognition" of one test word on the basis of one feature is predicated upon the absence of the other feature. Indeed, given that the subject identifies either of these two lures as old, he should not be expected to be able to identify the original target item as old any more readily than he identifies any test item possessing the critical features. In strictest terms, these implications depend upon all-or-none retention of the attributes and are based on decision rules like those conjectured by Bower (1967). Were the retention of each attribute a "more-or-less" matter of strength, then all patterns of false alarms to phonetic or semantic lures are possible, with probability of accepting a given lure as "old" varying directly with the retention level of its overlapping attributes and inversely with retention of the nonoverlapping attributes. In any case, for a given subject, one should expect a negative correlation in false positives to lures whose overlap with the target item is based on different features.

Another problem with reliance on false positive errors is that of the independence of or overlap between different features. For instance, in experiments concerned with the "acoustic" attribute, experimenters frequently use homophonic or rhyming words as test lures. Now, in most natural languages there is a high correlation between the pronunciation and the spelling of a word; therefore, when effects of "acoustic similarity" have been demonstrated with visual stimuli, the experimenter can not be sure that his results are not due to orthographic similarity instead. Indeed, some evidence has already been described, both with the false positive technique (Raser, 1972) and the clustering method (Jacoby & Goolkasian, 1973), suggesting that the confounding between acoustic and orthographic similarity has to be taken into account in interpreting outcomes of experiments.

The problem of information overlap between features becomes considerably more complicated when the features cannot be described with reference to identifiable properties of the physical stimulus. For instance, how are we to classify semantic information? How many different "kinds" of semantic information are there? Experimenters have sometimes distinguished between categories of semantic features, using contrasts such as synonyms versus antonyms (e.g., Anisfeld, 1970; Anisfeld & Knapp, 1968) and have found that the two types of semantic lures behave differently under different experimental conditions. But this sort of classification of semantic relations between words has only limited usefulness because most words have neither synonyms nor antonyms. What is needed is a satisfactory taxonomy of "semantic" information which can then be validated through memory experiments.

H. Clustering in Recall

When the material to be remembered consists of a collection of randomly selected items and the subjects are required only to remember the membership of items in the collection and to produce their responses in any convenient order ("free recall"), the actual

order that they use has sometimes been assumed to contain information about the characteristics of stored information. The logic
here is that when items share a common feature, that feature may
govern the ordering of the items in output, and that, therefore,
clustering of recall on the basis of an objectively identifiable characteristic of items is evidence for the presence of the corresponding
feature in the traces of items. For instance, Frost (1971) observed
clustering of pictorial items according to the spatial orientation of
objects depicted. She argued that information about pictures was
stored in "visual" form and that orientation of objects is one of the
dimensions of organization (we would say one of the features of
memory traces). Clustering scores were also used by Jacoby and
Goolkasian (1973) to argue that semantic coding is more effective
than (we would say, preferred to) acoustic coding in free recall.

Since clustering of items with respect to one attribute usually
precludes clustering on the basis of other attributes that nevertheless
might be represented in memory traces of retrieved items, the
method is not well suited for describing traces in all their presumed
richness and variety. Temporal succession of responses imposes, by
its very nature, a one-dimensional bottleneck on the amount of
information that can be gleaned from the data. Moreover, at present
there is little agreement as to what are "legitimate" measures of
clustering that should be used, and attempts to modify the method
to permit quantitative statements about clustering along several dimensions seem fruitless. The method may turn out to have some
usefulness, however, when used in conjunction with other methods,
as one of several converging operations.

I. Two-Component Analysis

This method has been used in attempts to distinguish between
primary and secondary memory (or short-term and long-term stores).
The method is often combined with the single-trial free-recall paradigm. Several different variants share the following general procedure. A serial position curve is constructed from the recall data
obtained under condition X and another one under condition Y.
For instance, condition X might be defined by a slow rate of presentation of words; condition Y, by a fast rate. Comparison of the
two curves shows no difference in recall of items from the last few
positions in the list, while items from earlier positions are better
recalled in the slow-rate condition (e.g., Murdock, 1962). As a second
illustration, condition X might be immediate recall, while Y might

be delayed recall (e.g., Glanzer & Cunitz, 1966): the finding here is that response probability for items from terminal positions is higher under X than Y, while response probability for preterminal items is not affected.

Logically it is clear that if a variable has an effect on recall of one component of performance (for instance, earlier list items) but not on that of another component (for instance, late items), the two components must in some way be different. Since recall of any item depends both on its trace and on the conditions under which recall takes place, however, it does not logically follow that the differential effect of a variable on two components of recall performance necessarily implicates traces of items making up the two components. The data are equally consistent with the possibility that retrieval information is differentially effective for the two components of recall, whereas their traces are indistinguishable.

Nevertheless, the two-component analysis has been used to supply evidence for the existence of two memory stores. We mention it in the present context because of the prevalence of the assumption that the properties of information in the two memory stores must be different. Most of these differences have usually been specified in terms of process models (for a reasonably complete listing, see Table 1 in Craik & Lockhart, 1972), but attempts have also been made to specify stored information in primary and secondary memory in terms of particular trace properties (e.g., Baddeley & Patterson, 1971; Kintsch & Buschke, 1969).

We do not quite understand the logic that ties the results of experiments based on two-component analyses to the postulated existence of different memory "stores." Many researchers seem to have assumed, on the basis of what to us appears an intuitive theory, that if a variable has an effect on one component of recall performance, but no effect or an opposite effect on the other, *and* if there is no other explanation for this result, then a store containing information of a sort that corresponds to the critical variable can be postulated to explain the dual effect of the variable. Thus, study time per item affects one component but not the other, but since there are many theories that can account for the effects of study time no one has proposed separate stores for fast and slowly presented items. Instead, the invariance of recall of late input items with changes in the rate of presentation is built into the theory as a defining characteristic of the short-term store (Atkinson & Shiffrin, 1968; Waugh & Norman, 1965). On the other hand, since there is no other theory that can account for the differences in recall between auditorily and visually presented items, separate stores for these two kinds of input are also postulated (e.g., Murdock & Walker, 1969). Similarly, if it is found that acoustic similarity affects recall of only one component, while semantic similarity affects recall of the other component, and no acceptable theory exists to accommodate these facts, two "stores" are created, one being primarily acoustic and the other being primarily semantic (Kintsch & Buschke, 1969). The exact reasoning bridging the data and theory in this case has always remained unspecified.

What seems to be sorely needed are unequivocal statements as to the assumptions that are made about processing of mnemonic information in a particular task and how this processing is affected by the nature of stored and available information to produce the observed outcome. In the absence of such statements, or an appropriate process model, inferences from the data to theory give rise to bothersome questions. Why, for instance, does the presence of an item in the early part of the list that is acoustically similar to an item in a late input position produce acoustic interference in the short-term store, if the information stored about the early item, at the time of retrieval, is primarily semantic (Kintsch & Buschke, 1969)? Why is it necessary to manipulate acoustic similarity among list items at all in order to demonstrate that acoustic interference occurs in retrieval of information about the terminal list items and their order?

J. Attribute Shifts

This is another extremely popular method, growing out of an experiment by Wickens, Born, and Allen (1963) and adopted by Wickens (1970, 1972) as the central methodological and conceptual tool for identifying and measuring encoding dimensions of stored materials, usually words. Since the method and its associated literature are widely known and readily accessible (Wickens, 1970, 1972), we will not recount the details of the method and the data. Some other comments, however, are in order.

Wickens' method provides an interesting example of a technique that works although no one is very sure why it does. The increase in recall on the shift trial has been referred to as a demonstration of "release from proactive inhibition," but this label is essentially an historical anachronism, related to initial attempts (e.g., Keppel & Underwood, 1962) to provide a theoretical interpretation of short-term forgetting observed in the Brown-Peterson paradigm in terms of the concept of proactive inhibition. Few people any longer hold the view that in the Wickens paradigm any proactive inhibition is "released." Since the label of "release from proactive inhibition" is cumbersome, we will refer to the method and paradigm as attribute shifts.

On what grounds can we assume that increments in recall on the shift trial signify the presence of information corresponding to shifted attributes as components of memory traces? Since the explanation of the shift effect is still obscure, the logic that ties data to theory is mostly intuitive. It contains at least two identifiable components. One, it depends on the absence of an obviously meaningful answer to the question about the alternative: if attribute shifts do not signify trace properties, what do they do? As long as the answer to the question is uncertain, the idea seems entirely reasonable that the "shift procedure may be used as something of a projective technique of organization in STM; a way of asking S what response classes are being employed without requiring him to identify and label them (Wickens & Clark, 1968, pp. 580–581)." The other component of the intuitive logic depends on the absence of an alternative explanation of the shift effect. Imagine, for instance, the outcome of the following thought experiment. The control group is tested on four trials with randomly selected trigrams, presented at the rate of 1 sec/item, and they show the typical "build-up of proactive inhibition" results. The experimental group is presented with the same materials under identical conditions, except that on the fourth critical trial the trigram is presented for a much longer study time, say 10 sec. Presumably the experimental group recalls that trigram better than the control group, thus producing a pattern of data that is identical with the "release" phenomenon. But since it is obvious that the increase simply reflects increased study time, the result is neither interesting nor informative with respect to composition of the underlying memory traces. Since an equally "obvious" explanation of the typical shift effects is lacking, the intuitive logic relating the effects to characteristics of encoding dimensions somehow becomes more respectable.

The standard explanation of the shift effects and their relevance to coding theory becomes complicated in the light of the data reported by Gardiner, Craik, and Birtwistle (1972) and recently replicated by Maureen O'Neill and Judith Sutcliffe at Toronto. These researchers demonstrated that it is possible to obtain large amounts of "release from proactive inhibition" under conditions where the changes in the presented material were identical for the experimental and the control groups on the critical trial. In addition to the standard control group, there were two experimental groups in the Gardiner *et al.* experiment. The two experimental groups and the control group were shown exactly the same material on all trials, including the critical "shift" trial. One experimental group was given special instructions about the nature of the input material on the shift trial, permitting the subjects in that group to encode the presented word triad differently from the encoding format presumably used by the control subjects. This experimental group showed a large increment in their recall on the shift trial. The second experimental group was given no special instructions at input on the critical trial. Subjects in this group, therefore, must have encoded the presented word triad identically with the control group, which also received no special instructions. But they were told about the special characteristics of the words presented on the critical trial just before they started to recall these words (for instance, that the words had all been names of garden flowers, rather than just flowers, or that the words referred to outdoor games, rather than just games). This group, too, showed a large increment in recall, that is, a typical shift effect.

The Gardiner *et al.* finding demonstrates several important points. First, the shift effects can be obtained in the Wickens paradigm even when the experimental group receives the same material on the critical trial as does the control group and even when the two groups encode this material identically. Thus, at least in this situation the shift effect must signify something other than the changes of the input along some encoding dimension represented in the memory trace. Unless we assume that the trace was modified through retrieval instructions—an assumption yet to be validated—we must conclude that shiftlike effects can occur independently of the format of stored information. This conclusion suggests the possibility that in typical shift studies, too, in which some aspect of the study material is changed on the shift trial, the shift effect signifies something more, or other, than the difference, along some encoding dimension, between traces of earlier presented materials and traces of the input on the shift trial.

The second implication of the Gardiner *et al.* results is that not all possible semantic encodings of to-be-remembered items are automatically activated when the items are presented. Calling subjects' attention to a particular feature of the critical word triad only at the time of retrieval permitted the subjects to recall the stored material more efficiently. This fact suggests that the typically observed "build-up of proactive inhibition" effects, such as those shown by control groups in the Wickens paradigm, may reflect a loss in the effectiveness of retrieval cues rather than less efficient storage of items on later trials. The extra retrieval information provided to the subjects at the time of recall could act either as a search restrictor or as an added discriminator to help the system find and select the specified recent-event traces in the episodic memory (cf. Bower, 1967, p. 318).

A final problem concerning the interpretation of attribute shift data from the point of view of description of internal representation of perceived events has to do with the independence or overlap among identified attributes. The problem is by no means unique to this method alone. A typical example is the observation that changing both the number of syllables per item and number of phonemes per item produces equal shift effects (Wickens, 1970). Since we know that a high correlation exists between these two attributes, we are not surprised to see one effective when the other one is. But the issue of independence becomes harder to decide with other attributes. For instance, shifting polarity of words as judged by the semantic differential, both within a dimension (e.g., Wickens & Clark, 1968) and between dimensions (Turvey & Fertig, 1970), and changing the taxonomic category on the shift trial (e.g., Loess, 1967), produce sizable shift effects. To what extent are these variables effective for the same reason? Do these manipulations tap roughly the same type of mnemonic information? It seems intuitively obvious that shifts in conceptual categories entail shifts in polarity of connotative meaning. Therefore, the finding of category shift effect may be redundant with the finding of the effect of the shift in connotative meaning, but the issue cannot be decided by armchair criteria. Some technique is needed by which overlap between encoding dimensions whose shifts are effective can be assessed and quantified. Evaluation of shift effects produced by variables X and Y individually as well as concurrently, as has been done by Goggin and Wickens (1971), for example, seems to provide one needed converging operation that may be useful in such assessment and quantification.

K. RETRIEVAL CUEING

The last technique we will consider is the method of retrieval cueing. The subject studies a list of items that includes a target T. Then he attempts to retrieve the trace of T in the presence of different retrieval cues. These cues vary in their effectiveness in providing access to the trace and thus producing the desired response. The effectiveness of a cue is assumed to reflect the informational overlap between the trace and the cue, and the trace can be described in terms of the pattern of effectiveness of various retrieval cues, that is, their informational overlap with the trace.

As an illustration, consider data from an experiment reported by Thomson and Tulving (1970). Subjects tried to recall target words that had appeared in a list either singly or in the company of other words, the list cues. Recall was measured (a) in the absence of any specific cues (in response only to free-recall instructions), (b) in the presence of the list cues, or (c) in the presence of strong associates of target words that had not appeared anywhere in the list. The recall probabilities, measures of cue effectiveness, are shown in Table I. The nominal target words were identical in all six experimental conditions. Recall probabilities shown in Table I, therefore, reflect only the effects of encoding and retrieval operations performed on target words.

The pattern of three retrieval probabilities associated with each of the two encoding conditions in Table I describes, although in a rather modest sense, the properties of the traces stored under those conditions. In Table I, data are pooled over many individual target words and cues, but they do illustrate the general assumptions underlying the method of retrieval cueing. First, the effectiveness of any cue—its informational overlap with the trace—depends on the properties of the trace as encoded rather than just the properties of the original to-be-remembered words. Second, the pattern of cue effectiveness provides more detailed information about the properties of the traces than would be available in retention tests in which the retrieval information is either unspecifiable, is held constant experimentally, or both. Third, similarities and differences between various traces manifest themselves in the patterns of cue effectiveness.

TABLE I

PROBABILITIES OF RETRIEVAL OF TARGET WORDS PRESENTED IN TWO ENCODING CONDITIONS AND RECALLED IN THREE RETRIEVAL CONDITIONS[a]

Encoding condition	Retrieval condition		
	No cues	List cues	Strong associates
Single targets	.49	.43	.68
Targets with list cues	.30	.83	.23

[a] Data from Thomson and Tulving (1970, Experiment 2, List 3).

Two traces may be compared to one another with respect to the effectiveness of any one of a number of specific retrieval cues.

Several researchers have already reported data on effectiveness of different types of retrieval cues (e.g., Anderson, 1972; Bahrick, 1969; Bregman, 1968; Ghatala & Hurlbut, 1973; Light, 1972; Nelson & Brooks, 1974), and a somewhat different variant of the method was used by Shulman (1970), but the technique has not yet been fully developed. For one thing, the work so far has all been done on the composite trace of many different items rather than identical items. Secondly, the method suffers from the shortcoming we have already met: the indeterminacy of independence of different cues. If a very large number of cues are effective to a smaller or larger extent in providing access to the trace, the description of the trace in terms of the pattern of cue effectiveness, in addition to being cumbersome, may be highly redundant in unknown ways. We might attribute to the trace a property X without knowing that it is the same as another assigned property Y, simply because two apparently different retrieval cues, X and Y, were effective in providing access to the trace. The problem is to estimate to what extent two cues, X and Y, contain the same information.

One method that can be used, in conjunction with the method of retrieval cueing, to assess the overlap among cues, with respect to a given trace, consists in probing the trace with two or more different cues in succession. We will refer to it as the *reduction method*. The basic idea is as follows. Given a trace T, it is probed first with Cue X and then with Cue Y. The same operation is also performed on the same trace in the opposite sequence—first with Cue Y, then with X. To the extent that the first cue X is effective, the informational content of the trace becomes known and the amount of unknown information in the trace is reduced. The effectiveness, or valence, of the second cue Y with respect to the reduced trace— the part of the original trace T not retrieved by Cue X—can be compared with its valence with respect to the original trace, that is, under conditions when it is used as the first cue. If the informational content of Cue Y entirely overlaps with, or is completely included in, the information contained in Cue X, Cue Y will be totally ineffective when applied to the trace reduced by Cue X, for the same reason that Cue X would be ineffective in retrieving that part of the trace with which it does not overlap. If, on the other hand, informational content of Cue Y has no overlap at all with Cue X, Cue Y is expected to be as effective with respect to the reduced trace as the original trace. Between these two extreme possibilities intermediate conditions of overlap or independence between X and Y can be imagined and quantitatively assessed.

A simple set of data from an imaginary experiment may help to clarify the relations between two Cues X and Y and illustrate the logic of the reduction method. The imaginary experiment is rather like the one reported by Tulving and Watkins (1974), except that it entails two successive cued-recall tests. Subjects study a list of five-letter words, such as GRAPH and STEAM, and are then tested for recall of these target words in the presence of either two or four initial letters of target words as retrieval cues. Let X designate the four-letter cues (GRAP-, STEA-) and Y the two letter cues (GR - - -, ST - - -). In one condition, subjects are first tested with Cue X, and then with Y, their task being in each case to retrieve target words specified by the cues, while in the other condition the first pass through the data store is done with Cue Y and the second pass with X. Logically, all information contained in Cue Y (e.g., GR - - -) is contained in the corresponding Cue X (GRAP-), and although we have reasons to believe, on the basis of some preliminary experiments done by Michael and Olga Watkins at Yale, that actual data may slightly depart from the logic, we will let the results of our imaginary experiment faithfully reflect the logical relations. These data are tabulated in Table II.

The left-hand panel of Table II gives the data for the condition where Cue X was presented first and Cue Y second, while the right-hand panel depicts the other sequence, Cue Y followed by Cue X. Each panel shows the probabilities of recall and nonrecall of target words in the presence of cues both in the first and in the second test. Thus, for instance, 70% of targets were recalled in the presence

TABLE II

EFFECTIVENESS OF TWO RETRIEVAL CUES IN TWO SUCCESSIVE TESTS
IN A HYPOTHETICAL EXPERIMENT[a,b]

| | | Second test | | | | | Second test | | |
| | | Cue Y: two letters | | | | | Cue X: four letters | | |
First test		R	$\bar{R}$	Total	First test		R	$\bar{R}$	Total
Cue X:	R	.28	.42	.70	Cue Y:	R	.28	.00	.28
Four letters	$\bar{R}$	.00	.30	.30	Two letters	$\bar{R}$	.42	.30	.72
	Total	.28	.72	1.00		Total	.70	.30	1.00

[a] Data are proportions of target items retrieved in the presence of given cues.
[b] R and $\bar{R}$ designate recall and nonrecall, respectively.

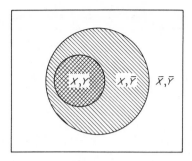

Fig. 1.   Venn diagram depicting informational overlap between the trace and two cues, X and Y. The diagram corresponds to the data shown in Table II. A part of the trace information overlaps with information in both cues (X, Y) and another part overlaps with Cue X but not Y $(X, \overline{Y})$. A certain amount of trace information overlaps with neither X nor Y $(\overline{X}, \overline{Y})$.

of four-letter cues, both when these cues were given first and when they were given second. In terms of the assumptions of the reduction method this means that 70% of the information contained in Cue X overlaps with the information contained in the (composite) trace of the target words. Two-letter cues were effective 28% of the time in both tests. (Such invariance is seldom observed in real experiments.) When two-letter cues had failed to retrieve target items, which happened 72% of the time, then, as can be seen in the right-hand panel, four-letter cues were nevertheless effective in .42/.72 or 58% of the cases. That is, the effectiveness of Cue X with respect to the trace reduced by Cue Y was 58%. This figure compares with the 70% effectiveness of Cue X with respect to the original trace. At the same time, no two-letter cue was effective after the four-letter cue had failed, as shown in the left-hand panel. Thus, in this particular example, the nature of the overlap between the two kinds of cue was such that all the information contained in two-letter cues was also contained in four-letter cues, while the latter contained some other information as well. This state of affairs can be expressed in the form of a Venn diagram as shown in Fig. 1. The total area represents the informational content of the original trace. The small circle (subset X, Y) corresponds to the information common to Cue X, Cue Y, and trace T; the area outside the small circle is the trace reduced by information in Cue Y; the large circle ($X,Y +$ X,Y) refers to the informational overlap between the trace and Cue X; and the area outside the large circle is the trace reduced by information in Cue X. The diagram also shows that all of the informational content of Cue Y (and the corresponding trace information) is included in the informational content of Cue X.

While the data from real experiments are more complex than those in our imaginary example, and while their interpretation entails many pesky problems that require solutions, the logic and reasoning is the same in all cases. Given any two cues, X and Y, their independence or informational overlap can be assessed by means of the reduction method. It does not matter what the cues are. The logic holds whether X is the set of "invisible" cues that can be assumed to be present in the free-recall situation or whether it is the literal copy of the target item in a recognition test. It is always possible to estimate to what extent informational content of one cue is included in the informational content of another. Indeed, the reduction method should in principle be capable of specifying the characteristics of retrieval information in situations in which these characteristics are not obvious, such as in free-recall tests. The retrieval information in the free-recall test, for instance, could be specified by the difference of effectiveness of various cues administered before and after the free-recall test.

We see the retrieval cueing as one of the more promising methods for studying properties of memory traces. It has obvious similarities to the method of false positive recognition errors, but it is more direct and hence more incisive. The false positive data are usually obtained as a by-product of recognition tests, their density is often very low, the subject makes such errors only to the extent that he has lost information about the actual input, and the experimenter does not really ever know for sure why the subject checks a new test item as "old." The method of retrieval cueing represents a task where subjects' responses reflect retention of stored information rather than its loss and where the experimenter can directly observe the products of retrieval. Moreover, the method of retrieval cueing can be combined with the reduction method to estimate overlap and independence among identified components of the trace. Quantitative assessment of such independence seems to be indispensable for an economical description of properties of memory traces.

III. Some Objectives of Trace Theory

The survey of approaches to the study of memory traces points to both accomplishments and problems that delineate further objectives for research. Some of the problems awaiting solution have already been mentioned in connection with specific methods. A major difficulty with a number of methods lies in the absence of clear rules for inferring properties of traces from the data. Ideally, these rules should be spelled out in the light of explicitly stated pretheoretical ideas about the nature of memory traces, and, more important, specified in conjunction with appropriate process models that describe how the trace information is used by the memory system. Another important problem concerns the development of a suitable language for describing memory traces. In this last section of the paper we will, after briefly considering the relation between trace information and the process of retrieval, say a few words about the taxonomy of trace attributes and the necessity of process models.

A. Traces and Retrieval

We began this review with a reference to the fundamental natural dichotomy between structure and function, between what things are and what they do, and we suggested that the dichotomy applies to memory, too. We did so in order to focus attention squarely on the problem of what is retained in memory after the original event is gone and before its recollection occurs, and how this something, memory trace, can be studied and described. Throughout this review we have referred to memory traces as entities having certain properties, as consisting of features and attributes, or as being made up of aggregates of informational elements of as yet unknown nature. We have, in short, talked about memory traces as things. We did so, too, in order to emphasize our concern with the aspect of the memory system that is not its activity but rather its "nonactive" part. But after having discussed the traces in this vein, we wish now to suggest that it probably will make little sense, in the long run, to persist in the attempts to define or characterize memory traces in terms of what they *are*. Rather, their description must be given in terms of what they *do*.

Once we adopt the attitude toward memory traces as a component of mental activity, it becomes immediately clear that memory traces do not do anything by themselves. They only act in combination with other processes. We do not yet know what all the other relevant processes are, but we have a fair idea that some of them are in an important way involved in retrieval, in utilization of stored information. Since memory traces do not possess independent existence and only manifest themselves in combination with retrieval processes, the interrelation between stored information and condi-

tions of retrieval cannot be ignored by anyone interested in the
format and characteristics of memory traces. To study the interrelation, conditions under which retrieval takes place must be systematically varied. The stratagem of postulating some "normal"
retrieval conditions, such as free recall or whole-item recognition,
and then observing the performance under these conditions, will
not do. Since the "old" item in the recognition test shares many
attributes with the target item, it cannot be known which one of
these, or which combination, is entered into the interaction with
stored information that will lead to retrieval of the trace. Moreover, recognition does not necessarily bypass retrieval processes to
directly assess what is available in the store (Tulving & Thomson,
1973). Nor is free recall a cue-free situation; rather, it is a condition
containing largely uncontrolled variations in the implicit cues on
which the system relies for retrieval. Performance in the presence
of experimentally manipulated retrieval cues, on the other hand,
provides different perspectives of a given memory trace. If the stored
event has any complexity at all, then its trace can be tapped in
various ways to yield a large variety of performances. It is the pattern
of performances, observed under systematically varied retrieval conditions, that provides a description of what a given trace does. The
trace thus becomes a hypothetical construct we use to pull together
this large list of relations between different questions directed at
the system and the output from the system.

The definition of the trace as a set of question-output relations
has obvious implications for methods used for studying properties
of traces. For one thing, methods that do not vary retrieval conditions are not likely to succeed. If output conditions are held constant, the characteristics of the trace can only be described in terms
of characteristics of the input, plus a single measure of performance.
The result is the copy theory, combined with the notion of
"strength" of the trace reflected in its retrievability. The impover-
ished picture of the memory trace emerging from such an approach
will have difficulty doing justice to the great variety of memory
phenomena and memory performances that describe the capabilities
of the system.

B.   Classifying Trace Attributes

An important challenge to trace theorists concerns the development of a language for talking about trace features, attributes, and
codes. The existing terminology, under the still pervasive influence

of the copy theory, divides these features and attributes roughly into three parts of "physicalistic" versus "linguistic" versus "semantic." The first category lists the possible physical properties of the event. A word in a memory test is presented in one or the other sensory modality, it has a spatial location, it may be typed in a particular type font, it may be spoken by a certain voice, and the like. The "linguistic" category includes a phonological description of the speech sound and the syntactic roles of the word. The "semantic" category includes a myriad of features concerned with the word's conceptual meaning as well as its referential imagery, emotional connotations, and other stray associations. This set of categories has not developed organically from studies on memory, but rather has been imported into such investigations from other domains. There is no guarantee that these are the optimal categories or that they will prove most useful for theoretical integration.

A second issue, one that we have mentioned several times before, concerns the overlap or independence of trace features, and the related issue of direct and derived information. Methods need to be developed for assessing the extent to which information of one kind is correlated with, and can be derived from, the information of another kind. Ideally the objective is the identification and specification of trace properties that are independent of each other. Work on this problem has recently been initiated. Noting the large correlation between phonetic and graphemic similarity of words, Jacoby and Goolkasian (1973) varied the two aspects of similarity separately, finding that graphemic overlap contributed considerably to memory confusions. Goggin and Wickens (1971) in a bilingual attribute shift study found that a shift of two attributes, language and conceptual category, produced more "release from PI" than either one alone, suggesting, perhaps not surprisingly, that the two attributes were at least to a certain extent independent. Bahrick and Bahrick (1971), Frost (1972), and Tversky (1974) have investigated the quasi-independence of memory for the name of a picture compared to its more detailed visual aspects. Instructions can bias which aspect receives more attention, and different test conditions are sensitive to one or another feature. Kintsch (1970) has obtained some evidence that, in a bilingual recognition memory task, retention of the language of the target word is independent of the retention of the concept represented by a word in one language and its translation in the other. And Kolers (1973) has separated information for semantic content of sentences from information about the physical format of the input in a recognition memory task.

In the fuzzier world of sentence meaning, Kosslyn and Bower (1974) have distinguished (via ratings) between sentence pairs on the basis of their conceptual similarity versus their imaginal similarity. Many sentence pairs express a conceptual difference which is not reflected in static imagery. For example, the distinctions between the words in brackets are primarily conceptual and not represented in static imagery: "The clerk [was really, appeared to be] [deliberately, accidentally] [competent, incompetent] [yesterday, today]." Kosslyn and Bower found that memory confusion errors for children were controlled largely by image similarity (though the children understood the conceptual differences) whereas memory confusion errors for adults were controlled to a greater degree by conceptual similarity of the item.

The development of a language that could be used to describe the relations between stored information and the corresponding characteristics of stimulus and response events is another one of the most pressing research objectives. Many investigators do not want to think and talk about traces of word events as being linguistic, or semantic, or verbal, or visual, or auditory, or pictorial, or whatever, but in the absence of suitable alternative concepts and terms they are frequently and reluctantly forced into using the copy-theory language. Some try to get around the problem by referring to stored information as conceptual or abstract, and while this is probably a small step in the right direction, the concept of abstract or conceptual information seems to be too broad for analytical purposes.

C.   TRACE THEORY AND PROCESS MODELS

Although ideally one might wish to specify properties of memory traces independently of any other part of the memory system, this ideal will probably never be realized. We have already stated why. Exactly what information can be extracted, or is extracted, from any given memory trace depends not only on the trace but also on many other conditions, including those prevailing at the time of retrieval. This simple fact has an important consequence for research into the nature of memory traces: explication of the logic that relates experimental outcomes to statements about properties of memory traces requires specific assumptions about how the stored information is processed when it is retrieved. It is only in the context of a particular process model that inferences can be meaningfully drawn from the experimental data. This restriction holds regardless of what method is used. When we noted, in discussing various methods, that the logic used was not entirely clear, the difficulty usually lay in the absence of a set of statements or assumptions about the principles governing the utilization of stored information at the time of retrieval. The process models that would help make sense out of data on trace features need not be complex or highly sophisticated or "correct." But they must enter the picture in some form. Even a bad process model is better than none at all. It would help make clear the logic of the method of specifying trace properties, aid communication, and facilitate cross-comparisons of data obtained with different methods. Moreover, it can be improved, revised, or replaced with a better one. A nonexistent model cannot.

D. CONCLUSION

We are told that the human brain is the most complicated piece of matter in the known universe. Its many capabilities border on the miraculous. The amount and complexity of knowledge stored in the brain of an adult human being will not be duplicated by artificial means for some time to come, perhaps never. The problem of describing the format and characteristics of this knowledge thus must be a problem of the highest order of difficulty. Obviously we cannot be very sanguine about prospects for rapid progress and great breakthroughs. The accomplishments that psychologists interested in memory traces can call their own so far have been rather modest. Perhaps the most important achievement to date has been the development of a reasonably consistent conceptual framework within which experimental work can be pursued and theoretical problems posed. Many researchers agree now that (a) traces of individual events can be studied and described, (b) they are usefully conceptualized as collections of more elementary components or features, (c) these features and components differ from one another in some sense qualitatively, (d) they are at least to some extent independently manipulable and variable, and (e) the extent to which a particular feature is represented in a memory trace can be quantitatively assessed. Initial experimental work that has been done has provided outcomes that can be readily fitted into this overall framework. While these accomplishments are not yet dazzling, the challenge has been clearly identified. Many will undoubtedly rise to meet it.

REFERENCES

Anderson, R. C. Semantic organization and retrieval of information from sentences. *Journal of Verbal Learning and Verbal Behavior,* 1972, **11,** 794–800.

Anisfeld, M. False recognition of adjective-noun phrases. *Journal of Experimental Psychology,* 1970, **86,** 120–122.

Anisfeld, M., & Knapp, M. Association, synonymity, and directionality in false recognition. *Journal of Experimental Psychology,* 1968, **77,** 171–179.

Atkinson, R. C., & Shiffrin, R. M. Human memory: A proposed system and its control processes. In K. W. Spence & J. T. Spence (Eds.), *The psychology of learning and motivation,* Vol. 2. New York: Academic Press, 1968.

Bach, M. J., & Underwood, B. J. Developmental changes in memory attributes. *Journal of Educational Psychology,* 1970, **61,** 292–296.

Baddeley, A. D. Short-term memory for word sequences as a function of acoustic, semantic and formal similarity. *Quarterly Journal of Experimental Psychology,* 1966, **18,** 362–365.

Baddeley, A. D., & Patterson, K. The relation between long-term and short-term memory. *British Medical Bulletin,* 1971, **27,** 237–242.

Bahrick, H. P. Measurement of memory by prompted recall. *Journal of Experimental Psychology,* 1969, **79,** 213–219.

Bahrick, H. P., & Bahrick, P. Independence of verbal and visual codes of the same stimuli. *Journal of Experimental Psychology,* 1971, **91,** 344–346.

Begg, I., & Paivio, A. Concreteness and imagery in sentence meaning. *Journal of Verbal Learning and Verbal Behavior,* 1969, **8,** 821–827.

Bem, D. Self-perception theory. In L. Berkowitz (Ed.), *Advances in experimental social psychology,* Vol. 6. New York: Academic Press, 1972.

Bower, G. A multicomponent theory of the memory trace. In K. W. Spence & J. T. Spence (Eds.), *The psychology of learning and motivation.* Vol. 1. New York: Academic Press, 1967.

Bransford, J. D., & Franks, J. J. The abstraction of linguistic ideas. *Cognitive Psychology,* 1971, **2,** 331–350.

Bregman, A. S. Forgetting curves with semantic, phonetic, graphic, and contiguity cues. *Journal of Experimental Psychology,* 1968, **78,** 539–546.

Bregman, A. S., & Chambers, D. W. All-or-none learning of attributes. *Journal of Experimental Psychology,* 1966, **71,** 785–793.

Cermak, G., Schnorr, J., Buschke, H., & Atkinson, R. C. Recognition memory as influenced by differential attention to semantic and acoustic properties of words. *Psychonomic Science,* 1970, **19,** 79–81.

Conrad, R. Acoustic confusions in immediate memory. *British Journal of Psychology,* 1964, **55,** 75–84.

Craik, F. I. M. A "levels of analysis" view of memory. In P. Pliner, L. Krames, & T. M. Alloway (Eds.), *Communication and affect: Language and thought.* New York: Academic Press, 1973.

Craik, F. I. M., & Lockhart, R. S. Levels of processing: A framework for memory research. *Journal of Verbal Learning and Verbal Behavior,* 1972, **11,** 671–684.

Eagle, M., & Ortof, E. The effect of level of attention upon "phonetic" recognition errors. *Journal of Verbal Learning and Verbal Behavior,* 1967, **6,** 226–231.

Elias, C. S., & Perfetti, C. A. Encoding task and recognition memory: The importance of semantic encoding. *Journal of Experimental Psychology,* 1973, **99,** 151–156.

Estes, W. K. Phonemic coding and rehearsal in short-term memory for letter strings. *Journal of Verbal Learning and Verbal Behavior*, 1973, **12**, 360–372.

Fillenbaum, S. Words as feature complexes: False recognition of antonyms and synonyms. *Journal of Experimental Psychology*, 1969, **82**, 400–402.

Frost, N. Clustering by visual shape in the free recall of pictorial stimuli. *Journal of Experimental Psychology*, 1971, **88**, 409–413.

Frost, N. Encoding and retrieval in visual memory tasks. *Journal of Experimental Psychology*, 1972, **95**, 317–326.

Gardiner, J. M., Craik, F. I. M., & Birtwistle, J. Retrieval cues and release from proactive inhibition. *Journal of Verbal Learning and Verbal Behavior*, 1972, **11**, 778–783.

Gazzaniga, M. S. One brain—two minds? *American Scientist*, 1972, **60**, 311–317.

Ghatala, E. S., & Hurlbut, N. L. Effectiveness of acoustic and conceptual retrieval cues in memory for words at two grade levels. *Journal of Experimental Psychology*, 1973, **64**, 261–266.

Glanzer, M., & Cunitz, A. R. Two storage mechanisms in free recall. *Journal of Verbal Learning and Verbal Behavior*, 1966, **5**, 351–360.

Goggin, J., & Wickens, D. D. Proactive interference and language change in short-term memory. *Journal of Verbal Learning and Verbal Behavior*, 1971, **10**, 453–458.

Hintzman, D. L. Articulatory coding in short-term memory. *Journal of Verbal Learning and Verbal Behavior*, 1967, **6**, 312–316.

Hintzman, D. L., & Block, R. A. Repetition and memory: Evidence for a multiple-trace hypothesis. *Journal of Experimental Psychology*, 1971, **88**, 297–306.

Hyde, T. S., & Jenkins, J. J. Differential effects of incidental tasks on the organization of recall of a list of highly associated words. *Journal of Experimental Psychology*, 1969, **82**, 472–481.

Jacoby, L. L., & Goolkasian, P. Semantic versus acoustic coding: Retention and conditions of organization. *Journal of Verbal Learning and Verbal Behavior*, 1973, **12**, 324–333.

Keppel, G., & Underwood, B. J. Proactive inhibition in short-term retention of single items. *Journal of Verbal Learning and Verbal Behavior*, 1962, **1**, 153–161.

Kintsch, W. Recognition memory in bilingual subjects. *Journal of Verbal Learning and Verbal Behavior*, 1970, **9**, 405–409.

Kintsch, W., & Buschke, H. Homophones and synonyms in short-term memory. *Journal of Experimental Psychology*, 1969, **80**, 403–407.

Kirsner, K. Modality differences in recognition memory for words and their attributes. *Journal of Experimental Psychology*, 1974, **102**, 579–584.

Kolers, P. A. Remembering operations. *Memory & Cognition*, 1973, **1**, 347–355.

Kosslyn, S. M., & Bower, G. H. The role of imagery in sentence memory: A developmental study, *Child Development*, 1974, **45**, 30–38.

Laurence, M. W. Role of homophones in transfer learning. *Journal of Experimental Psychology*, 1970, **86**, 1–7.

Light, L. L. Homonyms and synonyms as retrieval cues. *Journal of Experimental Psychology*, 1972, **96**, 255–262.

Light, L. L., Stansbury, C., Rubin, C., & Linde, S. Memory for modality of presentation: Within-modality discrimination. *Memory & Cognition*, 1973, **1**, 395–400.

Lively, B. Speed/accuracy trade off and practice as determinants of stage durations in a memory-search task. *Journal of Experimental Psychology*, 1972, **96**, 97–103.

Loess, H. Short-term memory, word class, and sequence of items. *Journal of Experimental Psychology*, 1967, **74**, 556–561.

Madigan, S. A. Intraserial repetition and coding processes in free recall. *Journal of Verbal Learning and Verbal Behavior*, 1969, **8**, 829–835.

Madigan, S. A., & Doherty, L. Retention of item attributes in free recall. *Psychonomic Science*, 1972, **27**, 233–235.

Morton, J. Repeated items and decay in memory. *Psychonomic Science*, 1968, **10**, 219–220.

Murdock, B. B., Jr. The serial position effect of free recall. *Journal of Experimental Psychology*, 1962, **64**, 482–488.

Murdock, B. B., Jr., & Walker, K. D. Modality effects in free recall. *Journal of Verbal Learning and Verbal Behavior*, 1969, **8**, 665–676.

Nelson, D. L., & Brooks, D. H. Relative effectiveness of rhymes and synonyms as retrieval cues. *Journal of Experimental Psychology*, 1974, **102**, 503–507.

Nelson, T. O., & Rothbart, R. Acoustic savings for items forgotten from long-term memory. *Journal of Experimental Psychology*, 1972, **93**, 357–360.

Norman, D. A. Toward a theory of memory and attention. *Psychological Review*, 1968, **75**, 522–536.

Paivio, A. Mental imagery in associative learning and memory. *Psychological Review*, 1969, **76**, 241–263.

Paivio, A. *Imagery and verbal processes*. New York: Holt, 1971.

Paivio, A., & Csapo, K. Picture superiority in free recall: Imagery or dual coding? *Cognitive Psychology*, 1973, **5**, 176–206.

Peterson, L. R., Johnson, S. T., & Coatrey, R. The effect of repeated occurrences on judgments of recency. *Journal of Verbal Learning and Verbal Behavior*, 1969, **8**, 591–596.

Posner, M. I. Abstraction and the process of recognition. In G. H. Bower & J. T. Spence (Eds.), *The psychology of learning and motivation*. Vol. 3. New York: Academic Press, 1969. (a)

Posner, M. I. Representational systems for storing information in memory. In G. A. Talland & N. C. Waugh (Eds.), *The pathology of memory*. New York: Academic Press, 1969. Pp. 173–194. (b)

Posner, M. I., Boies, I. J., Eichelman, W. H., & Taylor, R. L. Retention of visual and name codes of single letters. *Journal of Experimental Psychology Monograph*, 1969, **79**, 1–16.

Posner, M. I., & Keele, S. W. Decay of visual information from a single letter. *Science*, 1967, **158**, 137–139.

Posner, M. I., & Taylor, R. L. Subtractive method applied to separation of visual and name components of multiletter arrays. *Acta Psychologica*, 1969, **30**, 104–114.

Pylyshyn, Z. W. What the mind's eye tells the mind's brain: A critique of mental imagery. *Psychological Bulletin*, 1973, **80**, 1–24.

Raser, G. A. Recoding of semantic and acoustic information in short-term memory. *Journal of Verbal Learning and Verbal Behavior*, 1972, **11**, 692–697.

Ryle, G. *The concept of mind*. London: Hutchinson, 1949.

Sachs, J. S. Recognition memory for syntactic and semantic aspects of connected discourse. *Perception & Psychophysics*, 1967, **2**, 437–442.

Shulman, H. G. Encoding and retention of semantic and phonemic information in short-term memory. *Journal of Verbal Learning and Verbal Behavior*, 1970, **9**, 499–508.

Sternberg, S. High-speed scanning in human memory. *Science*, 1966, **153**, 652–654.

Sternberg, S. Memory-scanning: Mental process revealed by reaction-time experiments. *American Scientist*, 1969, **57**, 421–457.

Thomson, D. M., & Tulving, E. Associative encoding and retrieval: Weak and strong cues. *Journal of Experimental Psychology*, 1970, **86**, 255–262.

Till, R. E., & Jenkins, J. J. The effects of cued orienting tasks on the free recall of words. *Journal of Verbal Learning and Verbal Behavior*, 1973, **12**, 489–498.

Tulving, E. Episodic and semantic memory. In E. Tulving & W. Donaldson (Eds.), *Organization of memory*. New York: Academic Press, 1972.

Tulving, E., & Pearlstone, Z. Availability versus accessibility of information in memory for words. *Journal of Verbal Learning and Verbal Behavior*, 1966, **5**, 381–391.

Tulving, E., & Thomson, D. M. Encoding specificity and retrieval processes in episodic memory. *Psychological Review*, 1973, **80**, 352–373.

Tulving, E., & Watkins, M. J. Continuity between recall and recognition. *American Journal of Psychology*, 1974, in press.

Turvey, M. T., & Fertig, J. Polarity on the semantic differential and release from proactive interference in short-term memory. *Journal of Verbal Learning and Verbal Behavior*, 1970, **9**, 439–443.

Tversky, B. Eye fixations in prediction of recognition and recall. *Memory & Cognition*, 1974, **2**, 275–278.

Underwood, B. J. False recognition produced by implicit verbal responses. *Journal of Experimental Psychology*, 1965, **70**, 122–129.

Underwood, B. J. Attributes of memory. *Psychological Review*, 1969, **76**, 559–573.

Walter, D. A. The effect of sentence context on the stability of phonemic and semantic memory dimensions. *Journal of Verbal Learning and Verbal Behavior*, 1973, **12**, 185–192.

Waugh, N. C., & Norman, D. A. Primary memory. *Psychological Review*, 1965, **72**, 89–104.

Wickelgren, W. A. Acoustic similarity and intrusion errors in short-term memory. *Journal of Experimental Psychology*, 1965, **70**, 102–108.

Wickens, D. D. Encoding categories of words: An empirical approach to meaning. *Psychological Review*, 1970, **77**, 1–15.

Wickens, D. D. Characteristics of word encoding. In A. W. Melton & E. Martin (Eds.), *Coding processes in human memory*. Washington, D.C.: Winston, 1972.

Wickens. D. D., Born, D. G., & Allen, C. K. Proactive inhibition and item similarity in short-term memory. *Journal of Verbal Learning and Verbal Behavior*, 1963, **2**, 440–445.

Wickens, D. D., & Clark, S. Osgood dimensions as an encoding class in short-term memory. *Journal of Experimental Psychology*, 1968, **78**, 580–584.

SUBJECT INDEX